Life Application Bible Studies
LUKE

APPLICATION® BIBLE STUDIES

Part 1:
Complete text of Luke with study notes and features
from the *Life Application Study Bible*

Part 2:
Thirteen lessons for individual or group study

Study questions written and edited by

Linda Chaffee Taylor
Rev. David R. Veerman
Dr. James C. Galvin
Dr. Bruce B. Barton
Daryl J. Lucas

New Living
Translation®

Tyndale House Publishers, Inc.
Carol Stream, Illinois

luke

Visit Tyndale's exciting Web site at www.tyndale.com

New Living Translation, NLT, the New Living Translation logo, and *Life Application* are registered trademarks of Tyndale House Publishers, Inc.

Life Application Bible Studies: Luke

Copyright © 1999, 2009 by Tyndale House Publishers, Inc., Carol Stream, Illinois 60188. All rights reserved.

Life Application notes and features copyright © 1988, 1989, 1990, 1991, 1993, 1996, 2004 by Tyndale House Publishers, Inc., Carol Stream, Illinois 60188. Maps in text copyright © 1986, 1988 by Tyndale House Publishers, Inc. All rights reserved.

Cover photograph copyright © by Galina Barskaya/iStockphoto. All rights reserved.

ISBN 978-1-4143-2649-8

Printed in the United States of America

15 14 13 12 11 10 09
7   6   5   4   3   2   1

CONTENTS

A NOTE TO READERS

The *Holy Bible*, New Living Translation, was first published in 1996. It quickly became one of the most popular Bible translations in the English-speaking world. While the NLT's influence was rapidly growing, the Bible Translation Committee determined that an additional investment in scholarly review and text refinement could make it even better. So shortly after its initial publication, the committee began an eight-year process with the purpose of increasing the level of the NLT's precision without sacrificing its easy-to-understand quality. This second-generation text was completed in 2004 and is reflected in this edition of the New Living Translation. An additional update with minor changes was subsequently introduced in 2007.

The goal of any Bible translation is to convey the meaning and content of the ancient Hebrew, Aramaic, and Greek texts as accurately as possible to contemporary readers. The challenge for our translators was to create a text that would communicate as clearly and powerfully to today's readers as the original texts did to readers and listeners in the ancient biblical world. The resulting translation is easy to read and understand, while also accurately communicating the meaning and content of the original biblical texts. The NLT is a general-purpose text especially good for study, devotional reading, and reading aloud in worship services.

We believe that the New Living Translation—which combines the latest biblical scholarship with a clear, dynamic writing style—will communicate God's word powerfully to all who read it. We publish it with the prayer that God will use it to speak his timeless truth to the church and the world in a fresh, new way.

The Publishers
October 2007

INTRODUCTION TO THE
NEW LIVING TRANSLATION

Translation Philosophy and Methodology

English Bible translations tend to be governed by one of two general translation theories. The first theory has been called "formal-equivalence," "literal," or "word-for-word" translation. According to this theory, the translator attempts to render each word of the original language into English and seeks to preserve the original syntax and sentence structure as much as possible in translation. The second theory has been called "dynamic-equivalence," "functional-equivalence," or "thought-for-thought" translation. The goal of this translation theory is to produce in English the closest natural equivalent of the message expressed by the original-language text, both in meaning and in style.

Both of these translation theories have their strengths. A formal-equivalence translation preserves aspects of the original text—including ancient idioms, term consistency, and original-language syntax—that are valuable for scholars and professional study. It allows a reader to trace formal elements of the original-language text through the English translation. A dynamic-equivalence translation, on the other hand, focuses on translating the message of the original-language text. It ensures that the meaning of the text is readily apparent to the contemporary reader. This allows the message to come through with immediacy, without requiring the reader to struggle with foreign idioms and awkward syntax. It also facilitates serious study of the text's message and clarity in both devotional and public reading.

The pure application of either of these translation philosophies would create translations at opposite ends of the translation spectrum. But in reality, all translations contain a mixture of these two philosophies. A purely formal-equivalence translation would be unintelligible in English, and a purely dynamic-equivalence translation would risk being unfaithful to the original. That is why translations shaped by dynamic-equivalence theory are usually quite literal when the original text is relatively clear, and the translations shaped by formal-equivalence theory are sometimes quite dynamic when the original text is obscure.

The translators of the New Living Translation set out to render the message of the original texts of Scripture into clear, contemporary English. As they did so, they kept the concerns of both formal-equivalence and dynamic-equivalence in mind. On the one hand, they translated as simply and literally as possible when that approach yielded an accurate, clear, and natural English text. Many words and phrases were rendered literally and consistently into English, preserving essential literary and rhetorical devices, ancient metaphors, and word choices that give structure to the text and provide echoes of meaning from one passage to the next.

On the other hand, the translators rendered the message more dynamically when the literal rendering was hard to understand, was misleading, or yielded archaic or foreign wording. They clarified difficult metaphors and terms to aid in the reader's understanding. The translators first struggled with the meaning of the words and phrases in the ancient context; then they rendered the message into clear, natural English. Their goal was to be both faithful to the ancient texts and eminently readable. The result is a translation that is both exegetically accurate and idiomatically powerful.

Translation Process and Team

To produce an accurate translation of the Bible into contemporary English, the translation team needed the skills necessary to enter into the thought patterns of the ancient authors and then to render their ideas, connotations, and effects into clear, contemporary English.

To begin this process, qualified biblical scholars were needed to interpret the meaning of the original text and to check it against our base English translation. In order to guard against personal and theological biases, the scholars needed to represent a diverse group of evangelicals who would employ the best exegetical tools. Then to work alongside the scholars, skilled English stylists were needed to shape the text into clear, contemporary English.

With these concerns in mind, the Bible Translation Committee recruited teams of scholars that represented a broad spectrum of denominations, theological perspectives, and backgrounds within the worldwide evangelical community. Each book of the Bible was assigned to three different scholars with proven expertise in the book or group of books to be reviewed. Each of these scholars made a thorough review of a base translation and submitted suggested revisions to the appropriate Senior Translator. The Senior Translator then reviewed and summarized these suggestions and proposed a first-draft revision of the base text. This draft served as the basis for several additional phases of exegetical and stylistic committee review. Then the Bible Translation Committee jointly reviewed and approved every verse of the final translation.

Throughout the translation and editing process, the Senior Translators and their scholar teams were given a chance to review the editing done by the team of stylists. This ensured that exegetical errors would not be introduced late in the process and that the entire Bible Translation Committee was happy with the final result. By choosing a team of qualified scholars and skilled stylists and by setting up a process that allowed their interaction throughout the process, the New Living Translation has been refined to preserve the essential formal elements of the original biblical texts, while also creating a clear, understandable English text.

The New Living Translation was first published in 1996. Shortly after its initial publication, the Bible Translation Committee began a process of further committee review and translation refinement. The purpose of this continued revision was to increase the level of precision without sacrificing the text's easy-to-understand quality. This second-edition text was completed in 2004, and an additional update with minor changes was subsequently introduced in 2007. This printing of the New Living Translation reflects the updated 2007 text.

Written to Be Read Aloud

It is evident in Scripture that the biblical documents were written to be read aloud, often in public worship (see Nehemiah 8; Luke 4:16-20; 1 Timothy 4:13; Revelation 1:3). It is still the case today that more people will hear the Bible read aloud in church than are likely to read it for themselves. Therefore, a new translation must communicate with clarity and power when it is read publicly. Clarity was a primary goal for the NLT translators, not only to facilitate private reading and understanding, but also to ensure that it would be excellent for public reading and make an immediate and powerful impact on any listener.

The Texts behind the New Living Translation

The Old Testament translators used the Masoretic Text of the Hebrew Bible as represented in *Biblia Hebraica Stuttgartensia* (1977), with its extensive system of textual notes; this is an update of Rudolf Kittel's *Biblia Hebraica* (Stuttgart, 1937). The translators also further compared the Dead Sea Scrolls, the Septuagint and other Greek manuscripts, the Samaritan Pentateuch, the Syriac Peshitta, the Latin Vulgate, and any other versions or manuscripts that shed light on the meaning of difficult passages.

The New Testament translators used the two standard editions of the Greek New Testament: the *Greek New Testament*, published by the United Bible Societies (UBS, fourth revised edition, 1993), and *Novum Testamentum Graece*, edited by Nestle and Aland (NA, twenty-seventh edition, 1993). These two editions, which have the same text but differ in punctuation and textual notes, represent, for the most part, the best in modern textual scholarship. However, in cases where strong textual or other scholarly evidence supported the decision, the translators sometimes chose to differ from the UBS and NA Greek texts and followed variant readings found in other ancient witnesses. Significant textual variants of this sort are always noted in the textual notes of the New Living Translation.

Translation Issues

The translators have made a conscious effort to provide a text that can be easily understood by the typical reader of modern English. To this end, we sought to use only vocabulary and

language structures in common use today. We avoided using language likely to become quickly dated or that reflects only a narrow subdialect of English, with the goal of making the New Living Translation as broadly useful and timeless as possible.

But our concern for readability goes beyond the concerns of vocabulary and sentence structure. We are also concerned about historical and cultural barriers to understanding the Bible, and we have sought to translate terms shrouded in history and culture in ways that can be immediately understood. To this end:

- We have converted ancient weights and measures (for example, "ephah" [a unit of dry volume] or "cubit" [a unit of length]) to modern English (American) equivalents, since the ancient measures are not generally meaningful to today's readers. Then in the textual footnotes we offer the literal Hebrew, Aramaic, or Greek measures, along with modern metric equivalents.

- Instead of translating ancient currency values literally, we have expressed them in common terms that communicate the message. For example, in the Old Testament, "ten shekels of silver" becomes "ten pieces of silver" to convey the intended message. In the New Testament, we have often translated the "denarius" as "the normal daily wage" to facilitate understanding. Then a footnote offers: "Greek *a denarius,* the payment for a full day's wage." In general, we give a clear English rendering and then state the literal Hebrew, Aramaic, or Greek in a textual footnote.

- Since the names of Hebrew months are unknown to most contemporary readers, and since the Hebrew lunar calendar fluctuates from year to year in relation to the solar calendar used today, we have looked for clear ways to communicate the time of year the Hebrew months (such as Abib) refer to. When an expanded or interpretive rendering is given in the text, a textual note gives the literal rendering. Where it is possible to define a specific ancient date in terms of our modern calendar, we use modern dates in the text. A textual footnote then gives the literal Hebrew date and states the rationale for our rendering. For example, Ezra 6:15 pinpoints the date when the postexilic Temple was completed in Jerusalem: "the third day of the month Adar." This was during the sixth year of King Darius's reign (that is, 515 B.C.). We have translated that date as March 12, with a footnote giving the Hebrew and identifying the year as 515 B.C.

- Since ancient references to the time of day differ from our modern methods of denoting time, we have used renderings that are instantly understandable to the modern reader. Accordingly, we have rendered specific times of day by using approximate equivalents in terms of our common "o'clock" system. On occasion, translations such as "at dawn the next morning" or "as the sun was setting" have been used when the biblical reference is more general.

- When the meaning of a proper name (or a wordplay inherent in a proper name) is relevant to the message of the text, its meaning is often illuminated with a textual footnote. For example, in Exodus 2:10 the text reads: "The princess named him Moses, for she explained, 'I lifted him out of the water.' " The accompanying footnote reads: "*Moses* sounds like a Hebrew term that means 'to lift out.' "

  Sometimes, when the actual meaning of a name is clear, that meaning is included in parentheses within the text itself. For example, the text at Genesis 16:11 reads: "You are to name him Ishmael (*which means 'God hears'*), for the LORD has heard your cry of distress." Since the original hearers and readers would have instantly understood the meaning of the name "Ishmael," we have provided modern readers with the same information so they can experience the text in a similar way.

- Many words and phrases carry a great deal of cultural meaning that was obvious to the original readers but needs explanation in our own culture. For example, the phrase "they beat their breasts" (Luke 23:48) in ancient times meant that people were very upset, often in mourning. In our translation we chose to translate this phrase dynamically for clarity: "They went home *in deep sorrow.*" Then we included a footnote with the literal Greek, which reads: "Greek *went home beating their breasts.*" In other similar cases, however, we have sometimes chosen to illuminate the existing literal expression to make it immediately understandable. For example, here we might have expanded the literal Greek phrase to read: "They went home

beating their breasts *in sorrow.*" If we had done this, we would not have included
a textual footnote, since the literal Greek clearly appears in translation.

- Metaphorical language is sometimes difficult for contemporary readers to understand, so at times we have chosen to translate or illuminate the meaning of a
metaphor. For example, the ancient poet writes, "Your neck is *like* the tower of
David" (Song of Songs 4:4). We have rendered it "Your neck is *as beautiful as* the
tower of David" to clarify the intended positive meaning of the simile. Another
example comes in Ecclesiastes 12:3, which can be literally rendered: "Remember
him . . . when the grinding women cease because they are few, and the women
who look through the windows see dimly." We have rendered it: "Remember him
before your teeth—your few remaining servants—stop grinding; and before your
eyes—the women looking through the windows—see dimly." We clarified such
metaphors only when we believed a typical reader might be confused by the
literal text.

- When the content of the original language text is poetic in character, we have
rendered it in English poetic form. We sought to break lines in ways that clarify
and highlight the relationships between phrases of the text. Hebrew poetry often
uses parallelism, a literary form where a second phrase (or in some instances a third
or fourth) echoes the initial phrase in some way. In Hebrew parallelism, the subse-
quent parallel phrases continue, while also furthering and sharpening, the thought
expressed in the initial line or phrase. Whenever possible, we sought to represent
these parallel phrases in natural poetic English.

- The Greek term *hoi Ioudaioi* is literally translated "the Jews" in many English translations. In the Gospel of John, however, this term doesn't always refer to the Jewish
people generally. In some contexts, it refers more particularly to the Jewish religious
leaders. We have attempted to capture the meaning in these different contexts by
using terms such as "the people" (with a footnote: Greek *the Jewish people*) or "the
religious leaders," where appropriate.

- One challenge we faced was how to translate accurately the ancient biblical text that
was originally written in a context where male-oriented terms were used to refer to
humanity generally. We needed to respect the nature of the ancient context while
also trying to make the translation clear to a modern audience that tends to read
male-oriented language as applying only to males. Often the original text, though
using masculine nouns and pronouns, clearly intends that the message be applied
to both men and women. A typical example is found in the New Testament letters,
where the believers are called "brothers" (*adelphoi*). Yet it is clear from the content
of these letters that they were addressed to all the believers—male and female. Thus,
we have usually translated this Greek word as "brothers and sisters" in order to
represent the historical situation more accurately.

  We have also been sensitive to passages where the text applies generally to
human beings or to the human condition. In some instances we have used plural
pronouns (they, them) in place of the masculine singular (he, him). For example, a
traditional rendering of Proverbs 22:6 is: "Train up a child in the way he should go,
and when he is old he will not turn from it." We have rendered it: "Direct your children onto the right path, and when they are older, they will not leave it." At times, we
have also replaced third person pronouns with the second person to ensure clarity.
A traditional rendering of Proverbs 26:27 is: "He who digs a pit will fall into it, and
he who rolls a stone, it will come back on him." We have rendered it: "If you set a trap
for others, you will get caught in it yourself. If you roll a boulder down on others, it
will crush you instead."

  We should emphasize, however, that all masculine nouns and pronouns used to
represent God (for example, "Father") have been maintained without exception. All
decisions of this kind have been driven by the concern to reflect accurately the
intended meaning of the original texts of Scripture.

Lexical Consistency in Terminology

For the sake of clarity, we have translated certain original-language terms consistently, especially within synoptic passages and for commonly repeated rhetorical phrases, and within

certain word categories such as divine names and non-theological technical terminology (e.g., liturgical, legal, cultural, zoological, and botanical terms). For theological terms, we have allowed a greater semantic range of acceptable English words or phrases for a single Hebrew or Greek word. We have avoided some theological terms that are not readily understood by many modern readers. For example, we avoided using words such as "justification" and "sanctification," which are carryovers from Latin translations. In place of these words, we have provided renderings such as "made right with God" and "made holy."

The Spelling of Proper Names

Many individuals in the Bible, especially the Old Testament, are known by more than one name (e.g., Uzziah/Azariah). For the sake of clarity, we have tried to use a single spelling for any one individual, footnoting the literal spelling whenever we differ from it. This is especially helpful in delineating the kings of Israel and Judah. King Joash/Jehoash of Israel has been consistently called Jehoash, while King Joash/Jehoash of Judah is called Joash. A similar distinction has been used to distinguish between Joram/Jehoram of Israel and Joram/Jehoram of Judah. All such decisions were made with the goal of clarifying the text for the reader. When the ancient biblical writers clearly had a theological purpose in their choice of a variant name (e.g., Esh-baal/Ishbosheth), the different names have been maintained with an explanatory footnote.

For the names Jacob and Israel, which are used interchangeably for both the individual patriarch and the nation, we generally render it "Israel" when it refers to the nation and "Jacob" when it refers to the individual. When our rendering of the name differs from the underlying Hebrew text, we provide a textual footnote, which includes this explanation: "The names 'Jacob' and 'Israel' are often interchanged throughout the Old Testament, referring sometimes to the individual patriarch and sometimes to the nation."

The Rendering of Divine Names

All appearances of *'el, 'elohim,* or *'eloah* have been translated "God," except where the context demands the translation "god(s)." We have generally rendered the tetragrammaton (*YHWH*) consistently as "the LORD," utilizing a form with small capitals that is common among English translations. This will distinguish it from the name *'adonai,* which we render "Lord." When *'adonai* and *YHWH* appear together, we have rendered it "Sovereign LORD." This also distinguishes *'adonai YHWH* from cases where *YHWH* appears with *'elohim,* which is rendered "LORD God." When *YH* (the short form of *YHWH*) and *YHWH* appear together, we have rendered it "LORD GOD." When *YHWH* appears with the term *tseba'oth,* we have rendered it "LORD of Heaven's Armies" to translate the meaning of the name. In a few cases, we have utilized the transliteration, *Yahweh,* when the personal character of the name is being invoked in contrast to another divine name or the name of some other god (for example, see Exodus 3:15; 6:2-3).

In the New Testament, the Greek word *christos* has been translated as "Messiah" when the context assumes a Jewish audience. When a Gentile audience can be assumed, *christos* has been translated as "Christ." The Greek word *kurios* is consistently translated "Lord," except that it is translated "LORD" wherever the New Testament text explicitly quotes from the Old Testament, and the text there has it in small capitals.

Textual Footnotes

The New Living Translation provides several kinds of textual footnotes, all designated in the text with an asterisk:

- When for the sake of clarity the NLT renders a difficult or potentially confusing phrase dynamically, we generally give the literal rendering in a textual footnote. This allows the reader to see the literal source of our dynamic rendering and how our translation relates to other more literal translations. These notes are prefaced with "Hebrew," "Aramaic," or "Greek," identifying the language of the underlying source text. For example, in Acts 2:42 we translated the literal "breaking of bread" (from the Greek) as "the Lord's Supper" to clarify that this verse refers to the ceremonial practice of the church rather than just an ordinary meal. Then we attached a footnote to "the Lord's Supper," which reads: "Greek *the breaking of bread.*"

- Textual footnotes are also used to show alternative renderings, prefaced with the word "Or." These normally occur for passages where an aspect of the meaning is debated. On occasion, we also provide notes on words or phrases that represent a departure from long-standing tradition. These notes are prefaced with "Tradition-ally rendered." For example, the footnote to the translation "serious skin disease" at Leviticus 13:2 says: "Traditionally rendered *leprosy*. The Hebrew word used throughout this passage is used to describe various skin diseases."
- When our translators follow a textual variant that differs significantly from our stan-dard Hebrew or Greek texts (listed earlier), we document that difference with a foot-note. We also footnote cases when the NLT excludes a passage that is included in the Greek text known as the *Textus Receptus* (and familiar to readers through its transla-tion in the King James Version). In such cases, we offer a translation of the excluded text in a footnote, even though it is generally recognized as a later addition to the Greek text and not part of the original Greek New Testament.
- All Old Testament passages that are quoted in the New Testament are identified by a textual footnote at the New Testament location. When the New Testament clearly quotes from the Greek translation of the Old Testament, and when it differs signifi-cantly in wording from the Hebrew text, we also place a textual footnote at the Old Testament location. This note includes a rendering of the Greek version, along with a cross-reference to the New Testament passage(s) where it is cited (for example, see notes on Psalms 8:2; 53:3; Proverbs 3:12).
- Some textual footnotes provide cultural and historical information on places, things, and people in the Bible that are probably obscure to modern readers. Such notes should aid the reader in understanding the message of the text. For example, in Acts 12:1, "King Herod" is named in this translation as "King Herod Agrippa" and is iden-tified in a footnote as being "the nephew of Herod Antipas and a grandson of Herod the Great."
- When the meaning of a proper name (or a wordplay inherent in a proper name) is relevant to the meaning of the text, it is either illuminated with a textual footnote or included within parentheses in the text itself. For example, the footnote concerning the name "Eve" at Genesis 3:20 reads: "*Eve* sounds like a Hebrew term that means 'to give life.' " This wordplay in the Hebrew illuminates the meaning of the text, which goes on to say that Eve "would be the mother of all who live."

As WE SUBMIT this translation for publication, we recognize that any translation of the Scrip-tures is subject to limitations and imperfections. Anyone who has attempted to communi-cate the richness of God's Word into another language will realize it is impossible to make a perfect translation. Recognizing these limitations, we sought God's guidance and wisdom throughout this project. Now we pray that he will accept our efforts and use this translation for the benefit of the church and of all people.

We pray that the New Living Translation will overcome some of the barriers of history, cul-ture, and language that have kept people from reading and understanding God's Word. We hope that readers unfamiliar with the Bible will find the words clear and easy to understand and that readers well versed in the Scriptures will gain a fresh perspective. We pray that readers will gain insight and wisdom for living, but most of all that they will meet the God of the Bible and be forever changed by knowing him.

The Bible Translation Committee
October 2007

WHY THE
LIFE APPLICATION STUDY BIBLE
IS UNIQUE

Have you ever opened your Bible and asked the following:

- What does this passage really mean?
- How does it apply to my life?
- Why does some of the Bible seem irrelevant?
- What do these ancient cultures have to do with today?
- I love God; why can't I understand what he is saying to me through his word?
- What's going on in the lives of these Bible people?

Many Christians do not read the Bible regularly. Why? Because in the pressures of daily living they cannot find a connection between the timeless principles of Scripture and the ever-present problems of day-by-day living.

God urges us to apply his word (Isaiah 42:23; 1 Corinthians 10:11; 2 Thessalonians 3:4), but too often we stop at accumulating Bible knowledge. This is why the *Life Application Study Bible* was developed—to show how to put into practice what we have learned.

Applying God's word is a vital part of one's relationship with God; it is the evidence that we are obeying him. The difficulty in applying the Bible is not with the Bible itself, but with the reader's inability to bridge the gap between the past and present, the conceptual and practical. When we don't or can't do this, spiritual dryness, shallowness, and indifference are the results.

The words of Scripture itself cry out to us, "But don't just listen to God's word. You must do what it says. Otherwise, you are only fooling yourselves" (James 1:22). The *Life Application Study Bible* helps us to obey God's word. Developed by an interdenominational team of pastors, scholars, family counselors, and a national organization dedicated to promoting God's word and spreading the gospel, the *Life Application Study Bible* took many years to complete. All the work was reviewed by several renowned theologians under the directorship of Dr. Kenneth Kantzer.

The *Life Application Study Bible* does what a good resource Bible should: It helps you understand the context of a passage, gives important background and historical information, explains difficult words and phrases, and helps you see the interrelationship of Scripture. But it does much more. The *Life Application Study Bible* goes deeper into God's word, helping you discover the timeless truth being communicated, see the relevance for your life, and make a personal application. While some study Bibles attempt application, over 75 percent of this Bible is application oriented. The notes answer the questions "So what?" and "What does this passage mean to me, my family, my friends, my job, my neighborhood, my church, my country?"

Imagine reading a familiar passage of Scripture and gaining fresh insight, as if it were the first time you had ever read it. How much richer your life would be if you left each Bible reading with a new perspective and a small change for the better. A small change every day adds up to a changed life—and that is the very purpose of Scripture.

WHAT IS APPLICATION?

The best way to define application is to first determine what it is *not*. Application is *not* just accumulating knowledge. Accumulating knowledge helps us discover and understand facts and concepts, but it stops there. History is filled with philosophers who knew what the Bible said but failed to apply it to their lives, keeping them from believing and changing. Many think that understanding is the end goal of Bible study, but it is really only the beginning.

Application is *not* just illustration. Illustration only tells us how someone else handled a similar situation. While we may empathize with that person, we still have little direction for our personal situation.

Application is *not* just making a passage "relevant." Making the Bible relevant only helps us to see that the same lessons that were true in Bible times are true today; it does not show us how to apply them to the problems and pressures of our individual lives.

What, then, is application? Application begins by knowing and understanding God's word and its timeless truths. *But you cannot stop there*. If you do, God's word may not change your life, and it may become dull, difficult, tedious, and tiring. A good application focuses the truth of God's word, shows the reader what to do about what is being read, and motivates the reader to respond to what God is teaching. All three are essential to application.

Application is putting into practice what we already know (see Mark 4:24 and Hebrews 5:14) and answering the question "So what?" by confronting us with the right questions and motivating us to take action (see 1 John 2:5-6 and James 2:26). Application is deeply personal—unique for each individual. It makes a relevant truth a personal truth and involves developing a strategy and action plan to live your life in harmony with the Bible. It is the biblical "how to" of life.

You may ask, "How can your application notes be relevant to my life?" Each application note has three parts: (1) an *explanation*, which ties the note directly to the Scripture passage and sets up the truth that is being taught; (2) the *bridge*, which explains the timeless truth and makes it relevant for today; (3) the *application*, which shows you how to take the timeless truth and apply it to your personal situation. No note, by itself, can apply Scripture directly to your life. It can only teach, direct, lead, guide, inspire, recommend, and urge. It can give you the resources and direction you need to apply the Bible, but only you can take these resources and put them into practice.

A good note, therefore should not only give you knowledge and understanding but point you to application. Before you buy any kind of resource study Bible, you should evaluate the notes and ask the following questions: (1) Does the note contain enough information to help me understand the point of the Scripture passage? (2) Does the note assume I know more than I do? (3) Does the note avoid denominational bias? (4) Do the notes touch most of life's experiences? (5) Does the note help me apply God's word?

FEATURES OF THE
LIFE APPLICATION STUDY BIBLE

NOTES
In addition to providing the reader with many application notes, the *Life Application Study Bible* also offers several kinds of explanatory notes, which help the reader understand culture, history, context, difficult-to-understand passages, background, places, theological concepts, and the relationship of various passages in Scripture to other passages.

BOOK INTRODUCTIONS
Each book introduction is divided into several easy-to-find parts:

Timeline. A guide that puts the Bible book into its historical setting. It lists the key events and the dates when they occurred.

Vital Statistics. A list of straight facts about the book—those pieces of information you need to know at a glance.

Overview. A summary of the book with general lessons and applications that can be learned from the book as a whole.

Blueprint. The outline of the book. It is printed in easy-to-understand language and is designed for easy memorization. To the right of each main heading is a key lesson that is taught in that particular section.

Megathemes. A section that gives the main themes of the Bible book, explains their significance, and then tells you why they are still important for us today.

Map. If included, this shows the key places found in that book and retells the story of the book from a geographical point of view.

OUTLINE
The *Life Application Study Bible* has a new, custom-made outline that was designed specifically from an application point of view. Several unique features should be noted:

1. To avoid confusion and to aid memory work, the book outline has only three levels for headings. Main outline heads are marked with a capital letter. Subheads are marked by a number. Minor explanatory heads have no letter or number.

2. Each main outline head marked by a letter also has a brief paragraph below it summarizing the Bible text and offering a general application.

3. Parallel passages are listed where they apply.

PERSONALITY PROFILES
Among the unique features of this Bible are the profiles of key Bible people, including their strengths and weaknesses, greatest accomplishments and mistakes, and key lessons from their lives.

MAPS

The *Life Application Study Bible* has a thorough and comprehensive Bible atlas built right into the book. There are two kinds of maps: a book-introduction map, telling the story of the book, and thumbnail maps in the notes, plotting most geographic movements.

CHARTS AND DIAGRAMS

Many charts and diagrams are included to help the reader better visualize difficult concepts or relationships. Most charts not only present the needed information but show the significance of the information as well.

CROSS-REFERENCES

An updated, exhaustive cross-reference system in the margins of the Bible text helps the reader find related passages quickly.

TEXTUAL NOTES

Directly related to the text of the New Living Translation, the textual notes provide explanations on certain wording in the translation, alternate translations, and information about readings in the ancient manuscripts.

HIGHLIGHTED NOTES

In each Bible study lesson, you will be asked to read specific notes as part of your preparation. These notes have each been highlighted by a bullet (•) so that you can find them easily.

LUKE

LUKE

VITAL STATISTICS

PURPOSE:
To present an accurate account of the life of Christ and to present Christ as the perfect human and Savior

AUTHOR:
Luke—a doctor (Colossians 4:14), a Greek, and Gentile Christian. He is the only known Gentile author in the New Testament. Luke was a close friend and companion of Paul. He also wrote Acts, and the two books go together.

ORIGINAL AUDIENCE:
Theophilus ("one who loves God"), Gentiles

DATE WRITTEN:
About A.D. 60

SETTING:
Luke wrote from Rome or possibly from Caesarea.

KEY VERSES:
"Jesus responded, 'Salvation has come to this home today, for this man has shown himself to be a true son of Abraham. For the Son of Man came to seek and save those who are lost'" (19:9, 10).

KEY PEOPLE:
Jesus, Elizabeth, Zechariah, John the Baptist, Mary, the disciples, Herod the Great, Pilate, Mary Magdalene

KEY PLACES:
Bethlehem, Galilee, Judea, Jerusalem

SPECIAL FEATURES:
This is the most comprehensive of the Gospels. The general vocabulary and diction show that the author was educated. He makes frequent references to illnesses and diagnoses. Luke stresses Jesus' relationships with people; emphasizes prayer, miracles, and angels; records inspired hymns of praise; gives a prominent place to women. Most of 9:51–18:35 is not found in any other Gospel.

EVERY birth is a miracle, and every child is a gift from God. But nearly 20 centuries ago, the miracle of miracles occurred. A baby was born, but he was the Son of God. The Gospels tell of this birth, but Dr. Luke, as though he were the attending physician, provides most of the details surrounding this awesome occasion. With a divine Father and a human mother, Jesus entered history—God in the flesh.

Luke affirms Jesus' divinity, but the real emphasis of his book is on Jesus' humanity—Jesus, the Son of God, is also the Son of Man. As a doctor, Luke was a man of science, and as a Greek, he was a man of detail. It is not surprising, then, that he begins by outlining his extensive research and explaining that he is reporting the facts (1:1–4). Luke also was a close friend and traveling companion of Paul, so he could interview the other disciples, had access to other historical accounts, and was an eyewitness to the birth and growth of the early church. His Gospel and book of Acts are reliable, historical documents.

Luke's story begins with angels appearing to Zechariah and then to Mary, telling them of the upcoming births of their sons. From Zechariah and Elizabeth would come John the Baptist, who would prepare the way for Christ. And Mary would conceive a child by the Holy Spirit and bear Jesus, the Son of God. Soon after John's birth, Caesar Augustus declared a census, and so Mary and Joseph traveled to Bethlehem, the town of David, their ancient ancestor. There the child was born. Angels announced the joyous event to shepherds, who rushed to the manger. When the shepherds left, they went praising God and spreading the news. Eight days later, Jesus was circumcised and then dedicated to God in the Temple, where Simeon and Anna confirmed Jesus' identity as the Savior, their Messiah.

Luke gives us a glimpse of Jesus at age 12—discussing theology with the Jewish teachers of the law at the Temple (2:41–52). Eighteen years later Jesus went out in the wilderness to be baptized by John the Baptist before beginning his public ministry (3:1–23). At this point, Luke traces Jesus' genealogy on his stepfather Joseph's side, through David and Abraham back to Adam, underscoring Jesus' identity as the Son of Man (3:23–38).

After the Temptation (4:1–13), Jesus returned to Galilee to preach, teach, and heal (4:14ff). During this time, he began gathering his group of 12 disciples (5:1–11, 27–29). Later Jesus commissioned the disciples and sent them out to proclaim the Kingdom of God. When they returned, Jesus revealed to them his mission, his true identity, and what it meant to be his disciple (9:18–62). His mission would take him to Jerusalem (9:51–53), where he would be rejected, tried, and crucified.

While Jesus carried his own cross to Golgotha, some women in Jerusalem wept for him, but Jesus told them to weep for themselves and for their children (23:28). Luke's Gospel does not end in sadness, however. It concludes with the thrilling account of Jesus' resurrection from the dead, his appearances to the disciples, and his promise to send the Holy Spirit (24:1–53). Read Luke's beautifully written and accurate account of the life of Jesus, Son of Man and Son of God. Then praise God for sending the Savior—our risen and triumphant Lord—for all people.

THE BLUEPRINT

A. BIRTH AND PREPARATION OF JESUS, THE SAVIOR (1:1—4:13)

From an infant who could do nothing on his own, Jesus grew to become completely able to fulfill his mission on earth. He was fully human, developing in all ways like us. Yet he remained fully God. He took no shortcuts and was not isolated from the pressures and temptations of life. There are no shortcuts for us either as we prepare for lives of service to God.

B. MESSAGE AND MINISTRY OF JESUS, THE SAVIOR (4:14—21:38)
1. Jesus' ministry in Galilee
2. Jesus' ministry on the way to Jerusalem
3. Jesus' ministry in Jerusalem

Jesus taught great crowds of people, especially through parables, which are stories that illustrate great truths. But only those with ears to hear will understand. We should pray that God's Spirit would help us understand the implications of these truths for our lives so we can become more and more like Jesus.

C. DEATH AND RESURRECTION OF JESUS, THE SAVIOR (22:1—24:53)

The Savior of the world was arrested and executed. But death could not destroy him, and Jesus came back to life and ascended to heaven. In Luke's careful, historical account, we receive the facts about Jesus' resurrection. We must not only believe that these facts are true, but we must also trust Christ as our Savior. It is shortsighted to neglect the facts, but how sad it is to accept the facts and neglect the forgiveness that Jesus offers to each of us.

MEGATHEMES

THEME	EXPLANATION	IMPORTANCE
Jesus Christ, the Savior	Luke describes how God's Son entered human history. Jesus lived as the perfect example of a human. After a perfect ministry, he provided a perfect sacrifice for our sin so we could be saved.	Jesus is our perfect leader and Savior. He offers forgiveness to all who will accept him as Lord of their lives and believe that what he says is true.
History	Luke was a medical doctor and historian. He put great emphasis on dates and details, connecting Jesus to events and people in history.	Luke gives details so we can believe in the reliability of the history of Jesus' life. Even more important, we can believe with certainty that Jesus is God.
People	Jesus was deeply interested in people and relationships. He showed warm concern for his followers and friends—men, women, and children.	Jesus' love for people is good news for everyone. His message is for all people in every nation. Each one of us has an opportunity to respond to him in faith.
Compassion	As a perfect human, Jesus showed tender sympathy to the poor, the despised, the hurt, and the sinful. No one was rejected or ignored by him.	Jesus is more than a good teacher—he cares for you. Because of his deep love for you, he can satisfy your needs.
Holy Spirit	The Holy Spirit was present at Jesus' birth, baptism, ministry, and resurrection. As a perfect example for us, Jesus lived in dependence on the Holy Spirit.	The Holy Spirit was sent by God as confirmation of Jesus' authority. The Holy Spirit is given to enable people to live for Christ. By faith we can have the indwelling Holy Spirit's presence and power to witness and to serve.

A. BIRTH AND PREPARATION OF JESUS, THE SAVIOR (1:1—4:13)

Luke gives us the most detailed account of Jesus' birth. In describing Jesus' birth, childhood, and development, Luke lifts up the humanity of Jesus. Our Savior was the ideal human. Fully prepared, the ideal human was now ready to live the perfect life.

1:1-2
John 15:27
Acts 1:21-22
Heb 2:3
2 Pet 1:16
1 Jn 1:1-4

Luke's Purpose in Writing (1)

1 Many people have set out to write accounts about the events that have been fulfilled among us. ²They used the eyewitness reports circulating among us from the early

• **1:1, 2** Luke tells Jesus' story from the unique perspective of a Gentile, a physician, and the first historian of the early church. Though not an eyewitness of Jesus' ministry, Luke nevertheless was concerned that eyewitness accounts be preserved accurately and that the foundations of Christian belief be transmitted intact to the next generation. In Luke's Gospel are many of Jesus' parables. In addition, more than any other Gospel, it gives specific instances of Jesus' concern for women.

disciples.* ³Having carefully investigated everything from the beginning, I also have decided to write a careful account for you, most honorable Theophilus, ⁴so you can be certain of the truth of everything you were taught.

1:3
Acts 1:1

An Angel Promises the Birth of John to Zechariah (4)

⁵When Herod was king of Judea, there was a Jewish priest named Zechariah. He was a member of the priestly order of Abijah, and his wife, Elizabeth, was also from the priestly line of Aaron. ⁶Zechariah and Elizabeth were righteous in God's eyes, careful to obey all of the Lord's commandments and regulations. ⁷They had no children because Elizabeth was unable to conceive, and they were both very old.

1:5
1 Chr 24:10
2 Chr 31:2
Matt 2:1

⁸One day Zechariah was serving God in the Temple, for his order was on duty that week. ⁹As was the custom of the priests, he was chosen by lot to enter the sanctuary of the Lord and burn incense. ¹⁰While the incense was being burned, a great crowd stood outside, praying.

1:8
1 Chr 24:19
2 Chr 8:14
1:9
Exod 30:7

¹¹While Zechariah was in the sanctuary, an angel of the Lord appeared to him, standing to the right of the incense altar. ¹²Zechariah was shaken and overwhelmed with fear when he saw him. ¹³But the angel said, "Don't be afraid, Zechariah! God has heard your prayer. Your wife, Elizabeth, will give you a son, and you are to name him John. ¹⁴You will have great joy and gladness, and many will rejoice at his birth, ¹⁵for he will be great in the eyes of the Lord. He must never touch wine or other alcoholic drinks. He will be filled with the Holy Spirit, even before his birth.* ¹⁶And he will turn many Israelites to the Lord their God.

1:15
Num 6:3
Judg 13:4
Jer 1:5
Matt 11:11
1:16
Mal 4:5-6

1:2 Greek *from those who from the beginning were servants of the word.* **1:15** Or *even from birth.*

• **1:1-4** There was a lot of interest in Jesus, and many people had written firsthand accounts about him. Luke may have used these accounts and all other available resources as material for an accurate and complete account of Jesus' life, teachings, and ministry. Because truth was important to Luke, he relied heavily on eyewitness accounts. Christianity doesn't say, "Close your eyes and believe," but rather, "Check it out for yourself." The Bible encourages you to investigate its claims thoroughly (John 1:46; 21:24; Acts 17:11, 12) because your conclusion about Jesus is a life-and-death matter.

• **1:1-4** *Theophilus* means "one who loves God." The book of Acts, also written by Luke, is likewise addressed to Theophilus. This preface may be a general dedication to all Christian readers. Theophilus may have been Luke's patron, who helped to finance the book's writing. More likely, Theophilus was a Roman acquaintance of Luke's with a strong interest in the new Christian religion.

• **1:3, 4** As a medical doctor, Luke knew the importance of being thorough. He used his skills in observation and analysis to thoroughly investigate the stories about Jesus. His diagnosis: The Good News of Jesus Christ is true! You can read Luke's account of Jesus' life with confidence that it was written by a clear thinker and a thoughtful researcher. Because the Good News is founded on historical truth, our spiritual growth must involve careful, disciplined, and thorough investigation of God's Word so that we can understand how God has acted in history. If this kind of study is not part of your life, find a pastor, teacher, or even a book to help you get started and to guide you in this important part of Christian growth.

1:5 This was Herod the Great, confirmed by the Roman Senate as king of the Jews. Only half-Jewish himself and eager to please his Roman superiors, Herod expanded and beautified the Jerusalem Temple—but he placed a Roman eagle over the entrance. When he helped the Jews, it was for political purposes and not because he cared about their God. Later, Herod the Great would order a massacre of infants in a futile attempt to kill the infant Jesus, whom some were calling the new "king of the Jews" (Matthew 2:2).

1:5 A Jewish priest was a minister of God who worked at the Temple managing its upkeep, teaching the people the Scriptures, and directing the worship services. At this time there were about 20,000 priests throughout the country—far too many to minister in the Temple at one time. Therefore the priests were divided into 24 separate groups of about 1,000 each, according to David's instructions (1 Chronicles 24:3-19).

Zechariah was a member of the order of Abijah, on duty this particular week. Each morning a priest was to enter the Holy Place in the Temple and burn incense. The priests would cast lots to decide who would enter the inner sanctuary, and one day the lot fell to Zechariah. But it was not by chance that Zechariah was on duty that day and that he was chosen that day to enter the Holy Place—perhaps a once-in-a-lifetime opportunity. God was guiding the events of history to prepare the way for Jesus to come to earth.

1:6 Zechariah and Elizabeth didn't merely go through the motions in following God's laws; they backed up their outward compliance with inward obedience. Unlike the religious leaders whom Jesus called hypocrites, Zechariah and Elizabeth did not stop with the letter of the law. Their obedience was from the heart, and that is why they are called "righteous in God's eyes."

1:7 God answers prayer in his own way and in his own time. He worked in an "impossible" situation—Elizabeth's age and barrenness—to bring about the fulfillment of all the prophecies concerning the Messiah. If you want to have your prayers answered, you must be open to what God can do in impossible situations. And you must wait for God to work in his way and in his time.

1:9 Incense was burned in the Temple twice daily (Exodus 30:7-10). When the people saw the smoke from the burning incense, they prayed. The smoke drifting heavenward symbolized their prayers ascending to God's throne.

1:11, 12 Angels are spirit beings who live in God's presence and do his will. Only two angels are mentioned by name in Scripture—Michael and Gabriel—but there are many who act as God's messengers. Here, Gabriel (1:19) delivered a special message to Zechariah. This was not a dream or a vision. The angel appeared in visible form and spoke audible words to the priest.

• **1:13** While burning incense on the altar, Zechariah was also praying, most likely for the coming of the Messiah to his people. How odd it must have seemed that the angel would say that his prayer was answered and Zechariah would soon have a son. Yet the greatest desire of Zechariah's heart—to have a son—would come true. At the same time, the answer to the nation's prayer for the Messiah would also come true. Zechariah's son would grow up to prepare the way for the Messiah.

1:13 *John* means "the LORD is gracious," and *Jesus* means "the LORD saves." Both names were prescribed by God, not

KEY PLACES IN LUKE

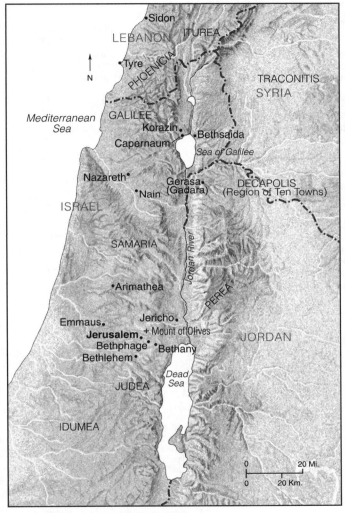

The broken lines (—·—·) indicate modern boundaries.

Luke begins his account in the Temple in Jerusalem, giving us the background for the birth of John the Baptist, then moves on to the town of Nazareth and the story of Mary, chosen to be Jesus' mother (1:26ff). As a result of Caesar's call for a census, Mary and Joseph had to travel to Bethlehem, where Jesus was born in fulfillment of prophecy (2:1ff). Jesus grew up in Nazareth and began his earthly ministry by being baptized by John (3:21, 22) and tempted by Satan (4:1ff). Much of his ministry focused on Galilee: He set up his "home" in Capernaum (4:31ff), and from there he taught throughout the region (8:1ff). Later he visited Gerasa (also called Gadara), where he healed a demon-possessed man (8:36ff). He fed more than 5,000 people with one lunch on the shores of the Sea of Galilee near Bethsaida (9:10ff). Jesus always traveled to Jerusalem for the major festivals, and he enjoyed visiting friends in nearby Bethany (10:38ff). He healed 10 men with leprosy on the border between Galilee and Samaria (17:11) and helped a dishonest tax collector in Jericho turn his life around (19:1ff). The little villages of Bethphage and Bethany on the Mount of Olives were Jesus' resting places during his last days on earth. He was crucified outside Jerusalem's walls, but he would rise again. Two of Jesus' followers walking on the road leading to Emmaus were among the first to see the resurrected Christ (24:13ff).

chosen by human parents. Throughout the Gospels, God acts graciously and saves his people. He will not withhold salvation from anyone who sincerely comes to him.

1:15 John was set apart for special service to God. He may have been forbidden to drink wine as part of the Nazirite vow, an ancient vow of consecration to God (see Numbers 6:1-8). Samson (Judges 13) was under the Nazirite vow, and Samuel may have been also (1 Samuel 1:11).

1:15 This is Luke's first mention of the Holy Spirit, the third Person of the Trinity; Luke refers to the Holy Spirit more than any other Gospel writer. Because Luke also wrote the book of Acts, we know he was thoroughly informed about the work of the

Holy Spirit. Luke recognized and emphasized the Holy Spirit's work in directing the beginnings of Christianity and in guiding the early church. The presence of the Spirit was God's gift to the entire church at Pentecost. Prior to that, God's Spirit was given to the faithful for special tasks. We need the Holy Spirit's help to do God's work effectively.

17He will be a man with the spirit and power of Elijah. He will prepare the people for the coming of the Lord. He will turn the hearts of the fathers to their children,* and he will cause those who are rebellious to accept the wisdom of the godly."

18Zechariah said to the angel, "How can I be sure this will happen? I'm an old man now, and my wife is also well along in years."

19Then the angel said, "I am Gabriel! I stand in the very presence of God. It was he who sent me to bring you this good news! 20But now, since you didn't believe what I said, you will be silent and unable to speak until the child is born. For my words will certainly be fulfilled at the proper time."

21Meanwhile, the people were waiting for Zechariah to come out of the sanctuary, wondering why he was taking so long. 22When he finally did come out, he couldn't speak to them. Then they realized from his gestures and his silence that he must have seen a vision in the sanctuary.

23When Zechariah's week of service in the Temple was over, he returned home. 24Soon afterward his wife, Elizabeth, became pregnant and went into seclusion for five months. 25"How kind the Lord is!" she exclaimed. "He has taken away my disgrace of having no children."

An Angel Promises the Birth of Jesus to Mary (5)

26In the sixth month of Elizabeth's pregnancy, God sent the angel Gabriel to Nazareth, a village in Galilee, 27to a virgin named Mary. She was engaged to be married to a man named Joseph, a descendant of King David. 28Gabriel appeared to her and said, "Greetings, favored woman! The Lord is with you!*"

29Confused and disturbed, Mary tried to think what the angel could mean. 30"Don't be afraid, Mary," the angel told her, "for you have found favor with God! 31You will conceive and give birth to a son, and you will name him Jesus. 32He will be very great and will be called the Son of the Most High. The Lord God will give him the throne of his ancestor David. 33And he will reign over Israel* forever; his Kingdom will never end!"

1:17 See Mal 4:5-6. **1:28** Some manuscripts add *Blessed are you among women.* **1:33** Greek *over the house of Jacob.*

1:17
Matt 17:11-13

1:18
Gen 18:11

1:19
Dan 8:16; 9:21

1:20
Ezek 3:26

1:25
Gen 30:23
Isa 4:1

1:26
Matt 2:23

1:27
Matt 1:16, 18
Luke 2:5

1:31
Isa 7:14
Matt 1:21-23

1:32
Isa 9:6-7; 16:5
Jer 23:5
Phil 2:10
1 Tim 6:15

1:33
Ps 89:3-4
Isa 9:7
Jer 33:17
Dan 2:44;
7:14, 27
Heb 1:8

• **1:17** John's role was to be almost identical to that of an Old Testament prophet: to encourage people to turn away from sin and back to God. John is often compared to the great prophet Elijah, who was known for standing up to evil rulers (Malachi 4:5; Matthew 11:14; 17:10-13). See Elijah's Profile in 1 Kings 17, p. 545.

• **1:18-20** When told he would have a son, Zechariah doubted the angel's word. From Zechariah's human perspective, his doubts were understandable—but with God, anything is possible. What God promises, he delivers. And God delivers *on time!* You can have complete confidence that God will keep his promises. Their fulfillment may not be the next day, but they will be "at the proper time." If you are waiting for God to answer some request or to fill some need, remain patient. No matter how impossible God's promises may seem, what he has said in his Word will come true at the right time.

1:21 The people were waiting outside for Zechariah to come out and pronounce the customary blessing upon them as found in Numbers 6:24-26.

1:25 Zechariah and Elizabeth were both godly people, yet they were suffering. Some Jews at that time did not believe in a bodily resurrection, so their hope of immortality was in their children. In addition, children cared for their parents in their old age and added to the family's financial security and social status. Children were considered a blessing, and childlessness was seen as a curse. Zechariah and Elizabeth had been childless for many years, and at this time they were too old to expect any change in their situation. They felt humiliated and hopeless. But God was waiting for the right time to encourage them and take away their disgrace.

1:26 Gabriel appeared not only to Zechariah and to Mary but also to the prophet Daniel more than 500 years earlier (Daniel 8:15-17; 9:21). Each time Gabriel appeared, he brought important messages from God.

1:26 Nazareth, Joseph and Mary's hometown, was a long way from Jerusalem, the center of Jewish life and worship. Located on a major trade route, Nazareth was frequently visited by Gentile merchants and Roman soldiers. It was known for its independent and aloof attitude. Jesus was born in Bethlehem but grew up in Nazareth. Nevertheless the people of Nazareth would reject him as the Messiah (4:22-30).

1:27, 28 Mary was young, poor, female—all characteristics that, to the people of her day, would make her seem unusable by God for any major task. But God chose Mary for one of the most important acts of obedience he has ever demanded of anyone. You may feel that your ability, experience, or education makes you an unlikely candidate for God's service. Don't limit God's choices. He can use you if you trust him.

1:30, 31 God's favor does not automatically bring instant success or fame. His blessing on Mary, the honor of being the mother of the Messiah, would lead to much pain: her peers would ridicule her; her fiancé would come close to leaving her; her son would be rejected and murdered. But through her son would come the world's only hope, and this is why Mary has been praised by countless generations. Her submission was part of God's plan to bring about our salvation. If sorrow weighs you down and dims your hope, think of Mary and wait patiently for God to finish working out his plan.

1:31 *Jesus,* a Greek form of the Hebrew name *Joshua,* was a common name meaning "the LORD saves." Just as Joshua had led Israel into the Promised Land (see Joshua 1:1, 2), so Jesus would lead his people into eternal life. The symbolism of his name was not lost on the people of his day, who took names seriously and saw them as a source of power. In Jesus' name, people were healed, demons were banished, and sins were forgiven.

1:32, 33 Centuries earlier, God had promised David that David's kingdom would last forever (2 Samuel 7:16). This promise was

1:35
Matt 1:20
Mark 1:1
John 1:34; 20:31
Rom 1:4

³⁴Mary asked the angel, "But how can this happen? I am a virgin."

³⁵The angel replied, "The Holy Spirit will come upon you, and the power of the Most High will overshadow you. So the baby to be born will be holy, and he will be called the Son of God. ³⁶What's more, your relative Elizabeth has become pregnant in her old age! People used to say she was barren, but she has conceived a son and is now in her sixth month. ³⁷For nothing is impossible with God.*"

1:37 Some manuscripts read *For the word of God will never fail.*

ZECHARIAH

Zechariah, a Jewish priest, was told before anyone else that God was setting in motion his own visit to earth. Zechariah and his wife, Elizabeth, were known for their personal holiness. They were well suited to doing a special work for God. But they shared the pain of not having children, and in Jewish culture this was considered not having God's blessing. Zechariah and Elizabeth were old, and they had stopped even asking for children.

One day while on duty at the Temple in Jerusalem, Zechariah received an unexpected blessing. He was chosen to be the priest who would enter the Holy Place to offer incense to God for the people. Suddenly, much to his surprise and terror, he found himself face to face with an angel. The angel's message was too good to be true! But the news of the coming Savior was eclipsed by doubts about his own ability to father the child the angel promised him. His age spoke more loudly than God's promise. As a result, God prevented Zechariah from speaking until the promise became a reality.

The record of the prayer in Luke 1 is our last glimpse of Zechariah. Like so many of God's most faithful servants, he passed quietly from the scene once his part was done. He becomes our hero for those times when we doubt God and yet are willing to obey. We gain hope from Zechariah's story that God can do great things through anyone who is available to him.

Strengths and accomplishments	• Known as a righteous man • Was a priest of God • One of the few people to be directly addressed by an angel • Fathered John the Baptist
Weakness and mistake	• Momentarily doubted the angel's promise of a son because of his own old age
Lessons from his life	• Physical limitations do not limit God • God accomplishes his will, often in unexpected ways
Vital statistics	• Occupation: Priest • Relatives: Wife: Elizabeth. Son: John the Baptist.
Key verses:	"Zechariah and Elizabeth were righteous in God's eyes, careful to obey all of the Lord's commandments and regulations. They had no children because Elizabeth was unable to conceive, and they were both very old" (Luke 1:6-7).

Zechariah's story is told in Luke 1.

---

fulfilled in the coming of Jesus, a direct descendant of David, whose Kingdom will never end.

1:34 The birth of Jesus to a virgin is a miracle that many people find hard to believe. These three facts can aid our faith: (1) Luke was a medical doctor, and he knew perfectly well how babies are made. It would have been just as hard for him to believe in a virgin birth as it is for us, yet he reports it as fact. (2) Luke was a painstaking researcher who based his Gospel on eyewitness accounts. Tradition holds that he talked with Mary about the events he recorded in the first two chapters. This is Mary's story, not a fictional invention. (3) Christians and Jews, who worship God as the Creator of the universe, should have no doubts that God has the power to create a child in a virgin's womb.

1:35 Why is the Virgin Birth important to the Christian faith? Jesus was born without the sin that entered the world through Adam. He was born holy, just as Adam was created sinless. In contrast to Adam, who disobeyed God, Jesus obeyed God and was thus able to face sin's consequences in our place and make us acceptable to God (Romans 5:14-19). Jesus Christ, God's Son, had to be free from the sinful nature passed on to all other human beings by Adam. Because Jesus was born of a woman, he was a human being; but as the Son of God, Jesus was born

without any trace of human sin. Jesus is both fully human and fully divine. Because Jesus lived as a man, human beings know that he fully understands their experiences and struggles (Hebrews 4:15-16). Because he is God, he has the power and authority to deliver people from sin (Colossians 2:13-15). People can tell Jesus all their thoughts, feelings, and needs. He has been where they are, and he has the ability to help.

38Mary responded, "I am the Lord's servant. May everything you have said about me come true." And then the angel left her.

Mary Visits Elizabeth (6)

39A few days later Mary hurried to the hill country of Judea, to the town 40where Zechariah lived. She entered the house and greeted Elizabeth. 41At the sound of Mary's greeting, Elizabeth's child leaped within her, and Elizabeth was filled with the Holy Spirit.

1:41
Gen 25:22
Luke 1:15

42Elizabeth gave a glad cry and exclaimed to Mary, "God has blessed you above all women, and your child is blessed. 43Why am I so honored, that the mother of my Lord should visit me? 44When I heard your greeting, the baby in my womb jumped for joy. 45You are blessed because you believed that the Lord would do what he said."

1:42
Judg 5:24

1:43
Luke 2:11

The Magnificat: Mary's Song of Praise

46Mary responded,

"Oh, how my soul praises the Lord.
47   How my spirit rejoices in God my Savior!
48 For he took notice of his lowly servant girl,
    and from now on all generations will call me blessed.
49 For the Mighty One is holy,
    and he has done great things for me.
50 He shows mercy from generation to generation
    to all who fear him.
51 His mighty arm has done tremendous things!
    He has scattered the proud and haughty ones.
52 He has brought down princes from their thrones
    and exalted the humble.
53 He has filled the hungry with good things
    and sent the rich away with empty hands.
54 He has helped his servant Israel
    and remembered to be merciful.
55 For he made this promise to our ancestors,
    to Abraham and his children forever."

1:46-55
1 Sam 2:1-10
Ps 34:2-3

1:47
1 Tim 1:1; 2:3
Titus 1:3; 2:10; 3:4

1:48
1 Sam 1:11

1:49
Ps 111:9

1:50
Ps 103:13, 17

1:51
2 Sam 22:28
Ps 89:10

1:52
Job 5:12;
12:19

1:53
1 Sam 2:5
Ps 107:9

1:54
Ps 98:3
Isa 41:8

1:55
Gen 17:7; 22:17

56Mary stayed with Elizabeth about three months and then went back to her own home.

1:38 A young unmarried girl who became pregnant risked disaster. Unless the father of the child agreed to marry her, she would probably remain unmarried for life. If her own father rejected her, she could be forced into begging or prostitution in order to earn her living. And Mary, with her story about becoming pregnant by the Holy Spirit, risked being considered crazy as well. Still Mary said, despite the possible risks, "May everything you have said about me come true." When Mary said that, she didn't know about the tremendous opportunity she would have. She only knew that God was asking her to serve him, and she willingly obeyed. Don't wait to see the bottom line before offering your life to God. Offer yourself willingly, even when the outcome seems disastrous.

• **1:38** God's announcement of the birth of a special child was met with various responses throughout Scripture. Sarah, Abraham's wife, laughed (Genesis 18:9-15). Zechariah doubted (Luke 1:18). By contrast, Mary graciously submitted. She believed the angel's words and agreed to bear the child, even under humanly impossible circumstances. God is able to do the impossible. Our response to his demands should not be laughter or doubt but willing acceptance.

1:41-43 Apparently the Holy Spirit told Elizabeth that Mary's child was the Messiah because Elizabeth called her young relative "the mother of my Lord" as she greeted her. As Mary rushed off to visit her relative, she must have been wondering if the events of the last few days had been real. Elizabeth's greeting must have strengthened her faith. Mary's pregnancy may have seemed impossible, but her wise relative believed in the Lord's faithfulness and rejoiced in Mary's blessed condition.

1:42, 43 Even though she herself was pregnant with a long-awaited son, Elizabeth could have envied Mary, whose son would

be even greater than her own. Instead, she was filled with joy that the mother of her Lord would visit her. Have you ever envied people whom God has apparently singled out for special blessing? A cure for jealousy is to rejoice with those individuals, realizing that God uses his people in ways best suited to his purpose.

1:46-55 This song is often called the *Magnificat*, the first word in the Latin translation of this passage. Mary's song has often been used as the basis for choral music and hymns. Like Hannah, the mother of Samuel (1 Samuel 2:1-10), Mary glorified God in song for what he was going to do for the world through her. Notice that in both songs, God is pictured as a champion of the poor, the oppressed, and the despised.

1:48 When Mary said, "From now on all generations will call me blessed," was she being proud? No, she was recognizing and accepting the gift God had given her. Pride is refusing to accept God's gifts or taking credit for what God has done; humility is accepting the gifts and using them to praise and serve God. Don't deny, belittle, or ignore your gifts. Thank God for them and use them to his glory.

1:54, 55 God kept his promise to Abraham to be merciful to God's people forever (Genesis 22:16-18). Christ's birth fulfilled the promise, and Mary understood this. She was not surprised when her special son eventually announced that he was the Messiah. She had known Jesus' mission from before his birth. Some of God's promises to Israel are found in 2 Samuel 22:50, 51; Psalms 89:2-4; 103:17, 18; Micah 7:18-20.

1:56 Because travel was difficult, long visits were customary. Mary must have been a great help to Elizabeth, who was experiencing the discomforts of a first pregnancy in old age.

John the Baptist Is Born (7)

57 When it was time for Elizabeth's baby to be born, she gave birth to a son. 58 And when her neighbors and relatives heard that the Lord had been very merciful to her, everyone rejoiced with her.

59 When the baby was eight days old, they all came for the circumcision ceremony. They wanted to name him Zechariah, after his father. 60 But Elizabeth said, "No! His name is John!"

61 "What?" they exclaimed. "There is no one in all your family by that name." 62 So they used gestures to ask the baby's father what he wanted to name him. 63 He motioned for a writing tablet, and to everyone's surprise he wrote, "His name is John." 64 Instantly Zechariah could speak again, and he began praising God.

65 Awe fell upon the whole neighborhood, and the news of what had happened spread throughout the Judean hills. 66 Everyone who heard about it reflected on these events and asked, "What will this child turn out to be?" For the hand of the Lord was surely upon him in a special way.

Zechariah's Prophecy

67 Then his father, Zechariah, was filled with the Holy Spirit and gave this prophecy:

68 "Praise the Lord, the God of Israel,
    because he has visited and redeemed his people.
69 He has sent us a mighty Savior*
    from the royal line of his servant David,
70 just as he promised
    through his holy prophets long ago.
71 Now we will be saved from our enemies
    and from all who hate us.
72 He has been merciful to our ancestors
    by remembering his sacred covenant—

1:69 Greek *has raised up a horn of salvation for us.*

Cross-references (left margin):

1:59 Gen 17:12; Lev 12:3; Luke 2:21; Phil 3:5

1:66 Luke 2:19; Acts 11:21

1:67 Joel 2:28

1:68 Pss 41:13; 72:18; 106:48; 111:9

1:69 1 Sam 2:1-10; Pss 18:2; 132:17; Ezek 29:21

1:70 Jer 23:5; Acts 3:21; Rom 1:2-4

1:71 Ps 106:10

1:72-73 Pss 105:8-9; 106:45-46

GOD'S UNUSUAL METHODS OF COMMUNICATING
One of the best ways to understand God's willingness to communicate to people is to note the various methods, some of them quite unexpected, that he has used to give his message.

Person/Group	Method	Reference
Jacob, Zechariah, Mary, shepherds	Angels	Genesis 32:22-32; Luke 1:13, 30; 2:10
Jacob, Joseph, a baker, a cup-bearer, Pharaoh, Isaiah, Joseph, the wise men	Dreams	Genesis 28:10-22; 37:5-10; 40:5; 41:7, 8; Isaiah 1:1; Matthew 1:20; 2:12, 13
Belshazzar	Writing on the wall	Daniel 5:5-9
Balaam	Talking donkey	Numbers 22:21-35
People of Israel	Pillars of cloud and fire	Exodus 13:21, 22
Jonah	Being swallowed by a fish	Jonah 2
Abraham, Moses, Jesus at his baptism, Paul	Verbally	Genesis 12:1-4; Exodus 7:8; Matthew 3:13-17; Acts 18:9
Moses	Fire	Exodus 3:2
Us	God's Son	Hebrews 1:1, 2

1:59 The circumcision ceremony was an important event to the family of a Jewish baby boy. God commanded circumcision when he was beginning to form his holy nation (Genesis 17:4-14), and he had reaffirmed it through Moses (Leviticus 12:1-3). This ceremony was a time of joy when friends and family members would celebrate the baby's becoming part of God's covenant nation.

1:59 Family lines and family names were important to the Jews. The people naturally assumed the child would receive Zechariah's name or at least a family name. They were surprised, therefore, that both Elizabeth and Zechariah wanted to name the boy John. This was the name the angel had given them (see 1:13).

1:62 Zechariah's relatives talked to him by gestures because he was apparently deaf as well as speechless and had not heard what his wife had said.

1:67-79 Zechariah praised God with his first words after months of silence. In a song that is often called the *Benedictus* after the first words in the Latin translation of this passage, Zechariah prophesied the coming of a Savior who would redeem his people and predicted that his son, John, would prepare the Messiah's way. All the Old Testament prophecies were coming true—no wonder Zechariah praised God! The Messiah would come in Zechariah's lifetime, and his son had been chosen to pave the way.

1:72, 73 This was God's promise to Abraham to bless all peoples through him (see Genesis 12:3). It would be fulfilled through the Messiah, Abraham's descendant.

73 the covenant he swore with an oath
 to our ancestor Abraham.
74 We have been rescued from our enemies
 so we can serve God without fear,
75 in holiness and righteousness
 for as long as we live.

76 "And you, my little son,
 will be called the prophet of the Most High,
 because you will prepare the way for the Lord.
77 You will tell his people how to find salvation
 through forgiveness of their sins.
78 Because of God's tender mercy,
 the morning light from heaven is about to break upon us,*
79 to give light to those who sit in darkness and in the shadow of death,
 and to guide us to the path of peace."

80 John grew up and became strong in spirit. And he lived in the wilderness until he began his public ministry to Israel.

1:73-74
Gen 22:16-18

1:75
Eph 4:24

1:76
Isa 40:3
Mal 3:1

1:77
Jer 31:34

1:78
Mal 4:2

1:79
Isa 9:2; 58:8;
60:1-2
Matt 4:16

1:80
Luke 2:40, 52

Jesus Is Born in Bethlehem (9)

2 At that time the Roman emperor, Augustus, decreed that a census should be taken throughout the Roman Empire. 2(This was the first census taken when Quirinius was governor of Syria.) 3All returned to their own ancestral towns to register for this census. 4And because Joseph was a descendant of King David, he had to go to Bethlehem in Judea, David's ancient home. He traveled there from the village of Nazareth in Galilee. 5He took with him Mary, his fiancée, who was now obviously pregnant.

2:1-7
Matt 1:18-25

2:5
Luke 1:27

1:78 Or *the Morning Light from Heaven is about to visit us.*

1:76 Zechariah had just recalled hundreds of years of God's sovereign work in history, beginning with Abraham and going on into eternity. Then, in tender contrast, he personalized the story. His son had been chosen for a key role in the drama of the ages. Although God has unlimited power, he chooses to work through frail humans who begin as helpless babies. Don't minimize what God can do through those who are faithful to him.

1:80 Why did John live out in the wilderness? Prophets used the isolation of the uninhabited wilderness to enhance their spiritual growth and to focus their message on God. By being in the wilderness, John remained separate from the economic and political powers so that he could aim his message against them. He also remained separate from the hypocritical religious leaders of his day. His message was different from theirs, and his life proved it.

THE JOURNEY TO BETHLEHEM
Caesar's decree for a census of the entire Roman Empire made it necessary for Joseph and Mary to leave their hometown, Nazareth, and journey the 70 miles to the Judean village of Bethlehem.

2:1 Luke is the only Gospel writer who related the events he recorded to world history. His account was addressed to a predominantly Greek audience that would have been interested in and familiar with the political situation. Palestine was under the rule of the Roman Empire with Emperor Caesar Augustus, the first Roman emperor, in charge. The Roman rulers, considered to be like gods, stood in contrast to the tiny baby in a manger who was truly God in the flesh.

2:1 A Roman census (registration) was taken to aid military conscription or tax collection. The Jews weren't required to serve in the Roman army, but they could not avoid paying taxes. Augustus's decree went out in God's perfect timing and according to God's perfect plan to bring his Son into the world.

2:1-6 The Romans ruled the civilized world at this time. By contrast, Joseph controlled very little. Against his better judgment and political convictions, he complied with the Roman order to make a long trip just to pay his taxes. His fiancée, who had to go with him, was about to give birth.

The Romans were in control insofar as human authority can get its way by exerting human power. But the Romans did not recognize their limitations. In reality, God controls the world. In all times and places, he works his will. By the decree of Emperor Augustus, Jesus was born in the very town prophesied for his birth (Micah 5:2), even though his parents did not live there. Joseph and Mary were both descendants of David. The Old Testament is filled with prophecies that the Messiah would be born in David's royal line (see, for example, Isaiah 11:1; Jeremiah 33:15; Ezekiel 37:24; Hosea 3:5). Rome made the decree, just as God intended.

2:4, 5 Sometimes we think to ourselves, "I'm being obedient, so why aren't things going better?" We face discomfort or inconvenience and immediately think either that we have misread God's will or that God has made a mistake. But watch this quiet couple as they head toward Bethlehem. God did not soften Joseph's bumpy road, but strengthened him. God did not provide a luxurious inn for Joseph and Mary, but brought his Son into the world in humble surroundings. When we do God's will, we are not guaranteed comfort and convenience. But we are

<table>
<tr><td>2:6
Matt 1:25
Gal 4:4</td><td>⁶And while they were there, the time came for her baby to be born. ⁷She gave birth to her first child, a son. She wrapped him snugly in strips of cloth and laid him in a manger, because there was no lodging available for them.</td></tr>
</table>

Shepherds Visit Jesus (10)

⁸That night there were shepherds staying in the fields nearby, guarding their flocks of sheep. ⁹Suddenly, an angel of the Lord appeared among them, and the radiance of the Lord's glory surrounded them. They were terrified, ¹⁰but the angel reassured them. "Don't be afraid!" he said. "I bring you good news that will bring great joy to all people. ¹¹The Savior—yes, the Messiah, the Lord—has been born today in Bethlehem, the city of David! ¹²And you will recognize him by this sign: You will find a baby wrapped snugly in strips of cloth, lying in a manger."

¹³Suddenly, the angel was joined by a vast host of others—the armies of heaven—praising God and saying,

¹⁴ "Glory to God in highest heaven,
    and peace on earth to those with whom God is pleased."

Left margin references:

2:9
Acts 5:19

2:11
John 4:42; 20:31

2:13
Ps 103:20
Rev 5:11

2:14
Isa 57:19
Luke 19:38

**DOUBTERS
IN THE BIBLE**

Doubter	Doubtful Moment	Reference
Abraham	When told he would be a father in old age	Genesis 17:17
Sarah	When she heard she would be a mother in old age	Genesis 18:12
Moses	When told to return to Egypt to lead the people	Exodus 3:10-15
Israelites	Whenever they faced difficulties in the wilderness	Exodus 16:1-3
Gideon	When told he would be a judge and leader	Judges 6:14-23
Zechariah	When told he would be a father in old age	Luke 1:18
Thomas	When told Jesus had risen from the dead	John 20:24, 25

Many of the people God used to accomplish great things started out as real doubters. With all of them, God showed great patience. Honest doubt was not a bad starting point as long as they didn't stay there. How great a part does doubt have in your willingness to trust God?

---

promised that everything, even discomfort and inconvenience, has meaning in God's plan. He will guide you and provide all you need. Like Joseph, live each day by faith, trusting that God is in charge.

2:7 Strips of cloth were used to keep a baby warm and give him a sense of security. These cloths were believed to protect his internal organs. The custom of wrapping infants this way is still practiced in many Mid-eastern countries.

2:7 This mention of the manger is the basis for the traditional belief that Jesus was born in a stable. Stables were often caves with feeding troughs (mangers) carved into the rock walls. Despite popular Christmas card pictures, the surroundings were dark and dirty. This was not the atmosphere the Jews expected as the birthplace of the Messiah-King. They thought their promised Messiah would be born in royal surroundings. We should not limit God by our expectations. He is at work wherever he is needed in our sindarkened and dirty world.

2:7 Although our first picture of Jesus is as a baby in a manger, it must not be our last. The Christ child in the manger is the subject of a beautiful Christmas scene, but we must not leave him there. This tiny, helpless baby lived an amazing life, died for us, ascended to heaven, and will return to earth as King of kings. Christ will rule the world and judge all people according to their decisions about him. Do you still picture Jesus as a baby in a manger—or is he your Lord? Make sure you don't underestimate Jesus. Let him grow up in your life.

• **2:8** God continued to reveal the news about his Son, but not to those we might expect. Luke records that Jesus' birth was announced to shepherds in the fields. These may have been the shepherds who supplied the lambs for the Temple sacrifices that were performed for the forgiveness of sin. Here the angels invited these shepherds to greet the Lamb of God (John 1:36), who would take away the sins of the world forever.

• **2:8-15** What a birth announcement! The shepherds were terrified, but their fear turned to joy as the angels announced the Messiah's birth. First the shepherds ran to see the baby; then they spread the word. Jesus is *your* Messiah, *your* Savior. Do you look forward to meeting him in prayer and in his Word each day? Have you discovered a Lord so wonderful that you can't help sharing your joy with your friends?

2:9, 10 The greatest event in history had just happened! The Messiah had been born! For ages the Jews had waited for this, and when it finally occurred, the announcement came to humble shepherds. The Good News about Jesus is that he comes to all, including the plain and the ordinary. He comes to anyone with a heart humble enough to accept him. Whoever you are, whatever you do, you can have Jesus in your life. Don't think you need extraordinary qualifications—he accepts you as you are.

2:11-14 Some of the Jews were waiting for a savior to deliver them from Roman rule; others hoped the Christ (Messiah) would deliver them from physical ailments. But Jesus, while healing their illnesses and establishing a spiritual Kingdom, delivered them from sin. His work is more far-reaching than anyone could imagine. Christ paid the price for sin and opened the way to peace with God. He offers us more than temporary political or physical changes—he offers us new hearts that will last for eternity.

2:14 The story of Jesus' birth resounds with music that has inspired composers for 2,000 years. The angels' song, often called the *Gloria* after its first word in the Latin translation, is the basis for many modern choral works, traditional Christmas carols, and ancient liturgical chants.

15When the angels had returned to heaven, the shepherds said to each other, "Let's go to Bethlehem! Let's see this thing that has happened, which the Lord has told us about."

16They hurried to the village and found Mary and Joseph. And there was the baby, lying in the manger. 17After seeing him, the shepherds told everyone what had happened and what the angel had said to them about this child. 18All who heard the shepherds' story were astonished, 19but Mary kept all these things in her heart and thought about them often. 20The shepherds went back to their flocks, glorifying and praising God for all they had heard and seen. It was just as the angel had told them.

2:17 Luke 2:10-12
2:19 Luke 2:51

Mary and Joseph Bring Jesus to the Temple (11)
21Eight days later, when the baby was circumcised, he was named Jesus, the name given him by the angel even before he was conceived.

22Then it was time for their purification offering, as required by the law of Moses after the birth of a child; so his parents took him to Jerusalem to present him to the Lord. 23The law of the Lord says, "If a woman's first child is a boy, he must be dedicated to the Lᴏʀᴅ."* 24So they offered the sacrifice required in the law of the Lord—"either a pair of turtledoves or two young pigeons."*

2:21 Gen 17:12 Lev 12:3 Matt 1:21
2:22 Lev 12:2-6
2:23 †Exod 13:2, 12, 15
2:24 †Lev 5:11; 12:8

The Prophecy of Simeon
25At that time there was a man in Jerusalem named Simeon. He was righteous and devout and was eagerly waiting for the Messiah to come and rescue Israel. The Holy Spirit was upon him 26and had revealed to him that he would not die until he had seen the Lord's Messiah. 27That day the Spirit led him to the Temple. So when Mary and Joseph came to present the baby Jesus to the Lord as the law required, 28Simeon was there. He took the child in his arms and praised God, saying,

2:25 †Isa 40:1; 49:13
2:26 Ps 89:48 John 8:51 Heb 11:5

29 "Sovereign Lord, now let your servant die in peace,
      as you have promised.
30 I have seen your salvation,
31   which you have prepared for all people.
32 He is a light to reveal God to the nations,
      and he is the glory of your people Israel!"

2:30-31 Isa 40:5; 52:10 Acts 4:12
2:32 Isa 42:6-7; 46:13; 49:6

33Jesus' parents were amazed at what was being said about him. 34Then Simeon blessed them, and he said to Mary, the baby's mother, "This child is destined to cause many in Israel to fall, but he will be a joy to many others. He has been sent as a sign from God, but many will oppose him. 35As a result, the deepest thoughts of many hearts will be revealed. And a sword will pierce your very soul."

2:34 Isa 8:14 1 Cor 1:23 1 Pet 2:7-8

2:23 Exod 13:2. **2:24** Lev 12:8.

2:21-24 Jewish families went through several ceremonies soon after a baby's birth: (1) *Circumcision.* Every boy was circumcised and named on the eighth day after birth (Leviticus 12:3; Luke 1:59, 60). Circumcision symbolized the Jews' separation from Gentiles and their unique relationship with God (see the note on 1:59). (2) *Redemption of the firstborn.* A firstborn son was presented to God one month after birth (Exodus 13:2, 11-16; Numbers 18:15, 16). The ceremony included buying back—"redeeming"—the child from God through an offering. This way, the parents acknowledged that the child belonged to God, who alone has the power to give life. (3) *Purification of the mother.* For 40 days after the birth of a son and 80 days after the birth of a daughter, the mother was ceremonially unclean and could not enter the Temple. At the end of her time of separation, the parents were to bring a lamb for a burnt offering and a dove or pigeon for a sin offering. The priest would sacrifice these animals and declare her to be clean. If a lamb was too expensive, the parents could bring a second dove or pigeon instead. This is what Mary and Joseph did.

Jesus was God's Son, but his family carried out these ceremonies according to God's law. Jesus was not born above the law; instead, he fulfilled it perfectly.

2:28-32 When Mary and Joseph brought Jesus to the Temple to be dedicated to God, they met an old man who told them what their child would become. Simeon's song is often called the *Nunc*

Dimittis, from the first words of its Latin translation. Simeon could die in peace because he had seen the Messiah.

2:32 The Jews were well acquainted with the Old Testament prophecies that spoke of the Messiah's blessings to their nation. They did not always give equal attention to the prophecies stating that he would bring salvation to the entire world, not just the Jews (see, for example, Isaiah 49:6). Many thought that Christ had come to save only his own people. Luke made sure his Greek audience understood that Christ had come to save *all* who believe, Gentiles as well as Jews.

2:33 Joseph and Mary were amazed when this old man took their son into his arms and spoke such stunning words. Simeon said that Jesus was a gift from God, and he recognized Jesus as the Messiah who would be a light to the entire world. This was at least the second time that Mary had been greeted with a prophecy about her son; the first time was when Elizabeth had welcomed her as the mother of her Lord (1:42-45).

2:34, 35 Simeon prophesied that Jesus would have a paradoxical effect on Israel. Some would fall because of him (see Isaiah 8:14, 15), while others would rise (see Malachi 4:2). With Jesus, there would be no neutral ground: People would either joyfully accept him or totally reject him. As Jesus' mother, Mary would be grieved by the widespread rejection he would face. This is the first note of sorrow in Luke's Gospel.

The Prophecy of Anna

2:37
1 Tim 5:5

2:38
Isa 52:9
Luke 1:68; 24:21

2:39
Matt 2:23

2:40
Luke 1:80

36Anna, a prophet, was also there in the Temple. She was the daughter of Phanuel from the tribe of Asher, and she was very old. Her husband died when they had been married only seven years. 37Then she lived as a widow to the age of eighty-four.* She never left the Temple but stayed there day and night, worshiping God with fasting and prayer. 38She came along just as Simeon was talking with Mary and Joseph, and she began praising God. She talked about the child to everyone who had been waiting expectantly for God to rescue Jerusalem.

39When Jesus' parents had fulfilled all the requirements of the law of the Lord, they returned home to Nazareth in Galilee. 40There the child grew up healthy and strong. He was filled with wisdom, and God's favor was on him.

Jesus Speaks with the Religious Teachers (15)

2:41
Exod 12:24-27
Deut 16:1-8

41Every year Jesus' parents went to Jerusalem for the Passover festival. 42When Jesus was twelve years old, they attended the festival as usual. 43After the celebration was over, they started home to Nazareth, but Jesus stayed behind in Jerusalem. His parents didn't miss him at first, 44because they assumed he was among the other travelers. But when he didn't show up that evening, they started looking for him among their relatives and friends.

45When they couldn't find him, they went back to Jerusalem to search for him there. 46Three days later they finally discovered him in the Temple, sitting among the religious teachers, listening to them and asking questions. 47All who heard him were amazed at his understanding and his answers.

2:47
Matt 7:28
John 7:15

2:37 Or *She had been a widow for eighty-four years.*

**TO FEAR OR
NOT TO FEAR**

Person	Reference	Person	Reference
Abraham	Genesis 15:1	Zechariah	Luke 1:13
Moses	Numbers 21:34	Mary	Luke 1:30
	Deuteronomy 3:2	Shepherds	Luke 2:10
Joshua	Joshua 8:1	Peter	Luke 5:10
Jeremiah	Lamentations 3:57	Paul	Acts 27:23, 24
Daniel	Daniel 10:12, 19	John	Revelation 1:17, 18

People in the Bible who were confronted by God or his angels all had one consistent response—fear. To each of them, God's response was always the same—don't be afraid. As soon as they sensed that God accepted them and wanted to communicate with them, their fear subsided. He had given them freedom to be his friends. He has given you the same freedom.

2:36 Although Simeon and Anna were very old, they had never lost their hope that they would see the Messiah. Led by the Holy Spirit, they were among the first to bear witness to Jesus. In the Jewish culture, elders were respected; thus, because of Simeon's and Anna's ages, their prophecies carried extra weight. In contrast, our society values youthfulness over wisdom, and contributions by the elderly are often ignored. As Christians, we should reverse those values wherever we can. Encourage older people to share their wisdom and experience. Listen carefully when they speak. Offer them your friendship, and help them find ways to continue to serve God.

2:36, 37 Anna was called a prophet, indicating that she was unusually close to God. Prophets did not necessarily predict the future. Their main role was to speak for God, proclaiming his truth.

2:39 Did Mary and Joseph return immediately to Nazareth, or did they remain in Bethlehem for a time (as implied in Matthew 2)? Apparently there is a gap of several years between verses 38 and 39—ample time for them to find a place to live in Bethlehem, flee to Egypt to escape Herod's wrath, and return to Nazareth when it was safe to do so.

2:41, 42 According to God's law, every male was required to go to Jerusalem three times a year for the great festivals (Deuteronomy 16:16). In the spring, the Passover was celebrated, followed immediately by the weeklong Festival of Unleavened Bread. Pass-over commemorated the night of the Jews' escape from Egypt when God had killed the Egyptian firstborn but had passed over Israelite homes (see Exodus 12:21-36). Passover was the most important of the three annual festivals.

2:43-45 At age 12, Jesus was considered almost an adult, so he probably didn't spend a lot of time with his parents during the festival. Those who attended these festivals often traveled in caravans for protection from robbers along the Palestine roads. The women and children usually would travel at the front of the caravan, with the men bringing up the rear. A 12-year-old boy conceivably could have been in either group, so both Mary and Joseph probably assumed that Jesus was with the other one. But when the caravan left Jerusalem, Jesus stayed behind, absorbed in his discussion with the religious leaders.

2:46, 47 The Temple courts were famous throughout Judea as a place of learning. The apostle Paul studied in Jerusalem, perhaps in the Temple courts, under Gamaliel, one of its foremost teachers (Acts 22:3). At the time of the Passover, the greatest rabbis of the land would assemble to teach and to discuss great truths among themselves. The coming Messiah would no doubt have been a popular discussion topic, for everyone was expecting him soon. Jesus would have been eager to listen and to ask probing questions. It was not his youth but the depth of his wisdom that astounded these teachers.

⁴⁸His parents didn't know what to think. "Son," his mother said to him, "why have you done this to us? Your father and I have been frantic, searching for you everywhere."

⁴⁹ "But why did you need to search?" he asked. "Didn't you know that I must be in my Father's house?"* ⁵⁰But they didn't understand what he meant.

⁵¹Then he returned to Nazareth with them and was obedient to them. And his mother stored all these things in her heart.

⁵²Jesus grew in wisdom and in stature and in favor with God and all the people.

John the Baptist Prepares the Way for Jesus (**16**/Matthew 3:1-12; Mark 1:1-8)

3 It was now the fifteenth year of the reign of Tiberius, the Roman emperor. Pontius Pilate was governor over Judea; Herod Antipas was ruler* over Galilee; his brother Philip was ruler* over Iturea and Traconitis; Lysanias was ruler over Abilene. ²Annas and Caiaphas were the high priests. At this time a message from God came to John son of Zechariah, who was living in the wilderness. ³Then John went from place to place on both sides of the Jordan River, preaching that people should be baptized to show that they had repented of their sins and turned to God to be forgiven. ⁴Isaiah had spoken of John when he said,

"He is a voice shouting in the wilderness,
'Prepare the way for the Lord's coming!
Clear the road for him!

2:48
Luke 3:23; 4:22
2:49
John 2:16
2:50
Mark 9:32
2:51
Luke 2:19
2:52
1 Sam 2:26
Prov 3:4
Luke 1:80
3:2
Luke 1:80
3:3
Acts 13:24; 19:4
3:4-6
†Isa 40:3-5

2:49 Or *"Didn't you realize that I should be involved with my Father's affairs?"*   **3:1a** Greek *Herod was tetrarch.* Herod Antipas was a son of King Herod.   **3:1b** Greek *tetrarch;* also in 3:1c.

2:48 Mary had to let go of her child and let him become a man, God's Son, the Messiah. Fearful that she hadn't been careful enough with this God-given child, she searched frantically for him. But she was looking for a boy, not the young man who was in the Temple astounding the religious leaders with his questions. Letting go of people or projects we have nurtured can be very difficult. It is both sweet and painful to see our children growing into adults, our students into teachers, our subordinates into managers, our inspirations into institutions. But when the time comes we must step back and let go—in spite of the hurt. Then our protégés can exercise their wings, take flight, and soar to the heights God intended for them.

• **2:49, 50** This is the first mention of Jesus' awareness that he was God's Son. But even though he knew his real Father, Jesus did not reject his earthly parents. He went back to Nazareth with them and lived under their authority for another 18 years. God's people do not despise human relationships or family responsibilities. If the Son of God obeyed his human parents, how much more should we honor our family members! Don't use commitment to God's work to justify neglecting your family.

2:50 Jesus' parents didn't understand what he meant about his Father's house. They didn't realize he was making a distinction between his earthly father and his heavenly Father. Jesus knew that he had a unique relationship with God. Although Mary and Joseph knew he was God's Son, they didn't understand what his mission would involve. Besides, they had to raise him, along with his brothers and sisters (Matthew 13:55, 56), as a normal child. They knew he was unique, but they did not know what was going on in his mind.

• **2:52** The Bible does not record any events of the next 18 years of Jesus' life, but Jesus undoubtedly was learning and maturing. As the oldest in a large family, he undoubtedly assisted Joseph in his carpentry work. Joseph may have died during this time, leaving Jesus to provide for the family. The normal routines of daily life gave Jesus a solid understanding of the Judean people.

• **2:52** The second chapter of Luke shows us that although Jesus was unique, he had a normal childhood and adolescence. In terms of development, he went through the same progression we do. He grew physically and mentally, he related to other people, and he was loved by God. A full human life is balanced. Thus it was important to Jesus—and it should be important to all believers—to develop fully and harmoniously in each of these key areas: physical, mental, social, and spiritual.

3:1 Tiberius, the Roman emperor, ruled from A.D. 14 to 37. Pilate

was the Roman governor responsible for the province of Judea; Herod Antipas and Philip were half brothers and sons of the cruel Herod the Great, who had been dead more than 20 years. Antipas, Philip, Pilate, and Lysanias apparently had equal powers in governing their separate territories. All were subject to Rome and responsible for keeping peace in their respective lands.

3:2 Jewish law provided for only one high priest. He was appointed from Aaron's line and held his position for life. By this time, however, the religious system had been corrupted, and the Roman government was appointing its own religious leaders to maintain greater control over the Jews. Apparently the Roman authorities had deposed the Jewish-appointed Annas and had replaced him with Annas's son-in-law, Caiaphas. Nevertheless Annas retained his title (see Acts 4:6) and probably also much of the power it carried. Because the Jews believed the high priest's position to be for life, they would have continued to call Annas their high priest.

3:2 This is John the Baptist, whose birth story is told in chapter 1. See his Profile in John 1, p. 1749.

3:2 Pilate, Herod, and Caiaphas were the most powerful leaders in Palestine, but they were upstaged by a wilderness prophet from rural Judea. God chose to speak through the loner, John the Baptist, who has gone down in history as greater than any of the rulers of his day. How often people judge others by the superficial standards of power, wealth, and beauty, and miss the truly great people through whom God works! Greatness is measured not by what you have but by your faith in God. Like John, give yourself entirely to God so God's power can work through you.

3:3 To turn to God to receive forgiveness from sins implies turning *away* from sins. We can't just say we believe and then live any way we choose (see 3:7, 8); neither can we simply live a morally correct life without a personal relationship with God because that cannot bring forgiveness from sin. Determine to rid your life of any sins God points out, and then determine to live in a way that pleases him.

3:4, 5 In John's day, before a king would take a trip, messengers would tell those he was planning to visit to prepare the roads for him. Similarly John told his listeners to make their lives ready so the Lord could come to them. This does not mean that you must get rid of all your sin or wrongdoing before you can accept Christ; rather, when you accept him, he takes care of all your sinfulness. To "prepare the way" means clearing aside the baggage of the past and the doubts of the present in order to let the King come into your life. He'll take it from there.

5 The valleys will be filled,
    and the mountains and hills made level.
The curves will be straightened,
    and the rough places made smooth.
6 And then all people will see
    the salvation sent from God.'"*

3:6
Luke 2:30-31
Acts 28:28
Titus 2:11

3:7
Matt 12:34; 23:33

3:8
John 8:33, 37, 39
Acts 3:25

7 When the crowds came to John for baptism, he said, "You brood of snakes! Who warned you to flee God's coming wrath? 8Prove by the way you live that you have repented of your

3:4-6 Isa 40:3-5 (Greek version).

In societies like Israel, in which a woman's value was largely measured by her ability to bear children, to be without children often led to personal hardship and public shame. For Elizabeth, a childless old age was a painful and lonely time but still she remained faithful to God.

Both Elizabeth and Zechariah came from priestly families. For two weeks each year, Zechariah had to go to the Temple in Jerusalem to attend to his priestly duties. After one of those trips, Zechariah returned home excited but speechless. He had to write down his good news, because he couldn't give it any other way. And what a wonderful surprise he had for his wife: Their faded dream would become an exciting reality! Soon Elizabeth became pregnant, and she knew her child was a long-hoped-for gift from God.

News traveled fast among the family. Seventy miles to the north, in Nazareth, Elizabeth's relative Mary also unexpectedly became pregnant. Within days after the angel's message that she would bear the Messiah, Mary went to visit Elizabeth. They were instantly bound together by the unique gifts God had given them. Elizabeth knew that Mary's son would be even greater than her own, for John would be the messenger for Mary's son.

When her baby was born, Elizabeth insisted on his God-given name: John. Zechariah's written agreement freed his tongue, and everyone in town wondered what would become of this obviously special child.

Elizabeth whispered her praise as she cared for God's gift. Knowing about Mary must have made her marvel at God's timing. Things had worked out even better than she could have planned. We, too, need to remember that God is in control of every situation. When did you last pause to recognize God's timing in the events of your life?

ELIZABETH

Strengths and accomplishments	• Known as a deeply spiritual woman • Showed no doubts about God's ability to fulfill his promise • Mother of John the Baptist • The first woman besides Mary to hear of the coming Savior
Lessons from her life	• God does not forget those who have been faithful to him • God's timetable and methods do not have to conform to what we expect
Vital statistics	• Occupation: Homemaker • Relatives: Husband: Zechariah. Son: John the Baptist. Relative: Mary. • Contemporaries: Joseph, Herod the Great
Key verses	"Why am I so honored, that the mother of my Lord should visit me? When I heard your greeting, the baby in my womb jumped for joy. You are blessed because you believed that the Lord would do what he said" (Luke 1:43-45).

Elizabeth's story is told in Luke 1:5-80.

3:6 This book was written to a non-Jewish audience. Luke quoted from Isaiah to show that salvation is for "all people," not just the Jews (Isaiah 40:3-5; 52:10). John the Baptist called everyone to prepare to meet Jesus. That includes you, no matter what your nationality, social standing, religious affiliation, or political position. God is calling to all people. Don't let feelings of being an outsider cause you to hold back. No one who wants to follow Jesus is an outsider in God's Kingdom.

3:7-9 Some people wanted to be baptized by John so they could escape eternal punishment, but they were not really repenting from sin nor were they willing to change the way they lived. John had harsh words for such people. He knew that God values reformation above ritual. Confession of sins and a changed life are inseparable. Faith without deeds is dead (James 2:14-26). Jesus also spoke harsh words to the respectable religious leaders who lacked the willingness to repent. They wanted to be known as religious authorities and they wanted eternal life, but they didn't want to repent of their sins. Thus, their lives were unproductive. Turning from sin must be tied to action. Following Jesus means more than saying the right words; it means acting on what he says.

3:8 Many of John's hearers were shocked when he said that being Abraham's descendants was not enough to ensure salvation. The religious leaders relied more on family lines than on faith for their standing with God. For them, religion was inherited. But a personal relationship with God cannot be handed down from parents to children. Everyone has to make a personal decision of whether or not to trust Christ. Don't rely on someone else's faith for your salvation. Have you made that personal decision to trust Christ?

sins and turned to God. Don't just say to each other, 'We're safe, for we are descendants of Abraham.' That means nothing, for I tell you, God can create children of Abraham from these very stones. 9Even now the ax of God's judgment is poised, ready to sever the roots of the trees. Yes, every tree that does not produce good fruit will be chopped down and thrown into the fire."

3:9
Matt 7:19
John 15:6

10The crowds asked, "What should we do?"

11John replied, "If you have two shirts, give one to the poor. If you have food, share it with those who are hungry."

3:11
Jas 2:15
1 Jn 3:17

12Even corrupt tax collectors came to be baptized and asked, "Teacher, what should we do?"

3:12
Luke 7:29

13He replied, "Collect no more taxes than the government requires."

3:13
Luke 19:8

14"What should we do?" asked some soldiers.

3:14
Exod 23:1
Lev 19:11

John replied, "Don't extort money or make false accusations. And be content with your pay."

15Everyone was expecting the Messiah to come soon, and they were eager to know whether John might be the Messiah. 16John answered their questions by saying, "I baptize you with* water; but someone is coming soon who is greater than I am—so much greater that I'm not even worthy to be his slave and untie the straps of his sandals. He will baptize you with the Holy Spirit and with fire.* 17He is ready to separate the chaff from the wheat with his winnowing fork. Then he will clean up the threshing area, gathering the wheat into his barn but burning the chaff with never-ending fire." 18John used many such warnings as he announced the Good News to the people.

3:16
Mark 1:4
John 1:26-27, 33
Acts 1:5; 2:3;
11:16; 13:25; 19:4

3:17
Matt 13:30

Herod Puts John in Prison (26)

19John also publicly criticized Herod Antipas, the ruler of Galilee,* for marrying Herodias, his brother's wife, and for many other wrongs he had done. 20So Herod put John in prison, adding this sin to his many others.

3:19-20
Matt 14:3
Mark 6:17

3:16a Or *in.* **3:16b** Or *in the Holy Spirit and in fire.* **3:19** Greek *Herod the tetrarch.*

3:11-14 John's message demanded at least three specific responses: (1) Share what you have with those who need it, (2) whatever your job is, do it well and with fairness, and (3) be content with your earnings. John had not been commissioned to bring comforting messages to those who lived sinful lives; he was calling the people to right living as he prepared the way for their Messiah. What changes can you make in sharing what you have, doing your work honestly and well, and being content?

3:12 Tax collectors were notorious for their dishonesty. Romans gathered funds for their government by farming out the collection privilege. Tax collectors earned their own living by adding a sizable sum—whatever they could get away with—to the total and keeping this money for themselves. Unless the people revolted and risked Roman retaliation, they had to pay whatever was demanded. Obviously the people hated the tax collectors, who were generally corrupt and greedy. Yet, said John, God would accept even these men; God desires to pour out mercy on those who confess their sins and then to give them strength to live changed lives.

3:12-14 John's message took root in unexpected places—among the poor, the dishonest, and even the hated occupation army. These people were painfully aware of their needs and they were honestly seeking to know what to do to change their lives. Did anyone follow John's advice? Surely some did, and their softened hearts became ready to receive the message of the One who was to come.

3:14 These soldiers were the Roman troops sent to keep peace in this distant province. Many of them oppressed the poor and used their power to take advantage of all the people. John called them to turn from their sins and change their ways.

• **3:15** Israel had not seen a prophet for more than 400 years. It was widely believed that when the Messiah would come, prophecy would reappear (Joel 2:28, 29; Malachi 3:1; 4:5). When John burst onto the scene, the people were excited. He was obviously a great prophet, and they were sure that the eagerly awaited age of the Messiah had come. Some, in fact, thought John himself was the

Messiah. John spoke like the prophets of old, saying that the people must turn from their sin to God to avoid punishment and to experience his mercy and approval. This is a message for all times and places, but John spoke it with particular urgency; he was preparing the people for the coming Messiah.

• **3:16** John's baptism with water symbolized the washing away of sins. His baptism followed his message of repentance and reformation. Jesus' baptism with fire equips one with power to do God's will. The baptism with the Holy Spirit was first given at Pentecost (Acts 2) when the Holy Spirit came upon believers in the form of tongues of fire, empowering them to proclaim Jesus' resurrection in many languages. The baptism with fire also symbolizes the work of the Holy Spirit in bringing God's judgment on those who refuse to repent.

3:17 John warned of impending judgment by comparing those who refuse to live for God to chaff, the useless outer husk of the grain. By contrast, John compared those who repent and reform their lives to the nourishing wheat itself. The winnowing fork was a pitchfork used to toss wheat so that the kernels would separate from the husks. Those who refuse to be used by God will be discarded because they have no value in furthering God's work. Those who repent and believe, however, hold great value in God's eyes because they are beginning a new life of productive service for him.

3:19, 20 In these two verses Luke flashes forward to continue his explanation about John the Baptist. (See the Harmony of the Gospels for the chronological order of events.) This is Herod Antipas (see Mark 6, p. 1629 for his Profile). Herodias was Herod's niece and also his brother's wife. She would treacherously plot John the Baptist's death (Matthew 14:1-12). The Herods were a murderous and deceitful family. Rebuking a tyrannical Roman official who could imprison and execute him was extremely dangerous, yet that is what John did. Herod seemingly would have the last word, but the story is not finished. At the Last Judgment, Herod, not John, will face God's punishment—for eternity.

The Baptism of Jesus (**17**/Matthew 3:13-17; Mark 1:9-11)

3:22
Gen 22:2
Ps 2:7
Isa 42:1
Matt 12:18; 17:5
Mark 9:7
Luke 9:35
2 Pet 1:17

²¹One day when the crowds were being baptized, Jesus himself was baptized. As he was praying, the heavens opened, ²² and the Holy Spirit, in bodily form, descended on him like a dove. And a voice from heaven said, "You are my dearly loved Son, and you bring me great joy.*"

3:22 Some manuscripts read *my Son, and today I have become your Father.*

SIMEON/ANNA

When Joseph and Mary took the eight-day-old Jesus to the Temple for his circumcision, they had two unexpected but delightful encounters. Well-worn examples of patient waiting met them—Simeon and Anna. Both of these godly saints recognized Jesus' identity as the Messiah. Simeon and Anna give us a picture of godly expectation in an environment ripe with expectations.

Simeon was certain he would see the Messiah before he died. We don't know how surprised he was to discover the Savior as a baby in Mary's arms. We do know that he recognized Jesus and gave God praise for his faithfulness. When Simeon saw the baby, he considered his life complete.

Simeon's exuberance caught Anna's attention. She was another regular in the Temple. Anna's brief marriage ended in widowhood and she spent the remainder of her eighty-four plus years serving as a prophetess. Anna overheard Simeon's prophecy about Jesus and immediately added her own excited words of praise for the Savior.

Anna discovered that God can make every passage of life meaningful and useful. The long years of widowhood were also effective years of worship and service. Both she and Simeon dedicated their lives to God and were rewarded in ways we can only fully appreciate if we are willing to live the same way.

As you interact with people at various stages of life today, think about the development of your relationship with God. When talking to a younger person, ask yourself: "How was God involved in my life at that age?" When noticing someone older ask: "How do I want my relationship with God to mature by that point in my life?"

Strengths and accomplishments	• Exercised faithful anticipation regarding God's promised Messiah • Did not hesitate to give praise to God for his work in the world • Both spoke from the powerful authority of their faith and age
Lessons from their lives	• God does give to some of his faithful followers a deeper insight and clarity about his plans • There were those in Israel who did recognize Jesus • Advancing age does not invalidate a person's usefulness in God's purposes
Vital statistics	• Where: Jerusalem • Contemporaries: Joseph, Mary, Herod the Great
Key verses	"The Holy Spirit was upon [Simeon] and had revealed to him that he would not die until he had seen the Lord's Messiah. . . . [Anna] never left the Temple but stayed there day and night, worshiping God with fasting and prayer" (Luke 2:25-26, 37).

Simeon and Anna's stories are told in Luke 2:21-38.

3:21 Luke emphasizes Jesus' human nature. Jesus was born to humble parents, a birth unannounced except to shepherds and foreigners. This baptism recorded here was the first public declaration of Jesus' ministry. Instead of going to Jerusalem and identifying with the established religious leaders, Jesus went to a river and identified with those who were repenting of sin. When Jesus, at age 12, had visited the Temple, he had understood his mission (2:49). Eighteen years later, at his baptism, he began carrying it out. And as Jesus prayed, God spoke and confirmed his decision to act. God was breaking into human history through Jesus the Christ.

3:21, 22 Theologians have long been troubled by Jesus' allowing himself to be baptized by John. After all, this baptism was for sinners. Why, then, did Jesus do it? He did it because he is both God and human—he underwent baptism and even death as only a human could; he lived a sinless life and rose from the dead as only God could. This baptism by John in the Jordan River was another step in his identification with us sinful people; and the arrival of the dove signifies God's approval. Now Jesus would officially begin his ministry as God's beloved Son walking

the dusty roads of Israel. When you are hurting, depressed, broken, remember: You have a Savior who understands your humanity. When you sin, remember: He has paid the price for your disobedience.

3:21, 22 This is one of several places in Scripture where all the members of the Trinity are mentioned—Father, Son, and Holy Spirit. In the traditional words of the church, the one God exists in three persons but one substance, coeternal and coequal. No explanation can adequately portray the power and intricacy of this unique relationship. There are no perfect analogies in nature because there is no other relationship like the Trinity.

The Record of Jesus' Ancestors (**3**/Matthew 1:1-17)

²³Jesus was about thirty years old when he began his public ministry.

> **3:23**
> Luke 4:22
> John 6:42

Jesus was known as the son of Joseph.
Joseph was the son of Heli.

²⁴ Heli was the son of Matthat.
Matthat was the son of Levi.
Levi was the son of Melki.
Melki was the son of Jannai.
Jannai was the son of Joseph.

²⁵ Joseph was the son of Mattathias.
Mattathias was the son of Amos.
Amos was the son of Nahum.
Nahum was the son of Esli.
Esli was the son of Naggai.

²⁶ Naggai was the son of Maath.
Maath was the son of Mattathias.
Mattathias was the son of Semein.
Semein was the son of Josech.
Josech was the son of Joda.

²⁷ Joda was the son of Joanan.
Joanan was the son of Rhesa.
Rhesa was the son of Zerubbabel.
Zerubbabel was the son of Shealtiel.
Shealtiel was the son of Neri.

> **3:27**
> 1 Chr 3:17
> Ezra 3:2

²⁸ Neri was the son of Melki.
Melki was the son of Addi.
Addi was the son of Cosam.
Cosam was the son of Elmadam.
Elmadam was the son of Er.

²⁹ Er was the son of Joshua.
Joshua was the son of Eliezer.
Eliezer was the son of Jorim.
Jorim was the son of Matthat.
Matthat was the son of Levi.

³⁰ Levi was the son of Simeon.
Simeon was the son of Judah.
Judah was the son of Joseph.
Joseph was the son of Jonam.
Jonam was the son of Eliakim.

³¹ Eliakim was the son of Melea.
Melea was the son of Menna.
Menna was the son of Mattatha.
Mattatha was the son of Nathan.
Nathan was the son of David.

> **3:31-33**
> Ruth 4:18-22
> 1 Sam 16:1, 13
> 2 Sam 5:14
> 1 Chr 2:9-12; 3:5

³² David was the son of Jesse.
Jesse was the son of Obed.
Obed was the son of Boaz.

• **3:23** Imagine the Savior of the world working in a small-town carpenter's shop until he was 30 years old! It seems incredible that Jesus would have been content to remain in Nazareth all that time, but he patiently trusted his Father's timing for his life and ministry. Thirty was the prescribed age for priests to begin their ministry (Numbers 4:3). Joseph was 30 years old when he began serving the king of Egypt (Genesis 41:46), and David was 30 years old when he began to reign over Judah (2 Samuel 5:4). Age 30, then, was a good time to begin an important task in the Jewish culture. Like Jesus, we need to resist the temptation to jump ahead before receiving the Spirit's direction. Are you waiting and wondering what your next step should be? Don't jump ahead—trust God's timing.

3:23-38 Matthew's genealogy goes back to Abraham and shows that Jesus was related to all Jews (Matthew 1). Luke's genealogy goes back to Adam, showing that Jesus is related to all human beings. This is consistent with Luke's picture of Jesus as the Savior of the whole world.

Boaz was the son of Salmon.*

Salmon was the son of Nahshon.

33 Nahshon was the son of Amminadab.

Amminadab was the son of Admin.

Admin was the son of Arni.*

Arni was the son of Hezron.

Hezron was the son of Perez.

Perez was the son of Judah.

3:34-36
Gen 11:10-26
1 Chr 1:24-27

34 Judah was the son of Jacob.

Jacob was the son of Isaac.

Isaac was the son of Abraham.

Abraham was the son of Terah.

Terah was the son of Nahor.

35 Nahor was the son of Serug.

Serug was the son of Reu.

Reu was the son of Peleg.

Peleg was the son of Eber.

Eber was the son of Shelah.

3:32 Greek *Sala,* a variant spelling of Salmon; also in 3:32b. See Ruth 4:22. **3:33** Some manuscripts read *Amminadab was the son of Aram. Arni* and *Aram* are alternate spellings of Ram. See 1 Chr 2:9-10.

MARY

Motherhood is a painful privilege. Young Mary of Nazareth had the unique privilege of being mother to the very Son of God. Yet the pains and pleasures of her motherhood can be understood by mothers everywhere. Mary was the only human present at Jesus' birth who also witnessed his death. She saw him arrive as her baby son, and she watched him die as her Savior.

Until Gabriel's unexpected visit, Mary's life was quite satisfactory. She had recently become engaged to a carpenter, Joseph, and was anticipating married life. But her life was about to change forever.

Angels don't usually make appointments before visiting. Feeling as if she were being congratulated for winning the grand prize in a contest she had never entered, Mary found the angel's greeting puzzling and his presence frightening. What she heard next was the news almost every woman in Israel hoped to hear—that her child would be the Messiah, God's promised Savior. Mary did not doubt the message but rather asked how pregnancy would be possible. Gabriel told her the baby would be God's Son. Her answer was the one God waits in vain to hear from so many other people: "I am the Lord's servant. May everything you have said about me come true" (Luke 1:38). Later her song of joy shows us how well she knew God, for her thoughts were filled with his words from the Old Testament.

When he was eight days old Jesus was taken to the Temple to be dedicated to God. There Joseph and Mary were met by two devout people, Simeon and Anna, who recognized the child as the Messiah and praised God. Simeon directed some words to Mary that must have come to her mind many times in the years that followed: "A sword will pierce your very soul" (Luke 2:35). A big part of her painful privilege of motherhood would be to see her son rejected and crucified by the people he came to save.

We can imagine that even if she had known all she would suffer as Jesus' mother, Mary would still have given the same response. Are you, like Mary, available to be used by God?

Strengths and accomplishments	• The mother of Jesus, the Messiah • The one human who was with Jesus from birth to death • Willing to be available to God • Knew and applied Old Testament Scriptures
Lessons from her life	• God's best servants are often ordinary people who make themselves available to him • God's plans involve extraordinary events in ordinary people's lives • A person's character is revealed by his or her response to the unexpected
Vital statistics	• Where: Nazareth, Bethlehem • Occupation: Homemaker • Relatives: Husband: Joseph. Relatives: Zechariah and Elizabeth. Children: Jesus, James, Joseph, Judas, Simon, and daughters.
Key verse	"Mary responded, 'I am the Lord's servant. May everything you have said about me come true.' And then the angel left her" (Luke 1:38).

Mary's story is told throughout the Gospels. She is also mentioned in Acts 1:14.

36 Shelah was the son of Cainan.
   Cainan was the son of Arphaxad.
   Arphaxad was the son of Shem.
   Shem was the son of Noah.
   Noah was the son of Lamech.
37 Lamech was the son of Methuselah.
   Methuselah was the son of Enoch.
   Enoch was the son of Jared.
   Jared was the son of Mahalalel.
   Mahalalel was the son of Kenan.
38 Kenan was the son of Enosh.*
   Enosh was the son of Seth.
   Seth was the son of Adam.
   Adam was the son of God.

3:36-38
Gen 4:25–5:32
1 Chr 1:1-4

3:38
Gen 1:26-27;
2:7; 5:1-2

Satan Tempts Jesus in the Wilderness (18/Matthew 4:1-11; Mark 1:12-13)

4 Then Jesus, full of the Holy Spirit, returned from the Jordan River. He was led by the Spirit in the wilderness,* ²where he was tempted by the devil for forty days. Jesus ate nothing all that time and became very hungry.

³Then the devil said to him, "If you are the Son of God, tell this stone to become a loaf of bread."

4:1
Isa 11:2; 61:1
4:2
Exod 34:28
1 Kgs 19:8
Heb 4:15

3:38 Greek *Enos*, a variant spelling of Enoch; also in 3:38b. See Gen 5:6.   **4:1** Some manuscripts read *into the wilderness.*

4:1 Sometimes we feel that if the Holy Spirit leads us, it will always be "beside peaceful streams" (Psalm 23:2). But that is not necessarily true. He led Jesus into the wilderness for a long and difficult time of testing, and he may also lead us into difficult situations. When facing trials, first make sure you haven't brought them on yourself through sin or unwise choices. If you find no sin to confess or unwise behavior to change, then ask God to strengthen you for your test. Finally, be careful to follow faithfully wherever the Holy Spirit leads.

4:1, 2 The devil, who tempted Adam and Eve in the garden, also tempted Jesus in the wilderness. Satan is a real being, a created but rebellious fallen angel, and not a symbol or an idea. He constantly fights against God and those who follow and obey God. Jesus was a prime target for the devil's temptations. Satan had succeeded with Adam and Eve, and he hoped to succeed with Jesus as well.

4:1-13 Knowing and obeying God's Word is an effective weapon against temptation, the only *offensive* weapon provided in the

Christian's "armor" (Ephesians 6:17). Jesus used Scripture to counter Satan's attacks, and so should we. But to use it effectively, we must have faith in God's promises because Satan also knows Scripture and is adept at twisting it to suit his purposes. Obeying the Scriptures is more important than simply having a verse to quote, so read them daily and apply them to your life. Then your "sword" will always be sharp.

• **4:2** Why was it necessary for Jesus to be tempted? First, temptation is part of the human experience. For Jesus to be fully human, for him to understand us completely, he had to face temptation (see Hebrews 4:15). Second, Jesus had to undo Adam's work. Adam, though created perfect, gave in to temptation and passed sin on to the whole human race. Jesus, by contrast, resisted Satan. His victory offers salvation to all of Adam's descendants (see Romans 5:12-19).

4:3 Satan may tempt us to doubt Christ's true identity. He knows that once we begin to question whether or not Jesus is God, it's far easier to get us to do what he wants. Times of questioning can help us sort out our beliefs and strengthen our faith, but those times can also be dangerous. If you are dealing with doubt, be aware that you are especially vulnerable to temptation. Even as you search for answers, protect yourself by meditating on the unshakable truths of God's Word.

4:3 Sometimes what we are tempted to do isn't wrong in itself. Turning a stone into bread wasn't necessarily bad. The sin was not in the act but in the reason behind it. The devil was trying to get Jesus to take a shortcut, to solve Jesus' immediate problem at the expense of his long-range goals, to seek comfort at the sacrifice of his discipline. Satan often works that way—persuading us to take action, even right action, for the wrong reason or at the wrong time. The fact that something is not wrong in itself does not mean that it is good for you at a given time. Many people sin by attempting to fulfill legitimate desires outside of God's will or ahead of his timetable. First ask: Is the Holy Spirit leading me to do this or is Satan trying to get me off the track?

4:3ff Often we are tempted not through our weaknesses, but through our strengths. The devil tempted Jesus where he was strong. Jesus had power over stones, the kingdoms of the world, and even angels, and Satan wanted him to use that power without regard for his mission. When we give in to the devil and wrongly use our strengths, we become proud and self-reliant. Trusting in our own powers, we feel little need of God. To avoid this trap, we

JESUS' TEMPTATION AND RETURN TO GALILEE

Jesus was tempted by Satan in the rough Judean wilderness before returning to his boyhood home, Nazareth. John's Gospel tells of Jesus' journeys in Galilee, Samaria, and Judea (see John 1–4) before he moved to Capernaum to set up his base of operations (see Matthew 4:12, 13).

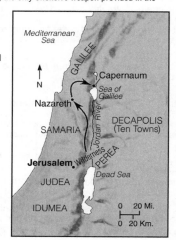

4:4
†Deut 8:3

4:6
Matt 28:18
John 12:31; 14:30
1 Jn 5:19
Rev 13:2

4:8
†Deut 6:13; 10:20

4:10-11
†Ps 91:11-12

4:12
†Deut 6:16

4:13
Heb 4:15

⁴But Jesus told him, "No! The Scriptures say, 'People do not live by bread alone.'*"

⁵Then the devil took him up and revealed to him all the kingdoms of the world in a moment of time. ⁶"I will give you the glory of these kingdoms and authority over them," the devil said, "because they are mine to give to anyone I please. ⁷I will give it all to you if you will worship me."

⁸Jesus replied, "The Scriptures say,

'You must worship the LORD your God
  and serve only him.'*"

⁹Then the devil took him to Jerusalem, to the highest point of the Temple, and said, "If you are the Son of God, jump off! ¹⁰For the Scriptures say,

'He will order his angels to protect and guard you.
¹¹ And they will hold you up with their hands
  so you won't even hurt your foot on a stone.'*"

¹²Jesus responded, "The Scriptures also say, 'You must not test the LORD your God.'*"
¹³When the devil had finished tempting Jesus, he left him until the next opportunity came.

B. MESSAGE AND MINISTRY OF JESUS, THE SAVIOR (4:14—21:38)

Luke accurately records the actions and teachings of Christ, helping us understand the way of salvation. Much unique material appears in Luke, especially the parables of Jesus. Jesus came to teach us how to live and how to find salvation. How carefully, then, we should study the words and life of our Savior.

1. Jesus' ministry in Galilee

Jesus Preaches in Galilee **(30**/Matthew 4:12-17; Mark 1:14-15; John 4:43-45)
¹⁴Then Jesus returned to Galilee, filled with the Holy Spirit's power. Reports about him spread quickly through the whole region. ¹⁵He taught regularly in their synagogues and was praised by everyone.

Jesus Is Rejected at Nazareth **(32)**
¹⁶When he came to the village of Nazareth, his boyhood home, he went as usual to the synagogue on the Sabbath and stood up to read the Scriptures. ¹⁷The scroll of Isaiah the prophet was handed to him. He unrolled the scroll and found the place where this was written:

4:4 Deut 8:3.   **4:8** Deut 6:13.   **4:10-11** Ps 91:11-12.   **4:12** Deut 6:16.

must realize that all our strengths are God's gifts to us, and we must dedicate those strengths to his service.

4:6, 7 The devil arrogantly hoped to succeed in his rebellion against God by diverting Jesus from his mission and winning his worship. "This world is mine, not God's," he was saying, "and if you hope to do anything worthwhile here, you'll need to follow my instructions." Jesus didn't argue with Satan about who owns the world, but Jesus refused to validate Satan's claim by worshiping him. Jesus knew that he would redeem the world through giving up his life on the cross, not through making an alliance with a corrupt angel.

4:9-11 Here the devil misinterpreted Scripture. The intention of Psalm 91 is to show God's protection of his people, not to incite them to use God's power for sensational or foolish displays.

4:13 Christ's defeat of the devil in the wilderness was decisive but not final. Throughout his ministry, Jesus would confront Satan in many forms. Too often we see temptation as once and for all. In reality, we need to be constantly on guard against the devil's ongoing attacks. Where are you most susceptible to temptation right now? How are you preparing to withstand it?

4:13 What would it take for you to "sell out"? What is there in life that would cause you to compromise your faith? Whatever it is—sexual temptation, financial inducement, fear of alienating or offending someone—it will be placed in your path at some point. The enemy wants to destroy believers or at least neutralize them through sin, shame, and guilt. When that temptation rears its seductive head, do what Jesus did: rely on the Word of God and stand fast in your commitment to worship God alone, above all else. No matter the cost or the sacrifice, no matter how

appealing the come-on, believers must follow Jesus' example and stand strong.

4:15, 16 Synagogues were very important in Jewish religious life. During the Exile when the Jews no longer had their Temple, synagogues were established as places of worship on the Sabbath and as schools for young boys during the week. Synagogues continued to exist even after the Temple was rebuilt. A synagogue could be set up in any town with at least 10 Jewish families. It was administered by one leader and an assistant. At the synagogue, the leader often would invite a visiting rabbi to read from the Scriptures and to teach. Itinerant rabbis, like Jesus, were always welcome to speak to those gathered each Sabbath in the synagogues. The apostle Paul also took advantage of this practice (see Acts 13:5; 14:1).

4:16 Jesus went to the synagogue "as usual." Even though he was the perfect Son of God and his local synagogue undoubtedly left much to be desired, Jesus attended services every week. His example makes our excuses for not attending church sound weak and self-serving. Make regular worship a part of your life.

4:17-21 Jesus was quoting from Isaiah 61:1, 2. Isaiah pictures the deliverance of Israel from exile in Babylon as a Year of Jubilee when all debts are cancelled, all slaves are freed, and all property is returned to original owners (Leviticus 25). But the release from Babylonian exile had not brought the expected fulfillment; they were still a conquered and oppressed people. So Isaiah must have been referring to a future messianic age. Jesus boldly announced, "The Scripture you've just heard has been fulfilled this very day!" Jesus was proclaiming himself as the one who would bring this Good News to pass, but he would do so in a way that the people were not yet able to grasp.

18 "The Spirit of the LORD is upon me,
    for he has anointed me to bring Good News to the poor.
He has sent me to proclaim that captives will be released,
    that the blind will see,
that the oppressed will be set free,
19   and that the time of the LORD's favor has come.*"

4:18-19
†Isa 61:1-2

20He rolled up the scroll, handed it back to the attendant, and sat down. All eyes in the synagogue looked at him intently. 21 Then he began to speak to them. "The Scripture you've just heard has been fulfilled this very day!"

4:19
Lev 25:8-10
2 Cor 6:2

22Everyone spoke well of him and was amazed by the gracious words that came from his lips. "How can this be?" they asked. "Isn't this Joseph's son?"

4:22
Luke 2:47
John 6:42; 7:15

23 Then he said, "You will undoubtedly quote me this proverb: 'Physician, heal yourself'—meaning, 'Do miracles here in your hometown like those you did in Capernaum.' 24But I tell you the truth, no prophet is accepted in his own hometown.

4:23
Matt 4:13; 11:23
Mark 1:21-28;
2:1-12

25 "Certainly there were many needy widows in Israel in Elijah's time, when the heavens were closed for three and a half years, and a severe famine devastated the land. 26 Yet Elijah was not sent to any of them. He was sent instead to a foreigner—a widow of Zarephath in the land of Sidon. 27And there were many lepers in Israel in the time of the prophet Elisha, but the only one healed was Naaman, a Syrian."

4:24
Matt 13:57
Mark 6:4
John 4:44

4:25-26
1 Kgs 17:1-9; 18:1
Jas 5:17

4:27
2 Kgs 5:1-14

28When they heard this, the people in the synagogue were furious. 29 Jumping up, they mobbed him and forced him to the edge of the hill on which the town was built. They intended to push him over the cliff, 30 but he passed right through the crowd and went on his way.

4:29
Num 15:35
Acts 7:58
Heb 13:12

4:30
John 8:59

Jesus Teaches with Authority (**34**/Mark 1:21-28)

31 Then Jesus went to Capernaum, a town in Galilee, and taught there in the synagogue every Sabbath day. 32 There, too, the people were amazed at his teaching, for he spoke with authority.

4:31
Matt 4:13-16
John 2:12

33Once when he was in the synagogue, a man possessed by a demon—an evil* spirit—began shouting at Jesus, 34"Go away! Why are you interfering with us, Jesus of Nazareth? Have you come to destroy us? I know who you are—the Holy One of God!"

4:32
Matt 7:28-29
John 7:46

4:34
Luke 4:41
John 6:69

35 Jesus cut him short. "Be quiet! Come out of the man," he ordered. At that, the demon threw the man to the floor as the crowd watched; then it came out of him without hurting him further.

4:35
Luke 4:39-41

36Amazed, the people exclaimed, "What authority and power this man's words possess! Even evil spirits obey him, and they flee at his command!" 37 The news about Jesus spread through every village in the entire region.

4:18-19 Or *and to proclaim the acceptable year of the LORD.* Isa 61:1-2 (Greek version); 58:6. **4:33** Greek *unclean;* also in 4:36.

• **4:24** Even Jesus himself was not accepted as a prophet in his hometown. Many people have a similar attitude. Don't be surprised if your Christian life and faith are not easily understood or accepted by those who know you well. Because they know your background, your failures, and your foibles, they may not see past those to the new person you have become. Let God work in your life, pray to be a positive witness for him, and be patient.

4:28 Jesus' remarks angered the people of Nazareth because he was saying that God sometimes chose to reach Gentiles rather than Jews. Jesus implied that his hearers were as unbelieving as the citizens of the northern kingdom of Israel in the days of Elijah and Elisha, a time notorious for its great wickedness.

4:31 Jesus had recently moved to Capernaum from Nazareth (Matthew 4:13). Capernaum was a thriving city with great wealth as well as great decadence. Because it was the headquarters for many Roman troops, word about Jesus could spread all over the Roman Empire from there.

4:33 A man possessed by a demon was in the synagogue where Jesus was teaching. This man made his way into the place of worship and verbally abused Jesus. It is naive to think that we will be sheltered from evil in the church. Satan is happy to invade our presence wherever and whenever he can. But Jesus' authority is much greater than Satan's, and where Jesus is present, demons cannot stay for long.

4:34-36 The people were amazed at Jesus' authority to drive out demons—evil spirits ruled by Satan and sent to harass people, tempt them to sin, and ultimately destroy them. Demons are fallen angels who have joined Satan in rebellion against God. Jesus faced many demons during his time on earth, and he always exerted authority over them. Not only did the evil spirit leave this man; Luke records that the man was not even injured.

While we may not often see cases of demon possession today, it does still exist. However, we would not doubt that evil permeates our world. We need not be fearful, however. Jesus' power is far greater than Satan's. The first step toward conquering fear of evil is to recognize Jesus' authority and power. He has overcome all evil, including Satan himself.

Jesus Heals Peter's Mother-in-Law and Many Others
(35/Matthew 8:14-17; Mark 1:29-34)

³⁸After leaving the synagogue that day, Jesus went to Simon's home, where he found Simon's mother-in-law very sick with a high fever. "Please heal her," everyone begged. ³⁹Standing at her bedside, he rebuked the fever, and it left her. And she got up at once and prepared a meal for them.

⁴⁰As the sun went down that evening, people throughout the village brought sick family members to Jesus. No matter what their diseases were, the touch of his hand healed every one. ⁴¹Many were possessed by demons; and the demons came out at his command, shouting, "You are the Son of God!" But because they knew he was the Messiah, he rebuked them and refused to let them speak.

Jesus Preaches throughout Galilee (36/Matthew 4:23-25; Mark 1:35-39)

⁴²Early the next morning Jesus went out to an isolated place. The crowds searched everywhere for him, and when they finally found him, they begged him not to leave them. ⁴³But he replied, "I must preach the Good News of the Kingdom of God in other towns, too, because that is why I was sent." ⁴⁴So he continued to travel around, preaching in synagogues throughout Judea.*

Jesus Provides a Miraculous Catch of Fish (37)

5 One day as Jesus was preaching on the shore of the Sea of Galilee,* great crowds pressed in on him to listen to the word of God. ²He noticed two empty boats at the water's edge, for the fishermen had left them and were washing their nets. ³Stepping into one of the boats, Jesus asked Simon,* its owner, to push it out into the water. So he sat in the boat and taught the crowds from there.

⁴When he had finished speaking, he said to Simon, "Now go out where it is deeper, and let down your nets to catch some fish."

⁵"Master," Simon replied, "we worked hard all last night and didn't catch a thing. But if you say so, I'll let the nets down again." ⁶And this time their nets were so full of fish they began to tear! ⁷A shout for help brought their partners in the other boat, and soon both boats were filled with fish and on the verge of sinking.

4:44 Some manuscripts read *Galilee.* **5:1** Greek *Lake Gennesaret*, another name for the Sea of Galilee.
5:3 *Simon* is called "Peter" in 6:14 and thereafter.

4:40-41
Matt 8:16-17
Mark 1:32-34
4:41
Mark 3:11

4:42-44
Matt 4:23
4:43
Luke 8:1
4:44
Matt 4:23
Mark 1:39

5:4
John 21:6

5:5
John 21:3
5:6
John 21:11

• **4:39** Jesus healed Simon's (Peter's) mother-in-law so completely that not only did the fever leave but her strength was restored, and immediately she got up and took care of others' needs. What a beautiful attitude of service she showed! God gives us health so that we may serve others.

• **4:40** The people came to Jesus when the sun was setting because this was the Sabbath (4:31), their day of rest. Sabbath lasted from sunset on Friday to sunset on Saturday. The people didn't want to break the law that prohibited travel on the Sabbath, so they waited until the sun set on the Sabbath before coming to Jesus. Then, as Luke the physician notes, they came with all kinds of diseases, and Jesus healed each one.

4:40 When you've faced a particularly difficult time, what helped you most? While some may have said kind words, most likely it was the presence of a friend and his or her touch. A hug, an arm around your shoulder, or even just a hand laid gently on top of yours—these simple wordless gestures mean so much to those in pain. In healing the sick and the demon possessed, Jesus had already demonstrated that he could heal with just a word (4:39). Yet here in Capernaum, Luke records that the touch of Jesus' hand healed the sick. Why not just speak a word and heal the whole crowd at once? Why go to all the trouble of treating each person individually, face-to-face? Because human touch is so very important. Does someone need a touch from you today?

4:41 Why didn't Jesus want the demons to reveal who he was? (1) Jesus commanded them to remain silent to show his authority over them. (2) Jesus wanted his listeners to believe he was the Messiah because of his words, not because of the demons' words. (3) Jesus was going to reveal his identity according to God's timetable, and he would not be pushed by Satan's evil

plans. The demons called Jesus "Son of God" or "the Holy One sent from God" (4:34) because they knew he was the Christ. But Jesus was going to show himself to be the suffering servant before he became the great King. To reveal his identity as King too soon would stir up the crowds with the wrong expectations of what he had come to do.

4:42 Jesus had to get up very early just to get some time alone. If Jesus needed solitude for prayer and refreshment, how much more is this true for us? Don't become so busy that life turns into a flurry of activity leaving no room for quiet fellowship alone with God. No matter how much you have to do, you should always have time for prayer.

4:43 The Kingdom of God is Good News! It was Good News to the Jews because they had been awaiting the coming of the promised Messiah ever since the Babylonian captivity. It is Good News for us also because it means freedom from slavery to sin and selfishness. The Kingdom of God is here and now because the Holy Spirit lives in the hearts of believers. Yet it is also in the future because Jesus will return to reign over a perfect Kingdom, where sin and evil will no longer exist.

5:2 Fishermen on the Sea of Galilee used nets, often bell-shaped ones with lead weights around the edges. A net would be thrown flat onto the water, and the lead weights would cause it to sink around the fish. Then the fishermen would pull on a cord, drawing the net around the fish. Nets had to be kept in good condition, so they would be washed to remove weeds and then mended.

⁸When Simon Peter realized what had happened, he fell to his knees before Jesus and said, "Oh, Lord, please leave me—I'm too much of a sinner to be around you." ⁹For he was awestruck by the number of fish they had caught, as were the others with him. ¹⁰His partners, James and John, the sons of Zebedee, were also amazed.

5:8
Gen 18:27
Job 42:5-6

Jesus replied to Simon, "Don't be afraid! From now on you'll be fishing for people!" ¹¹And as soon as they landed, they left everything and followed Jesus.

5:11
Matt 19:27

Jesus Heals a Man with Leprosy (38/Matthew 8:1-4; Mark 1:40-45)

¹²In one of the villages, Jesus met a man with an advanced case of leprosy. When the man saw Jesus, he bowed with his face to the ground, begging to be healed. "Lord," he said, "if you are willing, you can heal me and make me clean."

¹³Jesus reached out and touched him. "I am willing," he said. "Be healed!" And instantly the leprosy disappeared. ¹⁴Then Jesus instructed him not to tell anyone what had happened. He said, "Go to the priest and let him examine you. Take along the offering required in the law of Moses for those who have been healed of leprosy.* This will be a public testimony that you have been cleansed."

5:14
Lev 14:2-32

¹⁵But despite Jesus' instructions, the report of his power spread even faster, and vast crowds came to hear him preach and to be healed of their diseases. ¹⁶But Jesus often withdrew to the wilderness for prayer.

5:15
Matt 9:26

Jesus Heals a Paralyzed Man (39/Matthew 9:1-8; Mark 2:1-12)

¹⁷One day while Jesus was teaching, some Pharisees and teachers of religious law were sitting nearby. (It seemed that these men showed up from every village in all Galilee and Judea, as well as from Jerusalem.) And the Lord's healing power was strongly with Jesus.

¹⁸Some men came carrying a paralyzed man on a sleeping mat. They tried to take him inside to Jesus, ¹⁹but they couldn't reach him because of the crowd. So they went up to the roof and took off some tiles. Then they lowered the sick man on his mat down into the crowd, right in front of Jesus. ²⁰Seeing their faith, Jesus said to the man, "Young man, your sins are forgiven."

5:20
Luke 7:48

5:14 See Lev 14:2-32.

• **5:8** Simon Peter was awestruck at this miracle, and his first response was to realize his own insignificance in comparison to this man's greatness. Peter knew that Jesus had healed the sick and driven out demons, but he was amazed that Jesus cared about his day-to-day routine and understood his needs. God is interested not only in saving us but also in helping us in our daily activities.

• **5:11** God has two requirements for coming to him. Like Peter, we must recognize our own sinfulness. Then, like these fishermen, we must realize that we can't save ourselves and that we need help. If we know that Jesus is the only one who can help us, we will be ready to leave everything and follow him.

• **5:11** This was the disciples' second call. After the first call (Matthew 4:18-22; Mark 1:16-20), Peter, Andrew, James, and John had gone back to fishing. They continued to watch Jesus, however, as he established his authority in the synagogue, healed the sick, and drove out demons. Here he also established his authority in their lives—he met them on their level and helped them in their work. From this point on, they left their nets and remained with Jesus. For us, following Jesus means more than just acknowledging him as Savior. We must leave our past behind and commit our future to him.

5:12 Leprosy was a feared disease because there was no known cure for it, and some forms of it were highly contagious. Leprosy had a similar emotional impact and terror associated with it as AIDS does today. (Sometimes called Hansen's disease, leprosy still exists in a less contagious form that can be treated.) The priests monitored the disease, banishing lepers who were in a contagious stage to prevent the spread of infection and readmitting lepers whose disease was in remission. Because leprosy

destroys the nerve endings, lepers often would unknowingly damage their fingers, toes, and noses. This man with leprosy had an advanced case, so he undoubtedly had lost much bodily tissue. Still, he believed that Jesus could heal him of every trace of the disease. And Jesus did just that, reaching out to touch this untouchable, contagious, man in order to restore him. For more on the power of touch, see the second note on 4:40.

5:16 People were flocking to hear Jesus preach and to have their diseases healed, but Jesus made sure he often withdrew to quiet, solitary places to pray. Many things clamor for our attention, and we often run ourselves ragged attending to them. Like Jesus, however, we should take time to withdraw to a quiet and deserted place to pray. Strength comes from God, and we can only be strengthened by spending time with him.

5:17 The religious leaders spent much time defining and discussing the huge body of religious tradition that had been accumulating for more than 400 years since the Jews' return from exile. They were so concerned with these man-made traditions, in fact, that they often lost sight of Scripture. Here these leaders felt threatened because Jesus challenged their sincerity and because the people were flocking to him.

• **5:18, 19** In Bible times, houses were built of stone and had flat roofs made of mud mixed with straw. Outside stairways led to the roof. These men carried their friend up the stairs to the roof, where they took apart as much as was necessary to lower him in front of Jesus.

5:18-20 It wasn't the paralyzed man's faith that impressed Jesus but the faith of his friends. Jesus responded to their faith and healed the man. For better or worse, our faith affects others. We cannot make another person a Christian, but we can do much through our words, actions, and love to give him or her a chance to respond. Look for opportunities to bring your friends to the living Christ.

5:21
Isa 43:25; 55:7
Luke 7:49

5:22
Luke 6:8; 9:47

5:24-25
John 5:8-9

21But the Pharisees and teachers of religious law said to themselves, "Who does he think he is? That's blasphemy! Only God can forgive sins!"

22Jesus knew what they were thinking, so he asked them, "Why do you question this in your hearts? 23 Is it easier to say 'Your sins are forgiven,' or 'Stand up and walk'? 24 So I will prove to you that the Son of Man* has the authority on earth to forgive sins." Then Jesus turned to the paralyzed man and said, "Stand up, pick up your mat, and go home!"

25And immediately, as everyone watched, the man jumped up, picked up his mat, and went home praising God. 26Everyone was gripped with great wonder and awe, and they praised God, exclaiming, "We have seen amazing things today!"

Jesus Eats with Sinners at Matthew's House (**40**/Matthew 9:9-13; Mark 2:13-17)
27Later, as Jesus left the town, he saw a tax collector named Levi sitting at his tax collector's booth. "Follow me and be my disciple," Jesus said to him. 28So Levi got up, left everything, and followed him.

5:29-30
Luke 15:1-2

29Later, Levi held a banquet in his home with Jesus as the guest of honor. Many of Levi's fellow tax collectors and other guests also ate with them. 30But the Pharisees and their teachers of religious law complained bitterly to Jesus' disciples, "Why do you eat and drink with such scum?*"

31Jesus answered them, "Healthy people don't need a doctor—sick people do. 32 I have come to call not those who think they are righteous, but those who know they are sinners and need to repent."

Religious Leaders Ask Jesus about Fasting (**41**/Matthew 9:14-17; Mark 2:18-22)
33One day some people said to Jesus, "John the Baptist's disciples fast and pray regularly, and so do the disciples of the Pharisees. Why are your disciples always eating and drinking?"

5:34
John 3:29

5:35
Luke 9:22; 17:22

34Jesus responded, "Do wedding guests fast while celebrating with the groom? Of course not. 35But someday the groom will be taken away from them, and then they will fast."

36Then Jesus gave them this illustration: "No one tears a piece of cloth from a new garment and uses it to patch an old garment. For then the new garment would be ruined, and the new patch wouldn't even match the old garment.

5:24 "Son of Man" is a title Jesus used for himself.   **5:30** Greek *with tax collectors and sinners?*

• **5:21** When Jesus told the paralyzed man his sins were forgiven, the Jewish leaders accused Jesus of blasphemy—claiming to be God or to do what only God can do. In Jewish law, blasphemy was punishable by death (Leviticus 24:16). In labeling Jesus' claim to forgive sins blasphemous, the religious leaders showed they did not understand that Jesus *is* God, and that he has God's power to heal both the body and the soul. Forgiveness of sins was a sign that the messianic age had come (Isaiah 40:2; Joel 2:32; Micah 7:18, 19; Zechariah 13:1).

5:24 God offers the same forgiveness given to the paralytic to all who believe. The Greek word *aphiemi*, translated "forgiven," means to leave or let go, to give up a debt, to send away from oneself. Forgiveness means that a relationship has been renewed despite a wrong that has been done. But the act cannot be erased or changed. The notion of *aphiemi*, however, goes far beyond human forgiveness, for it includes the "putting away" of sin in two ways: (1) The law and justice are satisfied because Jesus paid the penalty that sin deserved; thus, sins can no longer be held against a believer. (2) The guilt caused by sin is removed and replaced with Christ's righteousness. Believers are so forgiven that, in God's eyes, it is as if they had never sinned. Do you carry a heavy burden for sins you have committed? Confess all to Christ and receive *aphiemi*—ultimate forgiveness.

5:27 For more about Levi (who was also named Matthew), the disciple and author of the Gospel of Matthew, see his Profile in Matthew 9, p. 1557.

• **5:28, 29** Levi left a lucrative, though probably dishonest, tax-collecting business to follow Jesus. Then he responded as Jesus would want all his followers to do. He held a banquet for his fellow tax collectors and other notorious "sinners" so they could meet Jesus, too. Levi, who left behind a material fortune in order to gain a spiritual fortune, was proud to be associated with Jesus.

5:30-32 The Pharisees wrapped their sin in respectability. They made themselves appear good by publicly doing good deeds and pointing at the sins of others. Jesus chose to spend time not with these proud, self-righteous religious leaders, but with people who sensed their own sin and knew that they were not good enough for God. In order to come to God, we must repent; in order to renounce our sin, we must first acknowledge it.

5:35 Jesus knew his death was coming. After that time, fasting would be in order. Although he was fully human, Jesus knew he was God and why he had come—to die for the sins of the world.

5:36-39 "Wineskins" were goatskins sewn together at the edges to form watertight bags. Because new wine expands as it ages, it had to be put in new, pliable wineskins. A used skin, having become more rigid, would burst and spill the wine. Like old wineskins, the Pharisees were too rigid to accept Jesus, who could not be contained in their traditions or rules. Christianity required new approaches, new traditions, new structures. Our church programs and ministries should not be so structured that they have no room for a fresh touch of the Spirit, a new method, or a new idea. We, too, must be careful that our heart does not become so rigid that it prevents us from accepting new ways of thinking that Christ brings. We need to keep our heart pliable so we can accept Jesus' life-changing message.

³⁷ "And no one puts new wine into old wineskins. For the new wine would burst the wineskins, spilling the wine and ruining the skins. ³⁸New wine must be stored in new wineskins. ³⁹But no one who drinks the old wine seems to want the new wine. 'The old is just fine,' they say."

The Disciples Pick Wheat on the Sabbath (45/Matthew 12:1-8; Mark 2:23-28)

6 One Sabbath day as Jesus was walking through some grainfields, his disciples broke off heads of grain, rubbed off the husks in their hands, and ate the grain. ²But some Pharisees said, "Why are you breaking the law by harvesting grain on the Sabbath?"

³Jesus replied, "Haven't you read in the Scriptures what David did when he and his companions were hungry? ⁴He went into the house of God and broke the law by eating the sacred loaves of bread that only the priests can eat. He also gave some to his companions." ⁵And Jesus added, "The Son of Man* is Lord, even over the Sabbath."

6:1
Deut 23:25

6:2
John 5:10

6:3-4
1 Sam 21:6

6:4
Lev 24:5-9

Jesus Heals a Man's Hand on the Sabbath (46/Matthew 12:9-14; Mark 3:1-6)

⁶On another Sabbath day, a man with a deformed right hand was in the synagogue while Jesus was teaching. ⁷The teachers of religious law and the Pharisees watched Jesus closely. If he healed the man's hand, they planned to accuse him of working on the Sabbath.

⁸But Jesus knew their thoughts. He said to the man with the deformed hand, "Come and stand in front of everyone." So the man came forward. ⁹Then Jesus said to his critics, "I have a question for you. Does the law permit good deeds on the Sabbath, or is it a day for doing evil? Is this a day to save life or to destroy it?"

¹⁰He looked around at them one by one and then said to the man, "Hold out your hand." So the man held out his hand, and it was restored! ¹¹At this, the enemies of Jesus were wild with rage and began to discuss what to do with him.

6:7
Luke 14:1

6:8
Luke 5:22; 9:47

Jesus Chooses the Twelve Disciples (48/Mark 3:13-19)

¹²One day soon afterward Jesus went up on a mountain to pray, and he prayed to God all night. ¹³At daybreak he called together all of his disciples and chose twelve of them to be apostles. Here are their names:

6:13
John 6:70

6:5 "Son of Man" is a title Jesus used for himself.

6:1, 2 Jewish legal tradition had 39 categories of activities forbidden on the Sabbath, and harvesting was one of them. The teachers of religious law even went so far as to describe different methods of harvesting. One method was to rub the heads of grain between the hands, as the disciples were doing here. God's law said farmers were to leave the edges of their fields unplowed so travelers and the poor could eat from this bounty (Deuteronomy 23:25); thus, the disciples were not guilty of stealing grain. Neither were they breaking the Sabbath by doing their daily work on it. In fact, though they may have been violating the Pharisees' rules, they were not breaking any divine law.

6:3-5 Each week 12 consecrated loaves of bread, representing the 12 tribes of Israel, would be placed on a table in the Temple. This bread was called the Bread of the Presence. After its use in the Temple, it was to be eaten only by priests. Jesus, accused of Sabbath breaking, referred to a well-known story about David (1 Samuel 21:1-6). On one occasion, when fleeing from Saul, David and his men had eaten this sacred bread. Their need had been more important than ceremonial regulations. Jesus was appealing to the same principle: Human need is more important than human regulations and rules. By comparing himself and his disciples with David and his men, Jesus was saying, "If you condemn me, you must also condemn David."

6:5 When Jesus said that he was "Lord, even over the Sabbath," he meant that he had the authority to overrule the Pharisees' traditions and regulations because he had created the Sabbath. The Creator is always greater than the creation.

6:6, 7 According to the tradition of the religious leaders, no healing could be done on the Sabbath. Healing, they said, was practicing medicine, and a person could not practice his or her profession on the Sabbath. The religious leaders were more concerned about protecting their laws than freeing a person from painful suffering. The religious leaders were more concerned with negatives: what

rules should not be broken, what activities should not be done. Jesus was positive: doing good and helping those in need.

Which would an objective observer say is more characteristic of your Christianity—the positives or the negatives? Are you more concerned about what people shouldn't be doing than you are about advancing God's Kingdom? Is your way of being a Christian the only way? And what about your church? The Pharisees thought their religious system had all the answers. They could not accept Jesus because he did not fit into their system. Beware of thinking that you or your church has all the answers. No religious system is big enough to contain Christ completely or to fulfill perfectly all his desires for the world. Christianity is the most positive force to ever hit this planet. Make sure you don't let it degenerate into a bunch of negatives.

6:11 Jesus' enemies were furious. Not only had he read their minds; he also had flouted their laws and exposed the hatred in their hearts. Ironically, their hatred, combined with their zeal for the law, drove them to plot murder—an act that was clearly against their law.

6:12 The Gospel writers note that before every important event in Jesus' life, he would take time to go off by himself and pray. This time Jesus was preparing to choose his inner circle, the 12 apostles. Make sure that all your important decisions are grounded in prayer.

6:13 Jesus had many *disciples* (learners), but he chose only 12 *apostles* (messengers). The apostles were his inner circle to whom he gave special training and whom he sent out with his own authority. These were the men who started the Christian church. In the Gospels these 12 men are usually called the disciples, but in the book of Acts they are called apostles.

6:13-16 Jesus selected "ordinary" men with a mixture of backgrounds and personalities to be his disciples. Today, God calls "ordinary" people together to build his church, teach salvation's

6:14-15
Acts 1:13

14 Simon (whom he named Peter),
   Andrew (Peter's brother),
   James,
   John,
   Philip,
   Bartholomew,
15 Matthew,
   Thomas,
   James (son of Alphaeus),
   Simon (who was called the zealot),
16 Judas (son of James),
   Judas Iscariot (who later betrayed him).

Jesus Gives the Beatitudes (49/Matthew 5:1-12)

17When they came down from the mountain, the disciples stood with Jesus on a large, level area, surrounded by many of his followers and by the crowds. There were people from all over Judea and from Jerusalem and from as far north as the seacoasts of Tyre and Sidon.

6:19
Matt 9:20
Mark 5:30

18They had come to hear him and to be healed of their diseases; and those troubled by evil* spirits were healed. 19Everyone tried to touch him, because healing power went out from him, and he healed everyone.

6:20-23
Matt 5:1-12

20Then Jesus turned to his disciples and said,

"God blesses you who are poor,
   for the Kingdom of God is yours.

6:21
Isa 55:1; 61:3
Rev 7:16-17

21 God blesses you who are hungry now,
   for you will be satisfied.
God blesses you who weep now,
   for in due time you will laugh.

6:22
John 15:19; 16:2
1 Pet 4:14

22What blessings await you when people hate you and exclude you and mock you and curse you as evil because you follow the Son of Man. 23 When that happens, be happy! Yes, leap for

6:23
2 Chr 36:16
Acts 5:41; 7:52
Jas 1:2

joy! For a great reward awaits you in heaven. And remember, their ancestors treated the ancient prophets that same way.

6:24
Jas 5:1

24 "What sorrow awaits you who are rich,
   for you have your only happiness now.

6:25
Isa 5:22; 65:13

25 What sorrow awaits you who are fat and prosperous now,
   for a time of awful hunger awaits you.
What sorrow awaits you who laugh now,
   for your laughing will turn to mourning and sorrow.

6:18 Greek *unclean.*

---

message, and serve others out of love. Alone we may feel unqualified to serve Christ effectively, but together we make up a group strong enough to serve God in any way. Ask for patience to accept the diversity of people in your church, and build on the variety of strengths represented in your group.

6:14-16 The disciples are not always listed by the same names. For example, Simon is sometimes called Peter or Cephas. Matthew is also known as Levi. Bartholomew is thought to be the same person as Nathanael (John 1:45). Judas the son of James is also called Thaddaeus.

6:19 Once word of Jesus' healing power spread, crowds gathered just to touch him. For many, he had become a magician or a symbol of good fortune. Instead of desiring God's pardon and love, they only wanted physical healing or a chance to see spectacular events. Some people still see God as a cosmic magician and consider prayer as a way to get God to do his tricks. But God is not a magician—he is the Master. Prayer is not a way for us to control God; it is a way for us to put ourselves under his control.

6:20ff This may be Luke's account of the sermon that Matthew records in Matthew 5–7, or it may be that Jesus gave similar sermons on several different occasions. Some believe that this was

not one sermon, but a composite based on Jesus' customary teachings.

• **6:20-23** These verses are called the *Beatitudes,* from the Latin word meaning "blessing." They describe what it means to be Christ's follower, give standards of conduct, and contrast Kingdom values with worldly values, showing what Christ's followers can expect from the world and what God will give them. In addition, they contrast fake piety with true humility. They also show how Old Testament expectations are fulfilled in God's Kingdom.

• **6:21** Some believe that the hunger about which Jesus spoke is a hunger for righteousness (Matthew 5:6). Others say this is physical hunger. In any case, in a nation where riches were seen as a sign of God's favor, Jesus startled his hearers by pronouncing blessings on the hungry. In doing so, however, he was in line with an ancient tradition. The Old Testament is filled with texts proclaiming God's concern for the poor and needy. See, for example, 1 Samuel 2:5; Psalm 146:7; Isaiah 58:6, 7; and Jesus' own mother's prayer in Luke 1:53.

• **6:24** If you are trying to find fulfillment only through riches, wealth may be the only reward you will ever get—and it does not last. We should not seek comfort now at the expense of eternal life.

[26] What sorrow awaits you who are praised by the crowds,
    for their ancestors also praised false prophets.

6:26
Jas 4:4

Jesus Teaches about Loving Enemies (57/Matthew 5:43-48)

[27] "But to you who are willing to listen, I say, love your enemies! Do good to those who hate you. [28] Bless those who curse you. Pray for those who hurt you. [29] If someone slaps you on one cheek, offer the other cheek also. If someone demands your coat, offer your shirt also. [30] Give to anyone who asks; and when things are taken away from you, don't try to get them back. [31] Do to others as you would like them to do to you.

[32] "If you love only those who love you, why should you get credit for that? Even sinners love those who love them! [33] And if you do good only to those who do good to you, why should you get credit? Even sinners do that much! [34] And if you lend money only to those who can repay you, why should you get credit? Even sinners will lend to other sinners for a full return.

[35] "Love your enemies! Do good to them. Lend to them without expecting to be repaid. Then your reward from heaven will be very great, and you will truly be acting as children of the Most High, for he is kind to those who are unthankful and wicked. [36] You must be compassionate, just as your Father is compassionate.

6:27
Prov 25:21
Rom 12:20
6:28
Rom 12:14
6:30
Deut 15:7-8, 10
6:31
Matt 7:12
6:33-35
Lev 25:35-36

6:36
Matt 5:48

Jesus Teaches about Judging Others (63/Matthew 7:1-6)

[37] "Do not judge others, and you will not be judged. Do not condemn others, or it will all come back against you. Forgive others, and you will be forgiven. [38] Give, and you will receive. Your gift will return to you in full—pressed down, shaken together to make room for more, running over, and poured into your lap. The amount you give will determine the amount you get back.*"

[39] Then Jesus gave the following illustration: "Can one blind person lead another? Won't they both fall into a ditch? [40] Students* are not greater than their teacher. But the student who is fully trained will become like the teacher.

[41] "And why worry about a speck in your friend's eye* when you have a log in your own? [42] How can you think of saying, 'Friend,* let me help you get rid of that speck in your eye,' when you can't see past the log in your own eye? Hypocrite! First get rid of the log in your own eye; then you will see well enough to deal with the speck in your friend's eye.

6:38
Ps 79:12
Mark 4:24

6:39
Matt 15:14
6:40
Matt 10:24-25
John 13:16; 15:20

Jesus Teaches about Fruit in People's Lives (66/Matthew 7:15-20)

[43] "A good tree can't produce bad fruit, and a bad tree can't produce good fruit. [44] A tree is identified by its fruit. Figs are never gathered from thornbushes, and grapes are not picked

6:44
Matt 12:33

6:38 Or *The measure you give will be the measure you get back.*   **6:40** Or *Disciples.*   **6:41** Greek *your brother's eye;* also in 6:42.   **6:42** Greek *Brother.*

• **6:26** Many false prophets lived during Old Testament times. They were praised by kings and crowds because their predictions—prosperity and victory in war—were exactly what the people wanted to hear. But popularity is no guarantee of truth, and human flattery does not bring God's approval. Sadness lies ahead for those who chase after the crowd's praise rather than God's truth.

• **6:27** The Jews despised the Romans because they oppressed God's people, but Jesus told the people to love these enemies. Such words turned many away from Christ. Jesus wasn't talking about having affection for enemies; he was talking about an act of the will. You can't "fall into" this kind of love—it takes conscious effort. Loving our enemies means acting in their best interests. We can pray for them, and we can think of ways to help them. Jesus loves the whole world, even though the world is in rebellion against God. Jesus asks us to follow his example by loving our enemies. Grant your enemies the same respect and rights as you desire for yourself.

• **6:37, 38** A forgiving spirit demonstrates that a person has received God's forgiveness. Jesus used the picture of measuring grain in a basket to ensure the full amount. If we are critical rather than compassionate, we will also receive criticism. If we treat others generously, graciously, and compassionately, however, these qualities will come back to us in full measure. We are to love others, not judge them.

6:39, 40 Make sure you're following the right teachers and leaders, because you will go no farther than they do. Look for leaders who will show you more about faith and whose guidance you can trust.

6:41 Jesus doesn't mean we should ignore wrongdoing, but we should not be so worried about others' sins that we overlook our own. We often rationalize our sins by pointing out the same mistakes in others. What kinds of specks in others' eyes are the easiest for you to criticize? Remember your own "logs" when you feel like criticizing, and you may find that you have less to say.

6:42 We should not be so afraid of the label *hypocrite* that we stand still in our Christian life, hiding our faith and making no attempts to grow. A person who tries to do right but often fails is not a hypocrite. Neither are those who fulfill their duty even when they don't feel like doing it. Often it is necessary and good to set aside our desires in order to do what needs to be done. It is not hypocrisy to be weak in faith. A hypocrite is a person who only puts on religious behavior in order to gain attention, approval, or admiration from others.

• **6:45** Jesus reminds us that our speech and actions reveal our true underlying beliefs, attitudes, and motivations. The good impressions we try to make cannot last if we are being deceptive. What is in your heart will come out in your speech and behavior.

from bramble bushes. 45A good person produces good things from the treasury of a good heart, and an evil person produces evil things from the treasury of an evil heart. What you say flows from what is in your heart.

Jesus Teaches about Building on a Solid Foundation (67/Matthew 7:21-29)

6:46
Mal 1:6
Matt 7:21

46 "So why do you keep calling me 'Lord, Lord!' when you don't do what I say? 47I will show you what it's like when someone comes to me, listens to my teaching, and then follows it. 48 It is like a person building a house who digs deep and lays the foundation on solid rock. When the floodwaters rise and break against that house, it stands firm because it is well built. 49 But anyone who hears and doesn't obey is like a person who builds a house without a foundation. When the floods sweep down against that house, it will collapse into a heap of ruins."

A Roman Officer Demonstrates Faith (68/Matthew 8:5-13)

7:2
John 4:47

7 When Jesus had finished saying all this to the people, he returned to Capernaum. 2At that time the highly valued slave of a Roman officer* was sick and near death. 3When the officer heard about Jesus, he sent some respected Jewish elders to ask him to come and heal his slave. 4So they earnestly begged Jesus to help the man. "If anyone deserves your help, he does," they said, 5 "for he loves the Jewish people and even built a synagogue for us."

7:5
Acts 10:2

6So Jesus went with them. But just before they arrived at the house, the officer sent some friends to say, "Lord, don't trouble yourself by coming to my home, for I am not worthy of such an honor. 7I am not even worthy to come and meet you. Just say the word from where you are, and my servant will be healed. 8I know this because I am under the authority of my superior officers, and I have authority over my soldiers. I only need to say, 'Go,' and they go, or 'Come,' and they come. And if I say to my slaves, 'Do this,' they do it."

7:7
Ps 107:20

9When Jesus heard this, he was amazed. Turning to the crowd that was following him, he said, "I tell you, I haven't seen faith like this in all Israel!" 10And when the officer's friends returned to his house, they found the slave completely healed.

7:2 Greek *a centurion;* similarly in 7:6.

6:46-49 Why would people build a house without a foundation? Perhaps to save time and avoid the hard work of preparing the stone. Possibly because the waterfront scenery is more attractive or because beach houses have higher social status than cliff houses. Perhaps because they want to join their friends who have already settled in sandy areas. Maybe because they haven't heard about the violent storms coming, because they have discounted the reports, or because they think disaster can't happen to them. Whatever their reason, those with no foundation are shortsighted, and they will be sorry. Obeying God is like building a house on a strong, solid foundation that stands firm when storms come. When life is calm, our foundations don't seem to matter. But when crises come, our foundations are tested. Be sure your life is built on the solid foundation of knowing and trusting Jesus Christ.

7:1ff This passage marks a turning point in Luke's account of Jesus' ministry. Up to this point, Jesus has dealt exclusively with the Jews; here he begins to include the Gentiles. Notice who the main characters are in this short drama: the Jewish elders, a Roman officer, and the officer's slave—very different racial and religious backgrounds, and vastly different standings on the social ladder. Jesus broke through all those barriers, all the way to the sick man's need. The gospel travels well across ethnic, racial, national, and religious barriers. Are you willing to work through them as well? Jesus was no respecter of artificial divisions, and we should follow his example. Reach out to those whom Jesus came to save.

7:2 This Roman officer was a centurion, meaning he was a captain in charge of 100 men. The officer heard about Jesus, so obviously also heard about Jesus' healing power. He sent a request through some of the Jewish elders on behalf of his slave. He may have heard about the healing of the Roman official's son (which probably occurred earlier, see John 4:46-54). He knew Jesus had the power to heal his slave.

7:3 Matthew 8:5 says the Roman officer visited Jesus himself, while Luke 7:3 says he sent Jewish elders to present his request to Jesus. In those days, dealing with a person's messengers was

considered the same as dealing with the one who had sent them. Thus, in dealing with the messengers, Jesus was dealing with the officer. For his Jewish audience, Matthew emphasized the Roman soldier's faith. For his Gentile audience, Luke highlighted the good relationship between the Jewish elders and the Roman officer. This army captain daily delegated work and sent groups on missions, so this was how he chose to get his message to Jesus.

7:9 The Roman officer didn't come to Jesus, and he didn't expect Jesus to come to him. Just as this officer did not need to be present to have his orders carried out, so Jesus didn't need to be present to heal. The officer's faith was especially amazing because he was a Gentile who had not been brought up to know a loving God. Hence Jesus' comment.

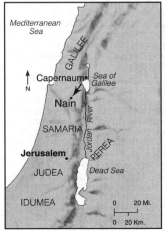

JESUS RAISES A WIDOW'S SON FROM THE DEAD
Jesus traveled to Nain and met a funeral procession leaving the village. A widow's only son had died, but Jesus brought the young man back to life. This miracle, recorded only in Luke, reveals Jesus' compassion for people's needs.

Jesus Raises a Widow's Son from the Dead (69)

¹¹Soon afterward Jesus went with his disciples to the village of Nain, and a large crowd followed him. ¹²A funeral procession was coming out as he approached the village gate. The young man who had died was a widow's only son, and a large crowd from the village was with her. ¹³When the Lord saw her, his heart overflowed with compassion. "Don't cry!" he said. ¹⁴Then he walked over to the coffin and touched it, and the bearers stopped. "Young man," he said, "I tell you, get up." ¹⁵Then the dead boy sat up and began to talk! And Jesus gave him back to his mother.

¹⁶Great fear swept the crowd, and they praised God, saying, "A mighty prophet has risen among us," and "God has visited his people today." ¹⁷And the news about Jesus spread throughout Judea and the surrounding countryside.

Jesus Eases John's Doubt (70/Matthew 11:1-19)

¹⁸The disciples of John the Baptist told John about everything Jesus was doing. So John called for two of his disciples, ¹⁹and he sent them to the Lord to ask him, "Are you the Messiah we've been expecting,* or should we keep looking for someone else?"

²⁰John's two disciples found Jesus and said to him, "John the Baptist sent us to ask, 'Are you the Messiah we've been expecting, or should we keep looking for someone else?'"

²¹At that very time, Jesus cured many people of their diseases, illnesses, and evil spirits, and he restored sight to many who were blind. ²²Then he told John's disciples, "Go back to John and tell him what you have seen and heard—the blind see, the lame walk, the lepers are cured, the deaf hear, the dead are raised to life, and the Good News is being preached to the poor. ²³And tell him, 'God blesses those who do not turn away because of me.*'"

²⁴After John's disciples left, Jesus began talking about him to the crowds. " What kind of man did you go into the wilderness to see? Was he a weak reed, swayed by every breath of wind? ²⁵Or were you expecting to see a man dressed in expensive clothes? No, people who wear beautiful clothes and live in luxury are found in palaces. ²⁶ Were you looking for a prophet? Yes, and he is more than a prophet. ²⁷ John is the man to whom the Scriptures refer when they say,

'Look, I am sending my messenger ahead of you,
and he will prepare your way before you.'*

²⁸I tell you, of all who have ever lived, none is greater than John. Yet even the least person in the Kingdom of God is greater than he is!"

7:19 Greek *Are you the one who is coming?* Also in 7:20.   **7:23** Or *who are not offended by me.*   **7:27** Mal 3:1.

Cross-references:
7:11-16 1 Kgs 17:17-24; 2 Kgs 4:32-37
7:13 Luke 8:52
7:14 Luke 8:54; John 11:43; Acts 9:40
7:16 Luke 1:65-68
7:19 Mal 3:1-3
7:22 †Isa 29:18-19; 35:5-6; 42:18; 61:1; Luke 4:18
7:26 Luke 1:76
7:27 †Exod 23:20; †Mal 3:1
7:28 Luke 1:15

• **7:11-15** The widow's situation was serious. She had lost her husband, and now her only son had died—her last means of support. The crowd of mourners would go home, and she would be left penniless and alone. The widow was probably past the age of childbearing and would not marry again. Unless a relative came to her aid, her future was bleak. She would be an easy prey for swindlers, and she would likely be reduced to begging for food. In fact, as Luke repeatedly emphasizes, this woman was just the kind of person Jesus had come to help—and help her he did. Jesus has great compassion on your pain, and he has the power to bring hope out of any tragedy.

7:11-17 This story illustrates salvation. The whole world was dead in sin (Ephesians 2:1), just as the widow's son was dead. Being dead, we could do nothing to help ourselves—we couldn't even ask for help. But God had compassion on us, and he sent Jesus to raise us to life with him (Ephesians 2:4-7). The dead man did not earn his second chance at life, and we cannot earn our new life in Christ. But we can accept God's gift of life, praise God for it, and use our lives to do his will.

7:12 Honoring the dead was important in Jewish tradition. A funeral procession, with relatives of the dead person following the body that was wrapped and carried on a kind of stretcher, would make its way through town, and bystanders would be expected to join the procession. In addition, hired mourners would cry aloud and draw attention to the procession. The family's mourning would continue for 30 days.

7:16 The people thought of Jesus as a prophet because, like the Old Testament prophets, he boldly proclaimed God's message and sometimes raised the dead. Both Elijah and Elisha raised children from the dead (1 Kings 17:17-24; 2 Kings 4:18-37). The people were correct in thinking that Jesus was a prophet, but he is much more—he was God himself.

7:18-23 John was confused because the reports he received about Jesus were unexpected and incomplete. John's doubts were natural, and Jesus didn't rebuke him for them. Instead, he responded in a way that John would understand: Jesus explained that he had accomplished what the Messiah was supposed to accomplish. God can handle our doubts, and he welcomes our questions. Do you have questions about Jesus—about who he is or what he expects of you? Admit them to yourself and to God, and begin looking for answers. Only as you face your doubts honestly can you begin to resolve them.

7:20-22 The proofs listed here for Jesus being the Messiah are significant. They consist of observable deeds, not theories—actions that Jesus' contemporaries saw and reported for us to read today. The prophets had said that the Messiah would do these very acts (see Isaiah 35:5, 6; 61:1). These physical proofs helped John—and will help all of us—to recognize who Jesus is.

7:28 Of all people, no one fulfilled his God-given purpose better than John. Yet in God's Kingdom, all who come after John have a greater spiritual heritage because they have clearer knowledge of the purpose of Jesus' death and resurrection. John was the last to

7:29-30
Matt 21:32
Luke 3:7, 12

29 When they heard this, all the people—even the tax collectors—agreed that God's way was right,* for they had been baptized by John. 30But the Pharisees and experts in religious law rejected God's plan for them, for they had refused John's baptism.

31 "To what can I compare the people of this generation?" Jesus asked. "How can I describe them? 32They are like children playing a game in the public square. They complain to their friends,

'We played wedding songs,
  and you didn't dance,
so we played funeral songs,
  and you didn't weep.'

7:33
Luke 1:15

7:35
1 Cor 1:24

33For John the Baptist didn't spend his time eating bread or drinking wine, and you say, 'He's possessed by a demon.' 34The Son of Man,* on the other hand, feasts and drinks, and you say, 'He's a glutton and a drunkard, and a friend of tax collectors and other sinners!' 35But wisdom is shown to be right by the lives of those who follow it.*"

A Sinful Woman Anoints Jesus' Feet (72)

7:36-50
Matt 26:6-13
Mark 14:3-9
John 12:1-8
7:37
Luke 8:2

36 One of the Pharisees asked Jesus to have dinner with him, so Jesus went to his home and sat down to eat.* 37When a certain immoral woman from that city heard he was eating there, she brought a beautiful alabaster jar filled with expensive perfume. 38Then she knelt behind him at his feet, weeping. Her tears fell on his feet, and she wiped them off with her hair. Then she kept kissing his feet and putting perfume on them.

7:39
Matt 21:11

39 When the Pharisee who had invited him saw this, he said to himself, "If this man were a prophet, he would know what kind of woman is touching him. She's a sinner!"

40Then Jesus answered his thoughts. "Simon," he said to the Pharisee, "I have something to say to you."

"Go ahead, Teacher," Simon replied.

7:42
Matt 18:27
Col 2:13

41 Then Jesus told him this story: "A man loaned money to two people—500 pieces of silver* to one and 50 pieces to the other. 42 But neither of them could repay him, so he kindly forgave them both, canceling their debts. Who do you suppose loved him more after that?"

43Simon answered, "I suppose the one for whom he canceled the larger debt."

7:44
Gen 18:4
1 Tim 5:10

"That's right," Jesus said. 44Then he turned to the woman and said to Simon, "Look at this woman kneeling here. When I entered your home, you didn't offer me water to wash the dust from my feet, but she has washed them with her tears and wiped them with her hair.

7:29 Or *praised God for his justice.*   **7:34** "Son of Man" is a title Jesus used for himself.   **7:35** Or *But wisdom is justified by all her children.*   **7:36** Or *and reclined.*   **7:41** Greek *500 denarii.* A denarius was equivalent to a laborer's full day's wage.

---

function like the Old Testament prophets, the last to prepare the people for the coming messianic age. Jesus was not contrasting the man John with individual Christians; he was contrasting life before Christ with life in the fullness of Christ's Kingdom.

7:29, 30 The common people, including the tax collectors (who embodied evil in most people's minds) heard John's message and repented. In contrast, the Pharisees and experts in the law—religious leaders—rejected his words. Wanting to live their own way, they justified their own point of view and refused to listen to other ideas. They "rejected God's plan for them." They were so close to Jesus, and yet so far away. The truth stood before them, and they rejected it. What have you done with the truth you read in God's Word?

7:31-35 The religious leaders hated both John and Jesus, but they did not bother to be consistent in their faultfinding. They criticized John the Baptist because he fasted and drank no wine; they criticized Jesus because he ate heartily and drank wine with tax collectors and sinners. Their real objection to both men, of course, had nothing to do with dietary habits. What the Pharisees and experts in the law couldn't stand was being exposed for their hypocrisy.

7:33, 34 The Pharisees weren't troubled by their inconsistency toward John the Baptist and Jesus. They were good at justifying their "wisdom." Most of us can find compelling reasons to do or believe whatever suits our purposes. If we do not examine our

ideas in the light of God's truth, however, we may be just as obviously self-serving as the Pharisees.

7:36ff A similar incident occurred later in Jesus' ministry (see Matthew 26:6-13; Mark 14:3-9; John 12:1-11).

7:38 Although the woman was not an invited guest, she entered the house anyway and knelt behind Jesus at his feet. In Jesus' day, it was customary to recline while eating. Dinner guests would lie on couches with their heads near the table, propping themselves up on one elbow and stretching their feet out behind them. The woman could easily anoint Jesus' feet without approaching the table.

• **7:44ff** Again Luke contrasts the Pharisees with sinners—and again the sinners come out ahead. Simon had committed several social errors in neglecting to wash Jesus' feet (a courtesy extended to guests because sandaled feet got very dirty), anoint his head with oil, and offer him the kiss of greeting. Did Simon perhaps feel that he was too good for Jesus? Was he trying to give Jesus a subtle put-down? Whatever the case, the contrast is vivid. The sinful woman lavished tears, expensive perfume, and kisses on her Savior. In this story it is the grateful immoral woman, and not the religious leader, whose sins were forgiven. Although God's grace through faith is what saves us, and not acts of love or generosity, this woman's act demonstrated her true faith, and Jesus honored her.

⁴⁵You didn't greet me with a kiss, but from the time I first came in, she has not stopped kissing my feet. ⁴⁶You neglected the courtesy of olive oil to anoint my head, but she has anointed my feet with rare perfume.

⁴⁷ "I tell you, her sins—and they are many—have been forgiven, so she has shown me much love. But a person who is forgiven little shows only little love." ⁴⁸Then Jesus said to the woman, "Your sins are forgiven."

⁴⁹The men at the table said among themselves, "Who is this man, that he goes around forgiving sins?"

⁵⁰And Jesus said to the woman, "Your faith has saved you; go in peace."

7:45
Rom 16:16
1 Cor 16:20
2 Cor 13:12
1 Thes 5:26
1 Pet 5:14
7:46
2 Sam 12:20
Ps 23:5
7:48-49
Luke 5:20-21
7:50
Matt 9:22

Women Accompany Jesus and the Disciples (73)

8 Soon afterward Jesus began a tour of the nearby towns and villages, preaching and announcing the Good News about the Kingdom of God. He took his twelve disciples with him, ²along with some women who had been cured of evil spirits and diseases. Among them were Mary Magdalene, from whom he had cast out seven demons; ³Joanna, the wife of Chuza, Herod's business manager; Susanna; and many others who were contributing from their own resources to support Jesus and his disciples.

8:1
Matt 4:23
8:2
Matt 27:55-56
Mark 15:40-41
Luke 23:49
8:3
Matt 14:1

Jesus Tells the Parable of the Four Soils (77/Matthew 13:1-9; Mark 4:1-9)

⁴One day Jesus told a story in the form of a parable to a large crowd that had gathered from many towns to hear him: ⁵ "A farmer went out to plant his seed. As he scattered it across his field, some seed fell on a footpath, where it was stepped on, and the birds ate it. ⁶Other seed fell among rocks. It began to grow, but the plant soon wilted and died for lack of moisture. ⁷Other seed fell among thorns that grew up with it and choked out the tender plants. ⁸Still other seed fell on fertile soil. This seed grew and produced a crop that was a hundred times as much as had been planted!" When he had said this, he called out, "Anyone with ears to hear should listen and understand."

Jesus Explains the Parable of the Four Soils (78/Matthew 13:10-23; Mark 4:10-25)

⁹His disciples asked him what this parable meant. ¹⁰He replied, "You are permitted to understand the secrets* of the Kingdom of God. But I use parables to teach the others so that the Scriptures might be fulfilled:

8:10
†Isa 6:9-10

'When they look, they won't really see.
When they hear, they won't understand.'*

8:10a Greek *mysteries.* **8:10b** Isa 6:9 (Greek version).

7:47 Overflowing love is the natural response to forgiveness and the appropriate consequence of faith. But only those who realize the depth of their sin can appreciate the complete forgiveness that God offers them. Jesus has rescued all of his followers, whether they were once extremely wicked or conventionally good, from eternal death. Do you appreciate the wideness of God's mercy? Are you grateful for his forgiveness?

7:49, 50 The Pharisees believed that only God could forgive sins, so they wondered why this man, Jesus, was saying that the woman's sins were forgiven. They did not grasp the fact that Jesus was indeed God. (See also 5:17-26 and notes there.)

• **8:2, 3** Jesus lifted women up from degradation and servitude to the joy of fellowship and service. In Jewish culture, women were not supposed to learn from rabbis. By allowing these women to travel with him, Jesus was showing that all people are equal under God. These women supported Jesus' ministry with their own money. They owed a great debt to him because he had driven demons out of some and had healed others.

8:2, 3 Here we catch a glimpse of a few of the people behind the scenes in Jesus' ministry. The ministry of those in the foreground is often supported by those whose work is less visible but just as essential. Offer your resources to God, whether or not you will be on center stage.

8:4 Jesus often communicated spiritual truth through short stories (called parables). These stories describe a familiar object or situation and give it a startling new twist. By linking the known with the hidden and forcing listeners to think, parables can point to spiritual truths. A parable compels listeners to discover the truth for themselves, and it conceals the truth from those too lazy or dull to understand it. In reading Jesus' parables, we must be careful not to read too much into them. Most have only one point and one meaning.

8:5 Why would a farmer allow precious seed to land on the footpath, on rocks, or among thorns? This is not an irresponsible farmer scattering seeds at random. He is using the acceptable method of seeding a large field—tossing it by handfuls as he walks through the field. His goal is to get as much seed as possible to take root in good soil, but waste is inevitable as some falls or is blown into less productive areas. That some of the seed produces no crop is not the fault of the faithful farmer or of the seed. The yield depends on the condition of the soil where the seed falls. It is our responsibility to spread the seed (God's message), but we should not give up when some of our efforts fail. Remember, not every seed falls on good soil.

8:10 Why didn't the crowds understand Jesus' words? Perhaps they were looking for a military leader or a political Messiah and could not fit his gentle teaching style into their preconceived idea. Perhaps they were afraid of pressure from religious leaders and did not want to look too deeply into Jesus' words. God told Isaiah that people would listen without understanding and watch without learning anything (Isaiah 6:9), and that kind of reaction confronted Jesus. The story of the farmer was an accurate picture of the people's reaction to the rest of his stories.

8:11
1 Pet 1:23
8:12
1 Cor 1:21

8:14
Matt 19:23
1 Tim 6:9, 10
2 Tim 4:10

8:16
Matt 5:15
Luke 11:33
8:17
Matt 10:26
8:18
Matt 25:29
Luke 19:26

11 "This is the meaning of the parable: The seed is God's word. 12The seeds that fell on the footpath represent those who hear the message, only to have the devil come and take it away from their hearts and prevent them from believing and being saved. 13The seeds on the rocky soil represent those who hear the message and receive it with joy. But since they don't have deep roots, they believe for a while, then they fall away when they face temptation. 14 The seeds that fell among the thorns represent those who hear the message, but all too quickly the message is crowded out by the cares and riches and pleasures of this life. And so they never grow into maturity. 15And the seeds that fell on the good soil represent honest, good-hearted people who hear God's word, cling to it, and patiently produce a huge harvest.

16 "No one lights a lamp and then covers it with a bowl or hides it under a bed. A lamp is placed on a stand, where its light can be seen by all who enter the house. 17 For all that is secret will eventually be brought into the open, and everything that is concealed will be brought to light and made known to all.

18 "So pay attention to how you hear. To those who listen to my teaching, more understanding will be given. But for those who are not listening, even what they think they understand will be taken away from them."

Jesus Describes His True Family (**76**/Matthew 12:46-50; Mark 3:31-35)
19Then Jesus' mother and brothers came to see him, but they couldn't get to him because of the crowd. 20Someone told Jesus, "Your mother and your brothers are outside, and they want to see you."

21Jesus replied, "My mother and my brothers are all those who hear God's word and obey it."

JESUS AND WOMEN

As a non-Jew recording the words and works of Jesus' life, Luke demonstrates a special sensitivity to other "outsiders" with whom Jesus came into contact. For instance, Luke records five events involving women that are not mentioned in the other Gospels. In first-century Jewish culture, women were usually treated as second-class citizens with few of the rights men had. But Jesus crossed those barriers, and Luke showed the special care Jesus had for women. Jesus treated all people with equal respect. The above passages tell of his encounters with women.

8:11-15 "Footpath" people, like many of the religious leaders, refuse to believe God's message. "Rocky soil" people, like many in the crowds who followed Jesus, believe his message but never get around to doing anything about it. "Thorn patch" people, overcome by worries and the lure of materialism, leave no room in their lives for God. "Good soil" people, in contrast to all the other groups, follow Jesus no matter what the cost. Which type of soil are you?

8:16, 17 When the light of the truth about Jesus illuminates us, we have the duty to shine that light to help others. Our witness for Christ should be public, not hidden. We should not keep the benefits for ourselves alone but pass them on to others. In order to be helpful, we need to be well placed. Seek opportunities to shine your light when unbelievers need help to see.

8:18 Applying God's Word helps us grow. This is a principle of growth in physical, mental, and spiritual life. For example,

a muscle, when exercised, will grow stronger, but an unused muscle will grow weak and flabby. If you are not growing stronger, you are growing weaker; it is impossible for you to stand still. How are you using what God has taught you?

8:21 Jesus' true family is comprised of those who hear *and* obey his words. Hearing without obeying is not enough. As Jesus loved his mother (see John 19:25-27), so he loves us. Christ offers us an intimate family relationship with him (Romans 8:14-16).

Jesus Calms the Storm (**87**/Matthew 8:23-27; Mark 4:35-41)

22One day Jesus said to his disciples, "Let's cross to the other side of the lake." So they got into a boat and started out. 23As they sailed across, Jesus settled down for a nap. But soon a fierce storm came down on the lake. The boat was filling with water, and they were in real danger.

24The disciples went and woke him up, shouting, "Master, Master, we're going to drown!"

When Jesus woke up, he rebuked the wind and the raging waves. Suddenly the storm stopped and all was calm. 25Then he asked them, "Where is your faith?"

The disciples were terrified and amazed. "Who is this man?" they asked each other. "When he gives a command, even the wind and waves obey him!"

Jesus Sends Demons into a Herd of Pigs (**88**/Matthew 8:28-34; Mark 5:1-20)

26So they arrived in the region of the Gerasenes,* across the lake from Galilee. 27As Jesus was climbing out of the boat, a man who was possessed by demons came out to meet him. For a long time he had been homeless and naked, living in a cemetery outside the town.

28As soon as he saw Jesus, he shrieked and fell down in front of him. Then he screamed, "Why are you interfering with me, Jesus, Son of the Most High God? Please, I beg you, don't torture me!" 29For Jesus had already commanded the evil* spirit to come out of him. This spirit had often taken control of the man. Even when he was placed under guard and put in chains and shackles, he simply broke them and rushed out into the wilderness, completely under the demon's power.

8:28
Matt 8:29
Mark 1:23-24

30Jesus demanded, "What is your name?"

"Legion," he replied, for he was filled with many demons. 31The demons kept begging Jesus not to send them into the bottomless pit.*

8:31
Rev 9:1-2, 11; 20:3

32There happened to be a large herd of pigs feeding on the hillside nearby, and the demons begged him to let them enter into the pigs.

So Jesus gave them permission. 33Then the demons came out of the man and entered the pigs, and the entire herd plunged down the steep hillside into the lake and drowned.

8:26 Other manuscripts read *Gadarenes;* still others read *Gergesenes;* also in 8:37. See Matt 8:28; Mark 5:1.
8:29 Greek *unclean.* **8:31** Or *the abyss,* or *the underworld.*

• **8:23** The Sea of Galilee (actually a large lake) is even today the scene of fierce storms, sometimes with waves as high as 20 feet. Jesus' disciples were not frightened without cause. Even though several of them were expert fishermen and knew how to handle a boat, their peril was real.

• **8:23-25** When caught in the storms of life, it is easy to think that God has lost control and that we're at the mercy of the winds of fate. In reality, God is sovereign. He controls the history of the world as well as our personal destiny. Just as Jesus calmed the waves, he can calm whatever storms you may face.

HEALING A DEMON-POSSESSED MAN
As he traveled through Galilee, Jesus told many parables and met many people, as recorded in Matthew and Mark. Later, from Capernaum, Jesus and the disciples set out in a boat, only to encounter a fierce storm. Jesus calmed the storm and, when they landed, exorcised a "legion" of demons.

8:26 The region of the Gerasenes was a Gentile region southeast of the Sea of Galilee, location of the Ten Towns. These were Greek cities that belonged to no country and were self-governing. Although Jews would not have raised pigs because the Jewish religion labeled them unclean, the Gentiles had no such aversion.

• **8:27, 28** These demons recognized Jesus and his authority immediately. They knew who Jesus was and what his great power could do to them. Demons, Satan's messengers, are powerful and destructive. Still active today, they attempt to distort and destroy people's relationship with God. Demons and demon possession are real. It is vital that believers recognize the power of Satan and his demons, but we shouldn't let curiosity lead us to get involved with demonic forces (Deuteronomy 18:10-12). Demons are powerless against those who trust in Jesus. If we resist the devil, he will leave us alone (James 4:7).

8:29-31 The demons begged Jesus to spare them from the bottomless pit, which is also mentioned in Revelation 9:1 and 20:1-3 as the place of confinement for Satan and his messengers. The demons, of course, knew all about this place of confinement, and they didn't want to go there.

• **8:30** The demon's name was Legion. A legion was the largest unit in the Roman army, having between 3,000 and 6,000 soldiers. The man was possessed by not one but many demons.

• **8:33** Why didn't Jesus just destroy these demons—or send them to the bottomless pit? Because the time for such work had not yet come. He healed many people of the destructive effects of demon possession, but he did not yet destroy demons. The same question could be asked today—why doesn't Jesus stop all the evil in the world? His time for that has not yet come. But it will come. The book of Revelation portrays the future victory of Jesus over Satan, his demons, and all evil.

8:33-37 A man had been freed from the devil's power, but the people in the town thought only about their livestock. People have

34When the herdsmen saw it, they fled to the nearby town and the surrounding countryside, spreading the news as they ran. 35People rushed out to see what had happened. A crowd soon gathered around Jesus, and they saw the man who had been freed from the demons. He was sitting at Jesus' feet, fully clothed and perfectly sane, and they were all afraid. 36Then those who had seen what happened told the others how the demon-possessed man had been healed. 37And all the people in the region of the Gerasenes begged Jesus to go away and leave them alone, for a great wave of fear swept over them.

8:37
Acts 16:39

So Jesus returned to the boat and left, crossing back to the other side of the lake. 38The man who had been freed from the demons begged to go with him. But Jesus sent him home, saying, 39 "No, go back to your family, and tell them everything God has done for you." So he went all through the town proclaiming the great things Jesus had done for him.

Jesus Heals a Bleeding Woman and Restores a Girl to Life
(89/Matthew 9:18-26; Mark 5:21-43)

40On the other side of the lake the crowds welcomed Jesus, because they had been waiting for him. 41Then a man named Jairus, a leader of the local synagogue, came and fell at Jesus' feet, pleading with him to come home with him. 42His only daughter,* who was about twelve years old, was dying.

8:43
Lev 15:25-30

As Jesus went with him, he was surrounded by the crowds. 43A woman in the crowd had suffered for twelve years with constant bleeding,* and she could find no cure. 44Coming up behind Jesus, she touched the fringe of his robe. Immediately, the bleeding stopped.

45 "Who touched me?" Jesus asked.

Everyone denied it, and Peter said, "Master, this whole crowd is pressing up against you."

8:46
Luke 5:17; 6:19

46But Jesus said, "Someone deliberately touched me, for I felt healing power go out from me." 47When the woman realized that she could not stay hidden, she began to tremble and fell to her knees in front of him. The whole crowd heard her explain why she had touched him and that she had been immediately healed. 48 "Daughter," he said to her, "your faith has made you well. Go in peace."

8:48
Matt 9:22
Mark 5:34
Luke 7:50; 17:19;
18:42

49While he was still speaking to her, a messenger arrived from the home of Jairus, the leader of the synagogue. He told him, "Your daughter is dead. There's no use troubling the Teacher now."

8:42 Or *His only child, a daughter.* **8:43** Some manuscripts add *having spent everything she had on doctors.*

---

always tended to value financial gain above needy people. Much injustice and oppression, both at home and abroad, is the direct result of some individual's or company's urge to get rich. People are continually being sacrificed to the god of money. Don't think more highly of "pigs" than of people.

8:38, 39 Often Jesus would ask those he healed to be quiet about the healing, but he urged this man to return to his family and tell them what God had done for him. Why? (1) Jesus knew the man would be an effective witness to those who knew his previous condition and could attest to the miraculous healing. (2) Jesus wanted to expand his ministry by introducing his message into this Gentile area. (3) Jesus knew that the Gentiles, since they were not expecting a Messiah, would not divert his ministry by trying to crown him king. (In fact, the people in this region had asked him to go away.) When God touches your life, don't be afraid to share the wonderful events with your family and friends.

8:41 The synagogue was the local center of worship. The synagogue leader was responsible for administration, building maintenance, and worship supervision. It would have been quite unusual for a respected synagogue leader to fall at the feet of an itinerant preacher and beg him to heal his little daughter. Jesus honored this man's humble faith (8:50, 54-56).

• **8:43-48** Many people surrounded Jesus as he made his way toward Jairus's house. It was virtually impossible to get through the multitude, but one woman fought her way desperately through the crowd in order to touch Jesus. As soon as she did so, she was healed. What a difference there is between the crowds that are curious about Jesus and the few who reach out and touch him! Today, many people are familiar with who Jesus

is, but nothing in their lives is changed by knowing he is God's Son. It is only faith in Christ that releases God's healing power. Are you just curious about God, or do you reach out to him in faith, knowing that his mercy will bring healing to your body, soul, and spirit?

• **8:45, 46** Certainly Jesus knew who had touched him—he knew that someone had intentionally touched him in order to receive some sort of healing. Jesus wanted the woman to step forward and identify herself. To let her slip away would have meant a lost opportunity for Jesus to teach her that his cloak did not have magical properties, it had been her faith in him that had healed her. He may also have wanted to teach the crowds a lesson. According to Jewish law, a man who touched a menstruating woman became ceremonially unclean (Leviticus 15:19-28). This was true whether her bleeding was normal or, as in this woman's case, the result of an abnormal condition. To protect themselves from such defilement, Jewish men carefully avoided touching, speaking to, or even looking at women. By contrast, Jesus proclaimed to hundreds of people that this "unclean" woman had touched him—and then he healed her. In Jesus' mind, this suffering woman was not to be overlooked. As God's creation, she deserved attention and respect.

⁵⁰But when Jesus heard what had happened, he said to Jairus, "Don't be afraid. Just have faith, and she will be healed."

⁵¹When they arrived at the house, Jesus wouldn't let anyone go in with him except Peter, John, James, and the little girl's father and mother. ⁵²The house was filled with people weeping and wailing, but he said, "Stop the weeping! She isn't dead; she's only asleep."

⁵³But the crowd laughed at him because they all knew she had died. ⁵⁴Then Jesus took her by the hand and said in a loud voice, "My child, get up!" ⁵⁵And at that moment her life* returned, and she immediately stood up! Then Jesus told them to give her something to eat. ⁵⁶Her parents were overwhelmed, but Jesus insisted that they not tell anyone what had happened.

8:52 Luke 7:13

8:54 Luke 7:14

8:56 Matt 8:4
Mark 7:36
Luke 5:14

Jesus Sends Out the Twelve Disciples (93/Matthew 10:1-15; Mark 6:7-13)

9 One day Jesus called together his twelve disciples* and gave them power and authority to cast out all demons and to heal all diseases. ²Then he sent them out to tell everyone about the Kingdom of God and to heal the sick. ³"Take nothing for your journey," he instructed them. "Don't take a walking stick, a traveler's bag, food, money,* or even a change of clothes. ⁴Wherever you go, stay in the same house until you leave town. ⁵And if a town refuses to welcome you, shake its dust from your feet as you leave to show that you have abandoned those people to their fate."

⁶So they began their circuit of the villages, preaching the Good News and healing the sick.

9:3 Luke 10:4; 22:35

9:4 Luke 10:5-7

9:5 Luke 10:10-11
Acts 13:51

Herod Kills John the Baptist (95/Matthew 14:1-12; Mark 6:14-29)

⁷When Herod Antipas, the ruler of Galilee,* heard about everything Jesus was doing, he was puzzled. Some were saying that John the Baptist had been raised from the dead. ⁸Others thought Jesus was Elijah or one of the other prophets risen from the dead.

9:8 Matt 11:14

8:55 Or *her spirit.*   **9:1** Greek *the Twelve;* other manuscripts read *the twelve apostles.*   **9:3** Or *silver coins.*
9:7 Greek *Herod the tetrarch.* Herod Antipas was a son of King Herod and was ruler over Galilee.

8:50 Anyone with a child can readily put himself or herself emotionally in Jairus's place. His daughter had died while they were on the way home. Luke did not record it, but the poor man probably cried out in grief. Jesus surely felt the father's very human grief. Jesus said, "Don't be afraid. Just have faith." Again, Luke didn't record Jairus's reaction to these words, but Jairus must have had at least some flicker of hope because he did complete his mission in bringing Jesus to his house. When you experience intense grief over the loss of a loved one, breakup of a marriage, loss of a job, or rejection of a close friend, don't abandon hope. Don't turn away from the one Person who can help you. Do what Jairus did: Don't be afraid; just have faith. Your hope is found in the resurrected Lord, the one with power over life and death.

• **8:56** Jesus told the parents not to talk about their daughter's healing because he knew the facts would speak for themselves. Jesus was concerned for his ministry. He did not want to be known as just a miracle worker; he wanted people to listen to his words that could heal their broken spiritual lives.

9:1-10 Note Jesus' methods of leadership. He empowered his disciples (9:1), gave them specific instructions so they knew what to do (9:3, 4), told them how to deal with tough times (9:5), and held them accountable (9:10). As you lead others, study the Master Leader's pattern. Which of these elements do you need to incorporate into your leadership?

9:2 Jesus announced his Kingdom by both preaching and healing, and he sent his disciples out to do the same. If he had limited himself to preaching, people might have seen his Kingdom as spiritual only. If he had healed without preaching, people might not have realized the spiritual importance of his mission. Most of his listeners expected a Messiah who would bring wealth and power to their nation; they preferred material benefits to spiritual discernment. The truth about Jesus is that he is both God and man, both spiritual and physical; and the salvation that he offers is both for the soul and the body. Any group or teaching that emphasizes soul at the expense of body, or body at the expense of soul, is in danger of distorting Jesus' Good News.

9:3, 4 Why were the disciples instructed to depend on others while they went from town to town preaching the Good News?

Their purpose was to blanket Judea with Jesus' message, and by traveling light they could move quickly. Their dependence on others had other good effects as well: (1) It clearly showed that the Messiah had not come to offer wealth to his followers. (2) It forced the disciples to rely on God's power and not on their own provision. (3) It involved the villagers and made them more eager to hear the message. This was an excellent approach for the disciples' short-term mission; it was not intended, however, to be a permanent way of life for them.

9:4 The disciples were told to stay in only one home in each town because they were not to offend their hosts by moving to a home that was more comfortable or socially prominent. To remain in one home was not a burden for the homeowner, because the disciples' stay in each community was short. (See also 10:7.)

9:5 Shaking the dust of certain towns from their feet had deep cultural implications. Pious Jews would do this after passing through Gentile cities to show their separation from Gentile practices. If the disciples were to shake the dust of a *Jewish* town from their feet, it would show their separation from Jews who rejected their Messiah. This action also would show that the disciples were not responsible for how the people responded to their message. Neither are we responsible if we have carefully and truthfully presented Christ but our message is rejected. Like the disciples, we must move on to others whom God desires to reach.

9:7 For more information on Herod Antipas, see his Profile in Mark 6, p. 1629.

9:7, 8 People found accepting Jesus as the Son of God so difficult that they tried to come up with other solutions—most of which sound quite unbelievable to us. Many thought that Jesus must be someone who had come back to life, perhaps John the Baptist or another prophet. Some suggested that he was Elijah, the great prophet who had not died but had been taken to heaven in a chariot of fire (2 Kings 2:1-11). Very few found the correct answer, as Peter did (9:20). Many people today still have difficulty accepting Jesus as the fully human yet fully divine Son of God. People are still trying to find alternate explanations—a great prophet, a radical political leader, a self-

Messiah sent form God.

9:9
Luke 23:8

⁹"I beheaded John," Herod said, "so who is this man about whom I hear such stories?" And he kept trying to see him.

Jesus Feeds Five Thousand (**96**/Matthew 14:13-21; Mark 6:30-44; John 6:1-15)
¹⁰When the apostles returned, they told Jesus everything they had done. Then he slipped quietly away with them toward the town of Bethsaida. ¹¹But the crowds found out where he was going, and they followed him. He welcomed them and taught them about the Kingdom of God, and he healed those who were sick.

¹²Late in the afternoon the twelve disciples came to him and said, "Send the crowds away to the nearby villages and farms, so they can find food and lodging for the night. There is nothing to eat here in this remote place."

Jesus singled out three of his 12 disciples for special training. James, his brother John, and Peter made up this inner circle. Each eventually played a key role in the early church. Peter became a great speaker, John became a major writer, and James was the first of the 12 disciples to die for his faith.

The fact that his name is always mentioned before John's indicates that James was the older brother. Zebedee, their father, owned a fishing business in which they worked alongside Peter and Andrew. When Peter, Andrew, and John left Galilee to see John the Baptist, James stayed back with the boats and fishing nets. Later, when Jesus called them, James was as eager as his partners to follow.

James enjoyed being in the inner circle of Jesus' disciples, but he misunderstood Jesus' purpose. He and his brother even tried to secure their role in Jesus' Kingdom by asking Jesus to promise them each a special position. Like the other disciples, James had a limited view of what Jesus was doing on earth, picturing only an earthly kingdom that would overthrow Rome and restore Israel's former glory. But above all, James wanted to be with Jesus. He had found the right leader, even though he was still on the wrong timetable. It took Jesus' death and resurrection to correct his view.

James was the first of the 12 disciples to die for the gospel. He was willing to die because he knew Jesus had conquered death, the doorway to eternal life. Our expectations about life will be limited if this life is all we can see. Jesus promised eternal life to those willing to trust him. If we believe this promise, he will give us the courage to stand for him even during dangerous times.

Strengths and accomplishments	• One of the 12 disciples • One of a special inner circle of three with Peter and John • First of the 12 disciples to be killed for his faith
Weaknesses and mistakes	• Two outbursts from James indicate struggles with temper (Luke 9:54) and selfishness (Mark 10:37). Both times, he and his brother, John, spoke as one
Lesson from his life	• Loss of life is not too heavy a price to pay for following Jesus
Vital statistics	• Where: Galilee • Occupations: Fisherman, disciple • Relatives: Father: Zebedee. Mother: Salome. Brother: John. • Contemporaries: Jesus, Pilate, Herod Agrippa
Key verses	"Then James and John, the sons of Zebedee, came over and spoke to him. 'Teacher,' they said, 'we want you to do us a favor.' 'What is your request?' he asked. They replied, 'When you sit on your glorious throne, we want to sit in places of honor next to you, one on your right and the other on your left'" (Mark 10:35-37).

James's story is told in the Gospels. He is also mentioned in Acts 1:13 and 12:2.

deceived rabble-rouser. None of these explanations can account for Jesus' miracles or especially his glorious resurrection. In the end, the attempts to explain away Jesus are far more difficult to believe than the truth.

9:9 For the story of why Herod had John beheaded, see Mark 6:14-29.

9:10, 11 Jesus had tried to slip quietly away from the crowds, but they found out where he was going and followed him. Instead of showing impatience at this interruption, Jesus welcomed the people and ministered to their needs. How do you see people who interrupt your schedule—as nuisances or as the reason for your life and ministry?

9:11 The Kingdom of God was a focal point of Jesus' teaching. He explained that it was not just a future Kingdom; it was among them, embodied in him, the Messiah. Even though the Kingdom will not be complete until Jesus comes again in glory, we do not have to wait to experience it. The Kingdom of God begins in the hearts of those who believe in Jesus (17:21). It is as present with us today as it was with the Judeans over 2,000 years ago.

¹³But Jesus said, "You feed them."

"But we have only five loaves of bread and two fish," they answered. "Or are you expecting us to go and buy enough food for this whole crowd?" ¹⁴For there were about 5,000 men there.

Jesus replied, "Tell them to sit down in groups of about fifty each." ¹⁵So the people all sat down. ¹⁶Jesus took the five loaves and two fish, looked up toward heaven, and blessed them. Then, breaking the loaves into pieces, he kept giving the bread and fish to the disciples so they could distribute it to the people. ¹⁷They all ate as much as they wanted, and afterward, the disciples picked up twelve baskets of leftovers!

9:17 2 Kgs 4:44

Peter Says Jesus Is the Messiah (109/Matthew 16:13-20; Mark 8:27-30)

¹⁸One day Jesus left the crowds to pray alone. Only his disciples were with him, and he asked them, "Who do people say I am?"

¹⁹"Well," they replied, "some say John the Baptist, some say Elijah, and others say you are one of the other ancient prophets risen from the dead."

²⁰Then he asked them, "But who do you say I am?"

Peter replied, "You are the Messiah* sent from God!"

9:19 Luke 9:7-8
9:20 John 6:68-69

Jesus Predicts His Death the First Time (110/Matthew 16:21-28; Mark 8:31–9:1)

²¹Jesus warned his disciples not to tell anyone who he was. ²²"The Son of Man* must suffer many terrible things," he said. "He will be rejected by the elders, the leading priests, and the teachers of religious law. He will be killed, but on the third day he will be raised from the dead."

²³Then he said to the crowd, "If any of you wants to be my follower, you must turn from your selfish ways, take up your cross daily, and follow me. ²⁴If you try to hang on to your life, you will lose it. But if you give up your life for my sake, you will save it. ²⁵And what do you benefit if you gain the whole world but are yourself lost or destroyed? ²⁶If anyone is ashamed of me and my message, the Son of Man will be ashamed of that person when he

9:23 Matt 10:38 Luke 14:27
9:24 Matt 10:39 Luke 17:33 John 12:25
9:26 Matt 10:33 Luke 12:9 2 Tim 2:12

9:20 Or *the Christ. Messiah* (a Hebrew term) and *Christ* (a Greek term) both mean "the anointed one." **9:22** "Son of Man" is a title Jesus used for himself.

• **9:13, 14** When the disciples expressed concern about where the crowd of thousands would eat, Jesus offered a surprising solution: "You feed them." The disciples protested, focusing their attention on what they didn't have (food and money). Do you think God would ask you to do something that you and he together couldn't handle? Don't let your lack of resources blind you to God's power.

• **9:16, 17** Why did Jesus bother to feed these people? He could just as easily have sent them on their way, but Jesus does not ignore needs. He is concerned with every aspect of life—the physical as well as the spiritual. As we work to bring wholeness to people's lives, we must never ignore the fact that all of us have both physical and spiritual needs. It is impossible to minister effectively to one type of need without considering the other.

9:18-20 The Christian faith goes beyond knowing what others believe. It requires us to hold beliefs for ourselves. When Jesus asks, "Who do you say I am?" he wants us to take a stand. Who do *you* say Jesus is?

9:21 Jesus told his disciples not to tell anyone that he was the Christ because at this point they didn't fully understand the significance of that confession—nor would anyone else. Everyone still expected the Messiah to come as a conquering king. But even though Jesus was the Messiah, he still had to suffer, be rejected by the leaders, be killed, and rise from the dead. When the disciples saw all this happen to Jesus, they would understand what the Messiah had come to do. Only then would they be equipped to share the Good News that the Messiah had come and brought his Kingdom to people's hearts.

9:22 This was the turning point in Jesus' instruction to his disciples. From then on he began teaching clearly and specifically what they could expect, so that they would not be surprised when it happened. He explained that he would not *now* be the

conquering Messiah because he first had to suffer, die, and rise again. But one day he would return in great glory to set up his eternal Kingdom.

9:23 To take up the cross meant to carry one's own cross to the place of crucifixion. Many Galileans had been killed that way by the Romans—and Jesus would face it as well. With this word picture, Christ presented a clear and challenging description of the Christian life. Being his disciple means putting aside selfish desires, shouldering one's "cross" every day, and following him. It is simple and yet so demanding. For the original Twelve, this meant literal suffering and death. For believers today, it means understanding that we belong to him and that we live to serve his purposes. Consider this: Do you think of your relationship with God primarily in terms of what's in it for you (which is considerable) or in terms of what you can do for him? Are you willing to deny yourself, take up your cross daily, and follow him? Anything less is not discipleship; it is merely superficial lip service. (See also the note on 14:27.)

9:24, 25 If this present life is most important to you, you will do everything you can to protect it. You will not want to do anything that might endanger your safety, health, or comfort. By contrast, if following Jesus is most important, you may find yourself in unsafe, unhealthy, and uncomfortable places. You may risk death, but you will not fear it because you know that Jesus will raise you to eternal life. Nothing material can compensate for the loss of eternal life. Jesus' disciples are not to use their lives on earth merely to please themselves; they should spend their lives serving God and others.

9:26 Luke's Greek audience would have had difficulty understanding a God who could die, just as Jesus' Jewish audience would have been perplexed by a Messiah who would let himself be captured and killed. Both would be ashamed of Jesus if they did not look past his death to his glorious resurrection and second coming. Then they would see Jesus, not as a loser,

returns in his glory and in the glory of the Father and the holy angels. 27 I tell you the truth, some standing here right now will not die before they see the Kingdom of God."

Jesus Is Transfigured on the Mountain (111/Matthew 17:1-13; Mark 9:2-13)

28 About eight days later Jesus took Peter, John, and James up on a mountain to pray. 29 And as he was praying, the appearance of his face was transformed, and his clothes became dazzling white. 30 Suddenly, two men, Moses and Elijah, appeared and began talking with Jesus.

9:31-32
2 Pet 1:15-16

31 They were glorious to see. And they were speaking about his exodus from this world, which was about to be fulfilled in Jerusalem.

32 Peter and the others had fallen asleep. When they woke up, they saw Jesus' glory and the two men standing with him. 33 As Moses and Elijah were starting to leave, Peter, not even knowing what he was saying, blurted out, "Master, it's wonderful for us to be here! Let's make three shelters as memorials*—one for you, one for Moses, and one for Elijah." 34 But even as he was saying this, a cloud overshadowed them, and terror gripped them as the cloud covered them.

9:35
Deut 18:15
Ps 2:7
Isa 42:1
Matt 3:17
2 Pet 1:17

35 Then a voice from the cloud said, "This is my Son, my Chosen One.* Listen to him." 36 When the voice finished, Jesus was there alone. They didn't tell anyone at that time what they had seen.

Jesus Heals a Demon-Possessed Boy (112/Matthew 17:14-21; Mark 9:14-29)

9:38
Luke 7:12

37 The next day, after they had come down the mountain, a large crowd met Jesus. 38 A man in the crowd called out to him, "Teacher, I beg you to look at my son, my only child. 39 An evil spirit keeps seizing him, making him scream. It throws him into convulsions so that he foams at the mouth. It batters him and hardly ever leaves him alone. 40 I begged your disciples to cast out the spirit, but they couldn't do it."

41 Jesus said, "You faithless and corrupt people! How long must I be with you and put up with you?" Then he said to the man, "Bring your son here."

42 As the boy came forward, the demon knocked him to the ground and threw him into a violent convulsion. But Jesus rebuked the evil* spirit and healed the boy. Then he gave him back to his father. 43 Awe gripped the people as they saw this majestic display of God's power.

Jesus Predicts His Death the Second Time (113/Matthew 17:22-23; Mark 9:30-32)

9:43b-45
2 Pet 1:16
9:44
Luke 18:32
9:45
Mark 9:32
Luke 18:34

While everyone was marveling at everything he was doing, Jesus said to his disciples, 44 "Listen to me and remember what I say. The Son of Man is going to be betrayed into the hands of his enemies." 45 But they didn't know what he meant. Its significance was hidden from them, so they couldn't understand it, and they were afraid to ask him about it.

9:33 Greek *three tabernacles.*   **9:35** Some manuscripts read *This is my dearly loved Son.*   **9:42** Greek *unclean.*

but as the Lord of the universe, who through his death brought salvation to those who believe.

• **9:27** When Jesus said some would not die without seeing the Kingdom, he may have been referring to: (1) Peter, James, and John, who would witness the Transfiguration eight days later; (2) all who would witness the Resurrection and Ascension; (3) all who would take part in the spread of the church after Pentecost. Jesus' listeners would not have to wait for another, future Messiah. The Kingdom was among them, and would soon come in power.

• **9:29, 30** Jesus took Peter, James, and John to the top of a mountain to show them who he really was—not merely a great prophet, but God's own Son. Moses, representing the Law, and Elijah, representing the Prophets, appeared with Jesus. Then God's voice singled out Jesus as the long-awaited Messiah, who possessed divine authority. Jesus would fulfill both the Law and the Prophets (Matthew 5:17).

9:33 When Peter suggested making three shelters, he may have been thinking of the Festival of Shelters, where shelters were set up to commemorate the Exodus, God's deliverance of the Israelites from slavery in Egypt. Peter wanted to keep Moses and Elijah with them, but this was not what God wanted. Peter's desire to build memorials for Jesus, Moses, and Elijah may also show his understanding that real faith is built on three cornerstones: the Law, the Prophets, and Jesus. But Peter grew in his understanding, and eventually he would write of Jesus as the "cornerstone" of the church (1 Peter 2:6).

9:35 As God's Son, Jesus has God's power and authority; thus, his words should be our final authority. If a person's teaching is true, it will agree with Jesus' teachings. Don't be hasty to seek advice and guidance from merely human sources and thereby neglect Christ's message. Test everything you hear against Jesus' words and you will not be led astray. If we believe he is God's Son, then we surely will want to do what he says.

9:37-39 Peter, James, and John experienced a wonderful moment on the mountain, and they probably didn't want to leave. Sometimes we too have such an inspiring experience that we want to stay where we are—away from the reality and problems of our daily life. Knowing that struggles await us in the valley encourages us to linger on the mountaintop. Yet staying on top of a mountain prohibits our ministering to others. Instead of becoming spiritual giants, we would soon become dwarfed by our self-centeredness. We need times of retreat and renewal but only so we can return to minister to the world. Our faith must make sense off the mountain as well as on it.

9:40 Why couldn't the disciples cast out the evil spirit? For a possible answer, see the note on Mark 9:18.

9:45, 46 The disciples didn't understand Jesus' words about his death. They still thought of Jesus as only an earthly king, and they were concerned about their places in the Kingdom he would set up. So they ignored Jesus' words about his death and began arguing about who would be the greatest.

Mark
9:29
footnote
in Bible

The Disciples Argue about Who Would Be the Greatest
(**115**/Matthew 18:1-6; Mark 9:33-37)

46Then his disciples began arguing about which of them was the greatest. 47But Jesus knew their thoughts, so he brought a little child to his side. 48Then he said to them, "Anyone who welcomes a little child like this on my behalf* welcomes me, and anyone who welcomes me also welcomes my Father who sent me. Whoever is the least among you is the greatest."

9:47
Matt 9:4
9:48
Matt 10:40
Luke 10:16

The Disciples Forbid Another to Use Jesus' Name (**116**/Mark 9:38-41)

49John said to Jesus, "Master, we saw someone using your name to cast out demons, but we told him to stop because he isn't in our group."

50But Jesus said, "Don't stop him! Anyone who is not against you is for you."

9:50
Matt 12:30
Luke 11:23

2. Jesus' ministry on the way to Jerusalem
Jesus Teaches about the Cost of Following Him (**122**/Matthew 8:18-22)

51As the time drew near for him to ascend to heaven, Jesus resolutely set out for Jerusalem. 52He sent messengers ahead to a Samaritan village to prepare for his arrival. 53But the people of the village did not welcome Jesus because he was on his way to Jerusalem. 54When James and John saw this, they said to Jesus, "Lord, should we call down fire from heaven to burn them up*?" 55But Jesus turned and rebuked them.* 56So they went on to another village.

9:51
Mark 16:19
Luke 13:22; 17:11;
18:31; 19:28
9:54
2 Kgs 1:10, 12

57As they were walking along, someone said to Jesus, "I will follow you wherever you go."

58But Jesus replied, "Foxes have dens to live in, and birds have nests, but the Son of Man has no place even to lay his head."

59He said to another person, "Come, follow me."

The man agreed, but he said, "Lord, first let me return home and bury my father."

60But Jesus told him, "Let the spiritually dead bury their own dead!* Your duty is to go and preach about the Kingdom of God."

9:60
Matt 3:2
9:61
1 Kgs 19:20
9:62
Phil 3:13

61Another said, "Yes, Lord, I will follow you, but first let me say good-bye to my family."

62But Jesus told him, "Anyone who puts a hand to the plow and then looks back is not fit for the Kingdom of God."

9:48 Greek *in my name.* **9:54** Some manuscripts add *as Elijah did.* **9:55** Some manuscripts add an expanded conclusion to verse 55 and an additional sentence in verse 56: *And he said, "You don't realize what your hearts are like.* 56*For the Son of Man has not come to destroy people's lives, but to save them."* **9:60** Greek *Let the dead bury their own dead.*

9:48 Our care for others is a measure of our greatness. How much concern do you show for others? This is a vital question that can accurately measure your greatness in God's eyes. How have you expressed your care for others lately, especially the helpless, the needy, the poor—those who can't return your love and concern? Your honest answer to that question will give you a good idea of your real greatness.

9:49, 50 The disciples were jealous. Nine of them together had been unable to cast out a single evil spirit (9:40), but when they saw a man who was not one of their group casting out demons, they told him to stop. Our pride is hurt when someone else succeeds where we have failed, but Jesus says there is no room for such jealousy in the spiritual warfare of his Kingdom. Share Jesus' open-arms attitude toward Christian workers outside your group. Rejoice when they are able to bring people to Christ.

• **9:51** Although Jesus knew he would face persecution and death in Jerusalem, he was determined to go there. That kind of resolve should characterize our lives as well. When God gives us a course of action, we must move steadily toward our destination, regardless of the potential hazards that await us there.

9:53 After Assyria invaded Israel, the northern kingdom, and resettled it with its own people (2 Kings 17:24-41), the mixed race that developed became known as the Samaritans. "Pure-bred" Jews hated these "half-breeds," and the Samaritans in turn hated the Jews. So many tensions arose between the two peoples that Jewish travelers between Galilee and southern Judea often would walk around rather than through Samaritan territory, even though this would lengthen their trip considerably. Jesus held no such prejudices, and he sent messengers ahead to get things ready in a Samaritan village. But the village refused to welcome these Jewish travelers who were headed for Jerusalem.

9:54 When the Samaritan village did not welcome Jesus and his disciples, James and John didn't want to stop at shaking the dust from their feet (9:5). They wanted to retaliate by calling down fire from heaven on the people, as Elijah had done on the servants of a wicked king of Israel (2 Kings 1). When others reject or scorn us, we, too, may feel like retaliating. We must remember that judgment belongs to God, and we must not expect him to use his power to carry out personal vendettas.

• **9:59** Luke does not say whether the father is already dead or terminally ill. It seems likely that if the father were dead, the son would have been fulfilling the burial duties. Jesus was saying that true discipleship requires instant action. Jesus did not teach people to forsake responsibilities to family, but he often gave commands to people in light of their real motives. Perhaps this man wanted to delay following Christ and was using his father as an excuse. Following Jesus has a cost, and each of us must be ready to serve, even when it requires sacrifice.

• **9:62** What does Jesus want from us? Total dedication, not half-hearted commitment. We can't pick and choose among Jesus' ideas and follow him selectively; we have to accept the cross along with the crown. We must count the cost and be willing to abandon everything else that has given us security—without looking back. With our focus on Jesus, we should allow nothing to distract us from following him.

Jesus Sends Out Seventy-Two Messengers (**130**)

10 The Lord now chose seventy-two* other disciples and sent them ahead in pairs to all the towns and places he planned to visit. ²These were his instructions to them: "The harvest is great, but the workers are few. So pray to the Lord who is in charge of the harvest; ask him to send more workers into his fields. ³Now go, and remember that I am sending you out as lambs among wolves. ⁴Don't take any money with you, nor a traveler's bag, nor an extra pair of sandals. And don't stop to greet anyone on the road.

⁵ "Whenever you enter someone's home, first say, 'May God's peace be on this house.' ⁶If those who live there are peaceful, the blessing will stand; if they are not, the blessing will return to you. ⁷Don't move around from home to home. Stay in one place, eating and drinking what they provide. Don't hesitate to accept hospitality, because those who work deserve their pay.

⁸ "If you enter a town and it welcomes you, eat whatever is set before you. ⁹Heal the sick, and tell them, 'The Kingdom of God is near you now.' ¹⁰But if a town refuses to welcome you, go out into its streets and say, ¹¹'We wipe even the dust of your town from our feet to show that we have abandoned you to your fate. And know this—the Kingdom of God is near!' ¹²I assure you, even wicked Sodom will be better off than such a town on judgment day.

10:1 Mark 6:7
10:2 Matt 9:37-38 John 4:35
10:3 Matt 10:16
10:4 2 Kgs 4:29 Luke 9:3
10:7 1 Cor 9:6-14 1 Tim 5:18
10:9 Matt 3:2
10:12 Gen 19:24-25 Matt 10:15

10:1 Some manuscripts read *seventy*; also in 10:17.

A COLLECTION OF ATTITUDES ABOUT OTHERS' NEEDS

To the expert in religious law . . . . the wounded man was a subject to discuss.

To the bandits . . . . the wounded man was someone to use and exploit.

To the religious men . . . . the wounded man was a problem to be avoided.

To the innkeeper · · · · · · · · · · · · · · · · · · the wounded man was a customer to serve for a fee.

To the Samaritan . . . . the wounded man was a human being worth being cared for and loved.

To Jesus . . . . all of them and all of us were worth dying for.

Confronting the needs of others brings out various attitudes in us. Jesus used the story of the good but despised Samaritan to make clear what attitude was acceptable to him. If we are honest, we often will find ourselves in the place of the expert in religious law, needing to learn again who our neighbor is. Note these different attitudes toward the wounded man.

10:1, 2 Far more than 12 people had been following Jesus. Here Jesus designated a group of 72 to prepare a number of towns for his later visit. These disciples were not unique in their qualifications. They were not better educated, more capable, or of higher status than Jesus' other followers. What prepared them for this mission was that they had been equipped with Jesus' power and a vision to reach all the people. It is important to dedicate our skills to God's Kingdom, but we must also be equipped with his power and have a clear vision of what he wants us to do.

10:2 Christian service has no unemployment. God has work enough for everyone. Jesus encouraged the disciples not just to do the work but also to pray for workers. Part of every missionary's job is to pray for new workers and to help newcomers learn the ropes. Whatever your role in God's work, pray today for more helpers. Believers are not always to work alone. God wants them to pray, recruit, and equip others to join them as they explore opportunities to serve Jesus. Some people, as soon as they understand the gospel, want to go to convert people immediately. Jesus gave a different approach: begin by mobilizing people to pray. And before praying for unsaved people, pray that other concerned disciples will join you in reaching out to them. God will lead you to an important responsibility, but prayer comes first.

• **10:3** Jesus said he was sending his disciples out "as lambs among wolves." They would have to be careful because they would surely meet with opposition. We, too, are sent into the world like lambs among wolves. Be alert, and remember to face your enemies, not with aggression but with love and gentleness. A dangerous mission requires sincere commitment.

10:7 Jesus' direction to stay in one house avoided certain problems. Shifting from house to house could offend the families who

first took them in. Some families might begin to compete for the disciples' presence, and some might think they weren't good enough to hear their message. If the disciples appeared not to appreciate the hospitality offered them, the town might not accept Jesus when he followed them there. In addition, by staying in one place, the disciples would not have to worry continually about getting good accommodations. They could settle down and focus on their appointed task. (See also 9:4.)

10:7 Jesus told his disciples to accept hospitality graciously because their work entitled them to it. Ministers of the Good News deserve to be supported, and our responsibility is to make sure they have what they need. There are several ways to encourage those who serve Jesus in his church: (1) See that they have an adequate salary; (2) see that they are supported emotionally—plan special times to express appreciation for something they have done; (3) lift their spirits with special surprises from time to time. Our ministers deserve to know we are giving to them cheerfully and generously.

10:8, 9 Jesus gave two rules for the disciples to follow as they traveled. They were to eat what was set before them—that is, they were to accept hospitality without being picky—and they were to heal the sick. Because of the healings, people would be willing to listen to the Good News.

10:12 Sodom was an evil city that God had destroyed because of its great sinfulness (Genesis 19). The city's name is often used to symbolize wickedness and immorality. Sodom will suffer on judgment day, but cities who saw the Messiah and rejected him will suffer even more.

13 "What sorrow awaits you, Korazin and Bethsaida! For if the miracles I did in you had been done in wicked Tyre and Sidon, their people would have repented of their sins long ago, clothing themselves in burlap and throwing ashes on their heads to show their remorse. 14 Yes, Tyre and Sidon will be better off on judgment day than you. 15And you people of Capernaum, will you be honored in heaven? No, you will go down to the place of the dead.*"

16Then he said to the disciples, "Anyone who accepts your message is also accepting me. And anyone who rejects you is rejecting me. And anyone who rejects me is rejecting God, who sent me."

The Seventy-Two Messengers Return (131)

17When the seventy-two disciples returned, they joyfully reported to him, "Lord, even the demons obey us when we use your name!"

18 "Yes," he told them, "I saw Satan fall from heaven like lightning! 19 Look, I have given you authority over all the power of the enemy, and you can walk among snakes and scorpions and crush them. Nothing will injure you. 20But don't rejoice because evil spirits obey you; rejoice because your names are registered in heaven."

21At that same time Jesus was filled with the joy of the Holy Spirit, and he said, "O Father, Lord of heaven and earth, thank you for hiding these things from those who think themselves wise and clever, and for revealing them to the childlike. Yes, Father, it pleased you to do it this way.

22 "My Father has entrusted everything to me. No one truly knows the Son except the Father, and no one truly knows the Father except the Son and those to whom the Son chooses to reveal him."

23Then when they were alone, he turned to the disciples and said, "Blessed are the eyes that see what you have seen. 24I tell you, many prophets and kings longed to see what you see, but they didn't see it. And they longed to hear what you hear, but they didn't hear it."

Jesus Tells the Parable of the Good Samaritan (132)

25One day an expert in religious law stood up to test Jesus by asking him this question: "Teacher, what should I do to inherit eternal life?"

26Jesus replied, "What does the law of Moses say? How do you read it?"

10:15 Greek to Hades.

10:13 Korazin was a city near the Sea of Galilee, probably about two miles north of Capernaum. Tyre and Sidon were cities destroyed by God as punishment for their wickedness (see Ezekiel 26–28).

10:15 Capernaum was Jesus' base for his Galilean ministry. The city was located at an important crossroads used by traders and the Roman army, so a message proclaimed in Capernaum was likely to go far. Many people of Capernaum did not understand Jesus' miracles or believe his teaching, however, and the city was included among those who would be judged for rejecting him.

10:17-20 The disciples had seen tremendous results as they ministered in Jesus' name and with his authority. They were elated by the victories they had witnessed, and Jesus shared their enthusiasm. He helped them get their priorities right, however, by reminding them of their most important victory—that their names were registered in heaven. This honor was more important than any of their accomplishments. As we see God's wonders at work in and through us, we should not lose sight of the greatest wonder of all—our heavenly citizenship.

10:18, 19 Jesus may have been looking ahead to his victory over Satan at the cross. John 12:31, 32 indicates that Satan would be judged and driven out at the time of Jesus' death. On the other hand, Jesus may have been warning his disciples against pride. Perhaps he was referring to Isaiah 14:12-17, which begins, "How you are fallen from heaven, O shining star, son of the morning!" Some interpreters identify this verse with Satan and explain that Satan's pride led to all the evil we see on earth today. To Jesus' disciples, who were thrilled with their power over evil spirits ("snakes and scorpions"), he may have been giving this stern

warning: "Yours is the kind of pride that led to Satan's downfall. Be careful!"

10:21 Jesus thanked God that spiritual truth was for everyone and not just for the elite. Many of life's rewards seem to go to the intelligent, the rich, the good looking, or the powerful, but the Kingdom of God is equally available to all, regardless of position or abilities. We come to Jesus, not through strength or brains, but through childlike trust. Jesus is not opposed to engaging in scholarly pursuits; he is opposed to spiritual pride (being wise in one's own eyes). Join Jesus in thanking God that we all have equal access to him. Trust in God's grace, not in your personal qualifications, for your citizenship in the Kingdom.

10:22 Christ's mission was to reveal God the Father to people. His words brought difficult ideas down to earth. He explained God's love through stories, teachings, and, most of all, his life. By examining Jesus' actions, principles, and attitudes, we can understand God more clearly.

● **10:23, 24** Old Testament men of God, such as David and Isaiah, made many God-inspired predictions that Jesus fulfilled. As Peter later wrote, these prophets wondered what their words meant and when they would be fulfilled (1 Peter 1:10-13). The disciples had the fantastic opportunity of being eyewitnesses to the fulfillment of those prophecies. For many months, however, they took Jesus for granted, not really listening to him or obeying him. We also have a privileged position: the legacy of 2,000 years of church history, the availability of the Bible in hundreds of languages and translations, and access to many excellent pastors and speakers. Yet often we take these for granted. Remember, with privilege comes responsibility. Because we are privileged to know so much about Christ, we must be careful to follow him.

10:27
†Deut 6:5
†Lev 19:18

10:28
Lev 18:5
Rom 10:5

10:29
Luke 16:15

27 The man answered, "'You must love the LORD your God with all your heart, all your soul, all your strength, and all your mind.' And, 'Love your neighbor as yourself.'"*

28 "Right!" Jesus told him. "Do this and you will live!"

29 The man wanted to justify his actions, so he asked Jesus, "And who is my neighbor?"

30 Jesus replied with a story: "A Jewish man was traveling from Jerusalem down to Jericho, and he was attacked by bandits. They stripped him of his clothes, beat him up, and left him half dead beside the road.

10:27 Deut 6:5; Lev 19:18.

MARTHA

Many older brothers and sisters have an irritating tendency to take charge, a habit developed while growing up. We can easily see this pattern in Martha, the older sister of Mary and Lazarus. She was used to being in control.

The fact that Martha, Mary, and Lazarus are remembered for their hospitality takes on added significance when we note that hospitality was a social requirement in their culture. It was considered shameful to turn anyone away from your door. Apparently Martha's family met this requirement very well.

Martha worried about details. She wished to please, to serve, to do the right thing—but she often succeeded in making everyone around her uncomfortable. Perhaps as the oldest she feared shame if her home did not measure up to expectations. She tried to do everything she could to make sure that wouldn't happen. As a result, she found it hard to relax and enjoy her guests and even harder to accept Mary's lack of cooperation in all the preparations. Martha's frustration was so intense that she finally asked Jesus to settle the matter. He gently corrected her attitude and showed her that her priorities, though good, were not the best. The personal attention she gave her guests should be more important than the comforts she tried to provide for them.

Later, following her brother Lazarus's death, Martha could hardly help being herself. When she heard Jesus was finally coming, she rushed out to meet him and expressed her inner conflict of disappointment and hope. Jesus pointed out that her hope was too limited. He was not only Lord over death; he was the resurrection and the life! Moments later, Martha again spoke without thinking, pointing out that four-day-old corpses are well on their way to decomposition. Her awareness of details sometimes kept her from seeing the whole picture, but Jesus was consistently patient with her.

In our last picture of Martha, she is once again serving a meal to Jesus and his disciples. She has not stopped serving. But the Bible records her silence this time. She has begun to learn that what her younger sister already knew—that worship begins with silence and listening.

Strengths and accomplishments	• Known as a hospitable homemaker • Believed in Jesus with growing faith • Had a strong desire to do everything exactly right
Weaknesses and mistakes	• Expected others to agree with her priorities • Was overly concerned with details • Tended to feel sorry for herself when her efforts were not recognized • Limited Jesus' power to this life
Lessons from her life	• Getting caught up in details can make us forget the main reasons for our actions • There is a proper time to listen to Jesus and a proper time to work for him
Vital statistics	• Where: Bethany • Relatives: Sister: Mary. Brother: Lazarus.
Key verse	"But Martha was distracted by the big dinner she was preparing. She came to Jesus and said, 'Lord, doesn't it seem unfair to you that my sister just sits here while I do all the work? Tell her to come and help me'" (Luke 10:40).

Martha's story is told in Luke 10:38-42 and John 11:17-45.

10:27 This expert in religious law was quoting Deuteronomy 6:5 and Leviticus 19:18. He correctly understood that the law demanded total devotion to God and love for one's neighbor. Jesus talked more about these laws elsewhere (see Matthew 19:16-22 and Mark 10:17-22).

• **10:27-37** The legal expert viewed the wounded man as a topic for discussion; the bandits, as an object to exploit; the priest, as a problem to avoid; and the Temple assistant, as an object of curiosity. Only the Samaritan treated him as a person to love.

From the illustration we learn three principles about loving our neighbor: (1) Lack of love is often easy to justify, even though it is never right; (2) our neighbor is anyone of any race, creed, or social background who is in need; (3) love means acting to meet the person's need. Wherever you live, needy people are close by. There is no good reason for refusing to help.

31 "By chance a priest came along. But when he saw the man lying there, he crossed to the other side of the road and passed him by. 32A Temple assistant* walked over and looked at him lying there, but he also passed by on the other side.

33"Then a despised Samaritan came along, and when he saw the man, he felt compassion for him. 34Going over to him, the Samaritan soothed his wounds with olive oil and wine and bandaged them. Then he put the man on his own donkey and took him to an inn, where he took care of him. 35The next day he handed the innkeeper two silver coins,* telling him, ' Take care of this man. If his bill runs higher than this, I'll pay you the next time I'm here.'

36 "Now which of these three would you say was a neighbor to the man who was attacked by bandits?" Jesus asked.

37 The man replied, "The one who showed him mercy."

Then Jesus said, "Yes, now go and do the same."

Jesus Visits Martha and Mary (133)

38As Jesus and the disciples continued on their way to Jerusalem, they came to a certain village where a woman named Martha welcomed him into her home. 39Her sister, Mary, sat at the Lord's feet, listening to what he taught. 40But Martha was distracted by the big dinner she was preparing. She came to Jesus and said, "Lord, doesn't it seem unfair to you that my sister just sits here while I do all the work? Tell her to come and help me."

41But the Lord said to her, "My dear Martha, you are worried and upset over all these details! 42There is only one thing worth being concerned about. Mary has discovered it, and it will not be taken away from her."

Jesus Teaches His Disciples about Prayer (134)

11 Once Jesus was in a certain place praying. As he finished, one of his disciples came to him and said, "Lord, teach us to pray, just as John taught his disciples." 2Jesus said, "This is how you should pray:*

"Father, may your name be kept holy.
May your Kingdom come soon.
3 Give us each day the food we need,*
4 and forgive us our sins,
as we forgive those who sin against us.
And don't let us yield to temptation.*"

10:31
Lev 21:1-3

10:38
John 11:1; 12:2-3

10:41
Matt 6:25-34
Luke 12:11, 22

10:42
Ps 27:4
Phil 3:13-14

11:1
Luke 3:21

11:2-4
Matt 6:9-13

11:4
Matt 18:35
Mark 11:25

10:32 Greek *A Levite*. 10:35 Greek *two denarii*. A denarius was equivalent to a laborer's full day's wage. 11:2 Some manuscripts add additional phrases from the Lord's Prayer as it reads in Matt 6:9-13. 11:3 Or *Give us each day our food for the day*; or *Give us each day our food for tomorrow*. 11:4 Or *And keep us from being tested*.

• **10:33** A deep hatred existed between Jews and Samaritans. The Jews saw themselves as pure descendants of Abraham, while the Samaritans were a mixed race produced when Jews from the northern kingdom intermarried with other peoples after Israel's exile (see also the note on 9:53). To this legal expert, the person least likely to act correctly would be the Samaritan. In fact, he did not even say the word *Samaritan* in answer to Jesus' question. This expert's attitude betrayed his lack of the very thing that he had earlier said the law commanded—love.

• **10:38-42** Mary and Martha both loved Jesus. On this occasion they were both serving him. But Martha thought Mary's style of serving was inferior to hers. She didn't realize that in her desire to serve, she was actually neglecting her guest. Are you so busy doing things *for* Jesus that you're not spending any time *with* him? Don't let your service become self-serving. Jesus did not blame Martha for being concerned about household chores. He was only asking her to set priorities. Service to Christ can degenerate into mere busywork that is totally devoid of devotion to God.

11:2-13 Notice the order in this prayer. First, Jesus praised God; then he made his requests. Praising God first puts us in the right frame of mind to tell him about our needs. Too often our prayers are more like shopping lists than conversations. These verses focus on three aspects of prayer: its content (11:2-4), our persistence (11:5-10), and God's faithfulness (11:11-13).

11:3 God's provision is daily, not all at once. We cannot store it up and then cut off communication with God. And we dare not be self-satisfied. If you are running low on strength, ask yourself, How long have I been away from the Source?

• **11:4** When Jesus taught his disciples to pray, he made forgiveness the cornerstone of their relationship with God. God has forgiven our sins; we must now forgive those who have wronged us. To remain unforgiving shows we have not understood that we

JESUS VISITS MARY AND MARTHA
After teaching throughout Galilee, Jesus returned to Jerusalem for the Festival of Shelters (John 7:2ff). He spoke in Jerusalem and then visited his friends Mary and Martha in Bethany, a tiny village on the eastern slope of the Mount of Olives.

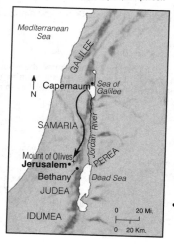

5 Then, teaching them more about prayer, he used this story: "Suppose you went to a friend's house at midnight, wanting to borrow three loaves of bread. You say to him, 6 'A friend of mine has just arrived for a visit, and I have nothing for him to eat.' 7 And suppose he calls out from his bedroom, 'Don't bother me. The door is locked for the night, and my family and I are all in bed. I can't help you.' 8 But I tell you this—though he won't do it for friendship's sake, if you keep knocking long enough, he will get up and give you whatever you need because of your shameless persistence.*

9 "And so I tell you, keep on asking, and you will receive what you ask for. Keep on seeking, and you will find. Keep on knocking, and the door will be opened to you. 10 For everyone who asks, receives. Everyone who seeks, finds. And to everyone who knocks, the door will be opened.

11 "You fathers—if your children ask* for a fish, do you give them a snake instead? 12 Or if they ask for an egg, do you give them a scorpion? Of course not! 13 So if you sinful people know how to give good gifts to your children, how much more will your heavenly Father give the Holy Spirit to those who ask him."

Jesus Answers Hostile Accusations (135)

14 One day Jesus cast out a demon from a man who couldn't speak, and when the demon was gone, the man began to speak. The crowds were amazed, 15 but some of them said, "No wonder he can cast out demons. He gets his power from Satan,* the prince of demons." 16 Others, trying to test Jesus, demanded that he show them a miraculous sign from heaven to prove his authority.

17 He knew their thoughts, so he said, "Any kingdom divided by civil war is doomed. A family splintered by feuding will fall apart. 18 You say I am empowered by Satan. But if Satan is divided and fighting against himself, how can his kingdom survive? 19 And if I am empowered by Satan, what about your own exorcists? They cast out demons, too, so they will condemn you for what you have said. 20 But if I am casting out demons by the power of God,* then the Kingdom of God has arrived among you. 21 For when a strong man like Satan is fully armed and guards his palace, his possessions are safe—22 until someone even stronger attacks and overpowers him, strips him of his weapons, and carries off his belongings.

23 "Anyone who isn't with me opposes me, and anyone who isn't working with me is actually working against me.

11:8 Or *in order to avoid shame*, or *so his reputation won't be damaged.* **11:11** Some manuscripts add *for bread, do you give them a stone? Or [if they ask].* **11:15** Greek *Beelzebub;* also in 11:18, 19. Other manuscripts read *Beezeboul;* Latin version reads *Beelzebub.* **11:20** Greek *by the finger of God.*

11:7
Matt 26:10
Luke 18:5
Gal 6:17
11:8
Luke 18:1-6

11:13
Jas 1:17

11:15
Matt 9:34

11:16
Matt 12:38; 16:1
11:17
Matt 9:4

11:20
Exod 8:19

11:22
Isa 49:24; 53:12

---

ourselves deeply need to be forgiven. Think of some people who have wronged you. Have you forgiven them? How will God deal with you if he treats you as you treat others?

11:8 Persistence, or boldness, in prayer overcomes *our* insensitivity, not God's. To practice persistence does more to change our heart and mind than his, and it helps us understand and express the intensity of our need. Persistence in prayer helps us recognize God's work.

11:13 Even though good fathers make mistakes, they treat their children well. How much better our perfect heavenly Father treats his children! The most important gift he could ever give us is the Holy Spirit (Acts 2:1-4), whom he promised to give all believers after his death, resurrection, and return to heaven (John 15:26).

11:14-23 A similar and possibly separate event is reported in Matthew 12:22-45 and Mark 3:20-30. The event described by Luke happened in Judea, while the other took place in Galilee. According to Luke, Jesus spoke to the crowds; in Matthew and Mark, he accused the Pharisees.

11:15-20 Some of the Pharisees' followers also were exorcists— that is, they drove out demons. The Pharisees' accusations were becoming more desperate. To accuse Jesus of being empowered by Satan, the prince of demons, because Jesus was driving out demons was also to say that the Pharisees' own exorcists were doing Satan's work. Jesus turned the religious leaders' accusation against them. Jesus first dismissed their claim as absurd (Why would the devil drive out his own demons?). Then he engaged in a little irony ("What about your own exorcists?"). Finally, he

concluded that his work of driving out demons proved that the Kingdom of God had arrived.

Satan, who had controlled the kingdom of this world for thousands of years, was now being controlled and overpowered by Jesus and the Kingdom of Heaven. Jesus' Kingdom began to come into power at Jesus' birth and grew as he resisted the wilderness temptations. It established itself through his teachings and healings, blossomed in victory at his resurrection and at Pentecost, and will become permanent and universal at his second coming.

11:21, 22 Jesus may have been referring to Isaiah 49:24-26. Regardless of how great Satan's power is, Jesus is stronger still. He will overpower Satan and dispose of him for eternity (see Revelation 20:2, 10).

11:23 How does this verse relate to 9:50: "Anyone who is not against you is for you"? In the earlier passage, Jesus was talking about a person who was driving out demons in Jesus' name. Those who fight evil, he was saying, are on the same side as the one driving out demons in Jesus' name. Here, by contrast, he was talking about the conflict between God and the devil. In this battle, if a person is not on God's side, he or she is on Satan's. There is no neutral ground. Because God has already won the battle, why be on the losing side? If you aren't actively for Christ, you are against him.

²⁴ "When an evil* spirit leaves a person, it goes into the desert, searching for rest. But when it finds none, it says, 'I will return to the person I came from.' ²⁵So it returns and finds that its former home is all swept and in order. ²⁶Then the spirit finds seven other spirits more evil than itself, and they all enter the person and live there. And so that person is worse off than before."

²⁷As he was speaking, a woman in the crowd called out, "God bless your mother—the womb from which you came, and the breasts that nursed you!"

²⁸Jesus replied, "But even more blessed are all who hear the word of God and put it into practice."

11:24-26
Matt 12:43-45

11:27
Luke 1:28, 42, 48

11:28
Luke 6:47; 8:21

Jesus Warns against Unbelief (136)

²⁹As the crowd pressed in on Jesus, he said, "This evil generation keeps asking me to show them a miraculous sign. But the only sign I will give them is the sign of Jonah. ³⁰ What happened to him was a sign to the people of Nineveh that God had sent him. What happens to the Son of Man* will be a sign to these people that he was sent by God.

³¹ "The queen of Sheba* will stand up against this generation on judgment day and condemn it, for she came from a distant land to hear the wisdom of Solomon. Now someone greater than Solomon is here—but you refuse to listen. ³² The people of Nineveh will also stand up against this generation on judgment day and condemn it, for they repented of their sins at the preaching of Jonah. Now someone greater than Jonah is here—but you refuse to repent.

11:29-32
Matt 12:38-42
1 Cor 1:22

11:30
Jon 1:17; 2:10

11:31
1 Kgs 10:1-10
2 Chr 9:1-12

11:32
Jon 3:5, 8, 10

Jesus Teaches about the Light Within (137)

³³ "No one lights a lamp and then hides it or puts it under a basket.* Instead, a lamp is placed on a stand, where its light can be seen by all who enter the house.

³⁴ "Your eye is a lamp that provides light for your body. When your eye is good, your whole body is filled with light. But when it is bad, your body is filled with darkness. ³⁵Make sure that the light you think you have is not actually darkness. ³⁶If you are filled with light, with no dark corners, then your whole life will be radiant, as though a floodlight were filling you with light."

11:33
Matt 5:15
Luke 8:16

11:34-36
Matt 6:22-23

Jesus Criticizes the Religious Leaders (138)

³⁷As Jesus was speaking, one of the Pharisees invited him home for a meal. So he went in and took his place at the table.* ³⁸His host was amazed to see that he sat down to eat without first performing the hand-washing ceremony required by Jewish custom. ³⁹Then the Lord said to him, "You Pharisees are so careful to clean the outside of the cup and the dish, but inside you are filthy—full of greed and wickedness! ⁴⁰ Fools! Didn't God make the inside as well as the outside? ⁴¹So clean the inside by giving gifts to the poor, and you will be clean all over.

11:38
Mark 7:3-4

11:39
Matt 23:25
Mark 7:20-23

11:41
Luke 12:33

11:24 Greek *unclean.*   **11:30** "Son of Man" is a title Jesus used for himself.   **11:31** Greek *The queen of the south.*   **11:33** Some manuscripts do not include *or puts it under a basket.*   **11:37** Or *and reclined.*

11:24-26 Jesus was illustrating an unfortunate human tendency: Our desire to reform often does not last long. In Israel's history, almost as soon as a good king would pull down idols, a bad king would set them up again. It is not enough to be emptied of evil; we must then be filled with the power of the Holy Spirit to accomplish God's new purpose in our life (see also Matthew 12:43-45; Galatians 5:22).

11:27, 28 Jesus was speaking to people who put extremely high value on family ties. Their genealogies were important guarantees that they were part of God's chosen people. A man's value came from his ancestors, and a woman's value came from the sons she bore. Jesus' response to the woman meant that a person's obedience to God is more important than his or her place on the family tree. Consistent obedience is more important than the honor of bearing a respected son.

11:29, 30 What was the sign of Jonah? God had asked Jonah to preach repentance to the Gentiles (non-Jews). Jesus was affirming Jonah's message. Salvation is not only for Jews but for all people. Matthew 12:40 adds another explanation: Jesus would die and rise after three days, just as the prophet Jonah was rescued after three days in the belly of the great fish.

11:29-32 The cruel, warlike men of Nineveh, capital of Assyria, repented when Jonah preached to them—and Jonah did not even care about them. The pagan queen of Sheba praised the God of

Israel when she heard Solomon's wisdom, and Solomon was full of faults. By contrast, Jesus, the perfect Son of God, came to people that he loved dearly—but they rejected him. Thus, God's chosen people made themselves more liable to judgment than either a notoriously wicked nation or a powerful pagan queen. Compare 10:12-15, where Jesus says the evil cities of Sodom, Tyre, and Sidon will be judged less harshly than the cities in Judea and Galilee that rejected Jesus' message.

11:31, 32 The people of Nineveh and the queen of Sheba had turned to God with far less evidence than Jesus was giving his listeners—and far less than we have today. We have eyewitness reports of the risen Jesus, the continuing power of the Holy Spirit unleashed at Pentecost, easy access to the Bible, and knowledge of 2,000 years of Christ's acts through his church. With the knowledge and insight available to us, our response to Christ ought to be even more complete and wholehearted.

11:33-36 The lamp is Christ; the eye represents spiritual understanding and insight. Evil desires make the eye less sensitive and blot out the light of Christ's presence. If you have a hard time seeing God at work in the world and in your life, check your vision. Are any sinful desires blinding you to Christ?

• **11:37-39** The hand-washing ceremony was done not for health reasons but as a symbol of washing away any contamination from touching anything unclean. Not only did the Pharisees make

11:42
Lev 27:30
Matt 23:23

11:43
Matt 23:6-7
Mark 12:38-39

11:44
Matt 23:27-28

11:46
Matt 23:4

11:47
Matt 23:29-32

11:48
Acts 7:51-53; 8:1

11:49-51
Matt 23:34-36
1 Cor 1:24, 30

11:51
Gen 4:8
2 Chr 24:20-21

11:52
Matt 23:13

11:54
Luke 20:20

42 "What sorrow awaits you Pharisees! For you are careful to tithe even the tiniest income from your herb gardens,* but you ignore justice and the love of God. You should tithe, yes, but do not neglect the more important things.

43 "What sorrow awaits you Pharisees! For you love to sit in the seats of honor in the synagogues and receive respectful greetings as you walk in the marketplaces. 44 Yes, what sorrow awaits you! For you are like hidden graves in a field. People walk over them without knowing the corruption they are stepping on."

45 "Teacher," said an expert in religious law, "you have insulted us, too, in what you just said."

46 "Yes," said Jesus, "what sorrow also awaits you experts in religious law! For you crush people with unbearable religious demands, and you never lift a finger to ease the burden. 47 What sorrow awaits you! For you build monuments for the prophets your own ancestors killed long ago. 48 But in fact, you stand as witnesses who agree with what your ancestors did. They killed the prophets, and you join in their crime by building the monuments! 49 This is what God in his wisdom said about you:* 'I will send prophets and apostles to them, but they will kill some and persecute the others.'

50 "As a result, this generation will be held responsible for the murder of all God's prophets from the creation of the world—51 from the murder of Abel to the murder of Zechariah, who was killed between the altar and the sanctuary. Yes, it will certainly be charged against this generation.

52 "What sorrow awaits you experts in religious law! For you remove the key to knowledge from the people. You don't enter the Kingdom yourselves, and you prevent others from entering."

53 As Jesus was leaving, the teachers of religious law and the Pharisees became hostile and tried to provoke him with many questions. 54 They wanted to trap him into saying something they could use against him.

11:42 Greek *tithe the mint, the rue, and every herb.*   **11:49** Greek *Therefore, the wisdom of God said.*

---

a public show of their washing, but they also commanded everyone else to follow a practice originally intended only for the priests.

• **11:41** The Pharisees loved to think of themselves as "clean," but their stinginess toward God and the poor proved that they were not as clean as they thought. How do you use the resources God has entrusted to you? Are you generous in meeting the needs around you? Your generosity reveals much about the purity of your heart.

11:42 Rationalizing not helping others is easy because we have already given to the church, but a person who follows Jesus should share with needy neighbors. While tithing is important to the life of the church, our compassion must not stop there. Where we can help, we should help.

• **11:42-52** Jesus criticized the Pharisees and the experts in religious law harshly because they (1) washed their outsides but not their insides, (2) remembered to give a tenth of even their garden herbs but neglected justice, (3) loved praise and attention, (4) loaded people down with burdensome religious demands, (5) would not accept the truth about Jesus, and (6) prevented others from believing the truth. They went wrong by focusing on outward appearances and ignoring the inner condition of their hearts. People do the same when their service comes from a desire to be seen rather than from a pure heart that is full of love for others. People may sometimes be fooled, but God isn't. Don't be a Christian on the outside only. Bring your inner life under God's control and your outer life will naturally reflect him.

• **11:44** The Old Testament laws said a person who touched a grave was unclean (Numbers 19:16). Jesus accused the Pharisees of making others unclean by their spiritual rottenness. Like unmarked graves hidden in a field, the Pharisees corrupted everyone who came in contact with them.

• **11:46** These "religious demands" were the details the Pharisees had added to God's law. To the commandment, "Remember to observe the Sabbath day by keeping it holy" (Exodus 20:8), for example, they had added instructions regarding how far a person

could walk on the Sabbath, which kinds of knots could be tied, and how much weight could be carried. Healing a person was considered unlawful work on the Sabbath although rescuing a trapped animal was permitted (14:5). No wonder Jesus condemned their additions to the law.

11:49 God's prophets have been persecuted and murdered throughout history. But this generation was rejecting more than a human prophet—they were rejecting God himself. This quotation is not from the Old Testament. Jesus, the greatest prophet of all, was directly giving them God's message.

11:51 Abel's death is recorded in Genesis 4:8. For more about him, see his Profile in Genesis 5, p. 15. Zechariah's death is recorded in 2 Chronicles 24:20-22 (the last book in the Hebrew canon). Why would all these sins come upon this particular generation? Because they were rejecting the Messiah himself, the one to whom all their history and prophecy were pointing.

• **11:52** How did the legal experts remove the "key to knowledge"? Through their erroneous interpretations of Scripture and their added man-made rules, they made God's truth hard to understand and practice. On top of that, these men were bad examples, arguing their way out of the demanding rules they placed on others. Caught up in a religion of their own making, they could no longer lead the people to God. They had closed the door of God's love to the people and had thrown away the key.

11:53, 54 The teachers of religious law and the Pharisees hoped to arrest Jesus for blasphemy, heresy, and lawbreaking. They were enraged by Jesus' words about them, but they couldn't arrest him for merely speaking words. They had to find a legal way to get rid of Jesus.

Jesus Speaks against Hypocrisy (**139**)

12 Meanwhile, the crowds grew until thousands were milling about and stepping on each other. Jesus turned first to his disciples and warned them, "Beware of the yeast of the Pharisees—their hypocrisy. ²The time is coming when everything that is covered up will be revealed, and all that is secret will be made known to all. ³Whatever you have said in the dark will be heard in the light, and what you have whispered behind closed doors will be shouted from the housetops for all to hear!

⁴"Dear friends, don't be afraid of those who want to kill your body; they cannot do any more to you after that. ⁵But I'll tell you whom to fear. Fear God, who has the power to kill you and then throw you into hell.* Yes, he's the one to fear.

⁶ "What is the price of five sparrows—two copper coins*? Yet God does not forget a single one of them. ⁷And the very hairs on your head are all numbered. So don't be afraid; you are more valuable to God than a whole flock of sparrows.

⁸ "I tell you the truth, everyone who acknowledges me publicly here on earth, the Son of Man* will also acknowledge in the presence of God's angels. ⁹But anyone who denies me here on earth will be denied before God's angels. ¹⁰Anyone who speaks against the Son of Man can be forgiven, but anyone who blasphemes the Holy Spirit will not be forgiven.

¹¹ "And when you are brought to trial in the synagogues and before rulers and authorities, don't worry about how to defend yourself or what to say, ¹²for the Holy Spirit will teach you at that time what needs to be said."

12:1 Matt 16:6, 11-12
12:2 Mark 4:22
12:4 John 15:14-15
12:5 Heb 10:31
12:8 Luke 15:10 / Rev 3:5
12:9 Mark 8:38 / Luke 9:26 / 2 Tim 2:12
12:10 Matt 12:31-32 / Mark 3:28-29 / 1 Jn 5:16
12:11-12 Matt 10:19-20 / Mark 13:11 / Luke 21:12-15

Jesus Tells the Parable of the Rich Fool (**140**)

¹³Then someone called from the crowd, "Teacher, please tell my brother to divide our father's estate with me."

12:5 Greek *Gehenna*.   **12:6** Greek *two assaria* [Roman coins equal to 1/16 of a denarius].   **12:8** "Son of Man" is a title Jesus used for himself.

• **12:1, 2** As Jesus watched the huge crowds waiting to hear him, he warned his disciples against hypocrisy—trying to appear holy when one's heart is far from God. The Pharisees could not keep their attitudes hidden forever. Their selfishness would act like yeast, and soon they would expose themselves for what they really were—power-hungry impostors, not devoted religious leaders. It is easy to be angry at the blatant hypocrisy of the Pharisees, but each of us must resist the temptation to settle for the appearance of respectability when our hearts are far from God.

12:1, 2 What are the signs of hypocrisy? (1) Hypocrisy is knowing the truth but not obeying it. People can say they follow Jesus, but not be obedient to his Word. (2) Hypocrisy is living a self-serving life. People may desire leadership only because they love position and control, not because they want to serve others. (3) Hypocrisy reduces faith to rigid rules. People can end up worshiping their own rules and regulations about what they think God wants instead of worshiping God himself. (4) Hypocrisy is outward conformity without inner reality. People can obey the details but still be disobedient in general behavior. For example, a person may carefully tithe his income, but be rude and obnoxious to his coworkers.

Many non-Christians use the supposed (or real) hypocrisy of Christians as an excuse to stay away from God and the church. Look carefully at your life. You are not perfect; therefore, at times an action or behavior might provide the ammunition for someone to label you a hypocrite. However, you must discern your own heart. Consider the signs of hypocrisy noted above and make sure you are not guilty. Then ask God to help you live rightly.

12:4, 5 Fear of opposition or ridicule can weaken our witness for Christ. Often we cling to peace and comfort, even at the cost of our walk with God. Jesus reminds us here that we should fear God who controls eternal, not merely temporal, consequences. Don't allow fear of a person or group to keep you from standing up for Christ.

12:7 Our true value is God's estimate of our worth, not our peers' estimate. Other people evaluate and categorize us according to how we perform, what we achieve, and how we look. But God cares for us, as he does for all of his creatures, because we belong to him. Thus, we can face life without fear; we are very valuable to God.

• **12:8, 9** We deny Jesus when we (1) hope no one will find out we are Christians, (2) decide *not* to speak up for what is right, (3) are silent about our relationship with God, (4) blend into society, and (5) accept our culture's non-Christian values. By contrast, we acknowledge him when we (1) live moral, upright, Christ-honoring lives, (2) look for opportunities to share our faith with others, (3) help others in need, (4) take a stand for justice, (5) love others, (6) acknowledge our loyalty to Christ, and (7) use our lives and resources to carry out his desires rather than our own.

12:10 Jesus said that blasphemy against the Holy Spirit is unforgivable. This has worried many sincere Christians, but it does not need to. The unforgivable sin is attributing to Satan the work that the Holy Spirit accomplishes (see the notes on Matthew 12:31, 32; Mark 3:28, 29). Thus, it is the deliberate and ongoing rejection of the Holy Spirit's work and even of God himself. A person who has committed this sin is far from God and totally unaware of any sin at all. If you fear you have committed this sin, be assured that your very concern shows that you have not sinned in this way.

12:11, 12 The disciples knew they could never get the upper hand in a religious dispute with the well-educated Jewish leaders. Nevertheless, they would not be left unprepared. Jesus promised that the Holy Spirit would give them the appropriate words in their time of need. The disciples' testimony might not make them look impressive, but it would still point out God's work in the world through Jesus' life. We need to pray for opportunities to witness for Christ, and then trust him to help us with our words. This promise of the Spirit's help, however, does not compensate for lack of preparation. Remember that these disciples had three years of personal instruction and practical application. We need to study God's Word. Then God will bring his truths to mind when we most need them, helping us present them in the most effective way.

12:13ff Problems like these were often brought to rabbis for them to settle. Jesus' response, though not directed to the topic, is not a change of subject. Rather, Jesus is pointing to a higher issue—a correct attitude toward the accumulation of wealth. Life is more than material goods; far more important is our relationship with God. Jesus put his finger on this questioner's heart. When we bring problems to God in prayer, he often responds in the same way, showing us how we need to change and grow in our attitude

12:14
Exod 2:14
Acts 7:27, 35
12:15
Job 20:20; 31:24
Ps 62:10
1 Tim 6:9-10
12:19
Prov 27:1
1 Cor 15:32
Jas 5:1-5
12:20
Job 27:8
Ps 39:6-7
12:24
Job 38:41
Ps 147:9
12:27
1 Kgs 10:1-10
12:30
Matt 6:8
12:32
Luke 22:29
12:33
Matt 19:21
Acts 2:45

¹⁴Jesus replied, "Friend, who made me a judge over you to decide such things as that?" ¹⁵Then he said, "Beware! Guard against every kind of greed. Life is not measured by how much you own."

¹⁶Then he told them a story: "A rich man had a fertile farm that produced fine crops. ¹⁷He said to himself, 'What should I do? I don't have room for all my crops.' ¹⁸Then he said, 'I know! I'll tear down my barns and build bigger ones. Then I'll have room enough to store all my wheat and other goods. ¹⁹And I'll sit back and say to myself, "My friend, you have enough stored away for years to come. Now take it easy! Eat, drink, and be merry!"'

²⁰"But God said to him, 'You fool! You will die this very night. Then who will get everything you worked for?'

²¹"Yes, a person is a fool to store up earthly wealth but not have a rich relationship with God."

Jesus Warns about Worry (141)
²²Then, turning to his disciples, Jesus said, "That is why I tell you not to worry about everyday life—whether you have enough food to eat or enough clothes to wear. ²³For life is more than food, and your body more than clothing. ²⁴Look at the ravens. They don't plant or harvest or store food in barns, for God feeds them. And you are far more valuable to him than any birds! ²⁵Can all your worries add a single moment to your life? ²⁶And if worry can't accomplish a little thing like that, what's the use of worrying over bigger things?

²⁷"Look at the lilies and how they grow. They don't work or make their clothing, yet Solomon in all his glory was not dressed as beautifully as they are. ²⁸And if God cares so wonderfully for flowers that are here today and thrown into the fire tomorrow, he will certainly care for you. Why do you have so little faith?

²⁹"And don't be concerned about what to eat and what to drink. Don't worry about such things. ³⁰These things dominate the thoughts of unbelievers all over the world, but your Father already knows your needs. ³¹Seek the Kingdom of God above all else, and he will give you everything you need.

³²"So don't be afraid, little flock. For it gives your Father great happiness to give you the Kingdom.

³³"Sell your possessions and give to those in need. This will store up treasure for you in heaven! And the purses of heaven never get old or develop holes. Your treasure will be safe;

toward the problem. This answer is often not the one we were looking for, but it is more effective in helping us trace God's hand in our life.

12:15 Jesus says that the good life has nothing to do with being wealthy, so be on guard against greed (desire for what we don't have). This is the exact opposite of what society usually says. Advertisers spend millions of dollars to entice us to think that if we buy more and more of their products, we will be happier, more fulfilled, more comfortable. How do you respond to the constant pressure to buy? Learn to tune out expensive enticements and concentrate instead on the truly fulfilled life—living in a relationship with God and doing his work.

12:16-21 The rich man in Jesus' story died before he could begin to use what was stored in his big barns. Planning for retirement—preparing for life *before* death—is wise, but neglecting life *after* death is disastrous. If you accumulate wealth only to enrich yourself, with no concern for helping others, you will enter eternity empty-handed.

12:18-20 Why do you save money? Are you saving for retirement? to buy more expensive cars or toys? to be secure? Jesus challenges us to think beyond earthbound goals and to use what we have been given for God's Kingdom. Faith, service, and obedience are the way to become rich toward God.

12:22-34 Jesus commands us not to worry. But how can we avoid it? Only faith can free us from the anxiety caused by greed and covetousness. Working and planning responsibly is good; dwelling on all the ways our planning could go wrong is bad. Worry is pointless because it can't fill any of our needs; worry is foolish because the Creator of the universe loves us and knows what we need. He promises to meet all our real needs but not necessarily all our desires.

Overcoming worry requires: (1) Simple trust in God, your heavenly Father. This trust is expressed by praying to him rather than worrying. (2) Perspective on your problems. This can be gained by developing a strategy for addressing and correcting your problems. (3) A support team to help. Find some believers who will pray for you to find wisdom and strength to deal with your worries.

12:31 Seeking the Kingdom of God above all else means making Jesus the Lord and King of your life. He must control every area—your work, play, plans, relationships. Is the Kingdom only one of your many concerns, or is it central to all you do? Are you holding back any areas of your life from God's control? As Lord and Creator, he wants to help provide what you need as well as guide how you use what he provides.

12:33 Money seen as an end in itself quickly traps us and cuts us off from both God and the needy. The key to using money wisely is to see how much we can use for God's purposes, not how much we can accumulate for ourselves. Does God's love touch your wallet? Does your money free you to help others? If so, you are storing up lasting treasures in heaven. If your financial goals and possessions hinder you from giving generously, loving others, or serving God, sell what you must to bring your life into line with his purposes.

no thief can steal it and no moth can destroy it. 34Wherever your treasure is, there the desires of your heart will also be.

Jesus Warns about Preparing for His Coming (142)

35"Be dressed for service and keep your lamps burning, 36 as though you were waiting for your master to return from the wedding feast. Then you will be ready to open the door and let him in the moment he arrives and knocks. 37The servants who are ready and waiting for his return will be rewarded. I tell you the truth, he himself will seat them, put on an apron, and serve them as they sit and eat! 38He may come in the middle of the night or just before dawn.* But whenever he comes, he will reward the servants who are ready.

39"Understand this: If a homeowner knew exactly when a burglar was coming, he would not permit his house to be broken into. 40You also must be ready all the time, for the Son of Man will come when least expected."

41Peter asked, "Lord, is that illustration just for us or for everyone?"

42And the Lord replied, "A faithful, sensible servant is one to whom the master can give the responsibility of managing his other household servants and feeding them. 43If the master returns and finds that the servant has done a good job, there will be a reward. 44I tell you the truth, the master will put that servant in charge of all he owns. 45But what if the servant thinks, 'My master won't be back for a while,' and he begins beating the other servants, partying, and getting drunk? 46The master will return unannounced and unexpected, and he will cut the servant in pieces and banish him with the unfaithful.

47"And a servant who knows what the master wants, but isn't prepared and doesn't carry out those instructions, will be severely punished. 48But someone who does not know, and then does something wrong, will be punished only lightly. When someone has been given much, much will be required in return; and when someone has been entrusted with much, even more will be required.

Jesus Warns about Coming Division (143)

49 "I have come to set the world on fire, and I wish it were already burning! 50I have a terrible baptism of suffering ahead of me, and I am under a heavy burden until it is accomplished. 51 Do you think I have come to bring peace to the earth? No, I have come to divide people against each other! 52From now on families will be split apart, three in favor of me, and two against—or two in favor and three against.

12:38 Greek *in the second or third watch.*

12:35-36
Matt 25:1-13
Mark 13:33-37
12:35
†Exod 12:11
12:37
Luke 17:7-8
John 13:4
12:39
1 Thes 5:2
Rev 16:15
12:40
Mark 13:33

12:47
Deut 25:2
Jas 4:17
12:48
Lev 5:17
Num 15:27-30

12:50
Mark 10:38-39

12:34 If you concentrate your money in your business, your thoughts will center on making the business profitable. If you direct it toward other people, you will become concerned with their welfare. Where do you put your time, money, and energy? What do you think about most? How should you change the way you use your resources in order to reflect Kingdom values more accurately?

12:35-40 Jesus repeatedly said that he would leave this world but would return at some future time (see Matthew 24–25; John 14:1-3). He also said that a Kingdom was being prepared for his followers. Many Greeks envisioned this as a heavenly, idealized, spiritual Kingdom. Jews—like Isaiah and John, the writer of Revelation—saw it as a restored earthly Kingdom.

12:40 Christ's return at an unexpected time is not a trap, a trick by which God hopes to catch us off guard. In fact, God is delaying his return so more people will have the opportunity to follow him (see 2 Peter 3:9). Before Christ's return, we have time to live out our beliefs and to reflect Jesus' love as we relate to others.

People who are ready for their Lord's return are (1) not hypocritical but sincere (12:1), (2) not fearful but ready to witness (12:4-9), (3) not worried but trusting (12:25, 26), (4) not greedy but generous (12:34), (5) not lazy but diligent (12:37). May your life be more like Christ's so that when he comes, you will be ready to greet him joyfully.

12:42-44 Jesus promises a reward for those who have been faithful to the Master. While we sometimes experience immediate and material rewards for our obedience to God, this is not always the case. If so, we would be tempted to boast about our achievements and only do good for what we get. Jesus said that if we look for rewards now, we will lose them later (see Mark 8:36). Our heavenly rewards will be the most accurate reflection of what we have done on earth, and they will be far greater than we can imagine.

12:48 Jesus has told us how to live until he comes: We must watch for him, work diligently, and obey his commands. Such attitudes are especially necessary for leaders. Watchful and faithful leaders will be given increased opportunities and responsibilities. The more resources, talents, and understanding we have, the more we are required to use them effectively. God will not hold us responsible for gifts he has not given us, but all of us have been given enough gifts and duties to keep us busy until Jesus returns.

12:50 The "baptism of suffering" to which Jesus referred was his coming crucifixion. Jesus was dreading the physical pain, of course, but even worse would be the spiritual pain of complete separation from God that would accompany his death for the sins of the world.

12:51-53 In these strange and unsettling words, Jesus revealed that his coming often results in conflict. Because he demands a response, families may be split apart when some choose to follow him and others refuse to do so. Jesus allows no middle ground. He demands loyalty and commitment, sometimes to the point of severing other relationships. Are you willing to risk your family's disapproval in order to follow the Lord?

12:54-57 For most of recorded history, the world's principal occupation was farming. The farmer depended directly on the weather for his livelihood. He needed just the right amounts of sun and rain—not too much, not too little—to make his living, and he grew skilled at interpreting natural signs. Jesus was

12:53
†Mic 7:6

53 'Father will be divided against son
　　　and son against father;
　mother against daughter
　　　and daughter against mother;
　and mother-in-law against daughter-in-law
　　　and daughter-in-law against mother-in-law.'*"

Jesus Warns about the Future Crisis (144)

12:54-56
Matt 16:2-3

54Then Jesus turned to the crowd and said, "When you see clouds beginning to form in the west, you say, 'Here comes a shower.' And you are right. 55When the south wind blows, you say, 'Today will be a scorcher.' And it is. 56You fools! You know how to interpret the weather signs of the earth and sky, but you don't know how to interpret the present times.

12:58-59
Matt 5:25-26

57"Why can't you decide for yourselves what is right? 58When you are on the way to court with your accuser, try to settle the matter before you get there. Otherwise, your accuser may drag you before the judge, who will hand you over to an officer, who will throw you into prison. 59And if that happens, you won't be free again until you have paid the very last penny.*"

Jesus Calls the People to Repent (145)

13:2
John 9:2-3
13:3
Ps 7:12
13:4
John 9:7, 11
13:6
Matt 21:19
Mark 11:12-14
13:7
Hab 3:17
Matt 3:10

13 About this time Jesus was informed that Pilate had murdered some people from Galilee as they were offering sacrifices at the Temple. 2 "Do you think those Galileans were worse sinners than all the other people from Galilee?" Jesus asked. "Is that why they suffered? 3Not at all! And you will perish, too, unless you repent of your sins and turn to God. 4And what about the eighteen people who died when the tower in Siloam fell on them? Were they the worst sinners in Jerusalem? 5No, and I tell you again that unless you repent, you will perish, too."

6Then Jesus told this story: "A man planted a fig tree in his garden and came again and again to see if there was any fruit on it, but he was always disappointed. 7Finally, he said to

12:53 Mic 7:6.　**12:59** Greek *last lepton* [the smallest Jewish coin].

SEVEN SABBATH MIRACLES

Jesus sends a demon out of a man . . . . Mark 1:21-28
Jesus heals Peter's mother-in-law. . . . . Mark 1:29-31
Jesus heals a lame man by the pool of Bethesda. . . . . John 5:1-18
Jesus heals a man with a deformed hand. . . . . Mark 3:1-6
Jesus restores a crippled woman . . . . Luke 13:10-17
Jesus heals a man with swollen arms and legs . . . . Luke 14:1-6
Jesus heals a man born blind . . . . John 9:1-16

Over the centuries, the Jewish religious leaders had added rule after rule to God's law. For example, God's law said the Sabbath is a day of rest (Exodus 20:10, 11). But the religious leaders added to that law, creating one that said, "You cannot heal on the Sabbath" because that is "work." Seven times Jesus healed people on the Sabbath. In doing this, he was challenging these religious leaders to look beyond their rules to their true purpose—to honor God by helping those in need. Would God have been pleased if Jesus had ignored these people?

---

announcing an earthshaking event that would be much more important than the year's crops—the coming of God's Kingdom. Just as dark clouds forewarn of a rainstorm, there were signs that the Kingdom would soon arrive. But Jesus' hearers, though skilled at interpreting weather signs, were intentionally ignoring the signs of the times.

13:1-5 Pilate may have killed the Galileans because he thought they were rebelling against Rome; those killed by the tower in Siloam may have been working for the Romans on an aqueduct there. The Pharisees, who were opposed to using force to deal with Rome, would have said that the Galileans killed by Pilate deserved to die for rebelling. The Zealots, a group of anti-Roman terrorists, would have said the aqueduct workers deserved to die for cooperating. Jesus dismissed the idea that accidents or human cruelties were God's judgment on especially bad sinners. Neither the Galileans nor the workers should be blamed for their calamities. Whether a person is killed in a tragic accident or

miraculously survives is not a measure of righteousness. Everyone has to die. Jesus did not explain why some live and some die tragically; instead he pointed to everyone's need for repentance. No matter how or when it occurs, death is not the end. Jesus promises that those who believe in him will not perish but have eternal life (John 3:16).

13:6-9 In the Old Testament, a fruitful tree was often used as a symbol of godly living (see, for example, Psalm 1:3 and Jeremiah 17:7, 8). Jesus pointed out what would happen to the other kind of tree—the kind that took valuable time and space and still produced nothing for the patient gardener. By this illustration Jesus warned his listeners that God would not tolerate forever their lack of productivity. (Luke 3:9 records John the Baptist's version of the same message.) Have you been enjoying God's special treatment without giving anything in return? If so, respond to the Gardener's patient care and begin to bear the fruit God has created you to produce.

his gardener, 'I've waited three years, and there hasn't been a single fig! Cut it down. It's just taking up space in the garden.'

8 "The gardener answered, 'Sir, give it one more chance. Leave it another year, and I'll give it special attention and plenty of fertilizer. 9If we get figs next year, fine. If not, then you can cut it down.'"

13:8
2 Pet 3:9, 15

Jesus Heals the Crippled Woman (146)

10One Sabbath day as Jesus was teaching in a synagogue, 11he saw a woman who had been crippled by an evil spirit. She had been bent double for eighteen years and was unable to stand up straight. 12When Jesus saw her, he called her over and said, "Dear woman, you are healed of your sickness!" 13Then he touched her, and instantly she could stand straight. How she praised God!

13:10
Matt 4:23

13:13
Mark 5:23

14But the leader in charge of the synagogue was indignant that Jesus had healed her on the Sabbath day. "There are six days of the week for working," he said to the crowd. "Come on those days to be healed, not on the Sabbath."

15But the Lord replied, "You hypocrites! Each of you works on the Sabbath day! Don't you untie your ox or your donkey from its stall on the Sabbath and lead it out for water? 16This dear woman, a daughter of Abraham, has been held in bondage by Satan for eighteen years. Isn't it right that she be released, even on the Sabbath?"

17This shamed his enemies, but all the people rejoiced at the wonderful things he did.

13:14
Exod 20:9-10
Deut 5:13-14
Matt 12:10
Mark 3:2
Luke 6:7
John 5:16

13:15
Luke 14:5

13:16
Luke 19:9

Jesus Teaches about the Kingdom of God (147)

18Then Jesus said, "What is the Kingdom of God like? How can I illustrate it? 19 It is like a tiny mustard seed that a man planted in a garden; it grows and becomes a tree, and the birds make nests in its branches."

20He also asked, "What else is the Kingdom of God like? 21It is like the yeast a woman used in making bread. Even though she put only a little yeast in three measures of flour, it permeated every part of the dough."

Jesus Teaches about Entering the Kingdom (153)

22Jesus went through the towns and villages, teaching as he went, always pressing on toward Jerusalem. 23Someone asked him, "Lord, will only a few be saved?"

He replied, 24"Work hard to enter the narrow door to God's Kingdom, for many will try to enter but will fail. 25When the master of the house has locked the door, it will be too late. You will stand outside knocking and pleading, 'Lord, open the door for us!' But he will reply, 'I don't know you or where you come from.' 26Then you will say, 'But we ate and drank with you, and you taught in our streets.' 27And he will reply, 'I tell you, I don't know you or where you come from. Get away from me, all you who do evil.'

13:24
Mark 10:25
1 Tim 6:12

13:25
Matt 25:10-11

13:27
†Ps 6:8
Matt 25:12

• **13:10-17** Why was healing considered work? The religious leaders saw healing as part of a doctor's profession, and practicing one's profession on the Sabbath was prohibited. The synagogue leader could not see beyond the law to Jesus' compassion in healing this crippled woman. Jesus shamed him and the other leaders by pointing out their hypocrisy. They would untie their animals and care for them, but they refused to rejoice when a human being was freed from Satan's bondage.

13:16 In our fallen world, disease and disability are common. Their causes are many and often multiple—inadequate nutrition, contact with a source of infection, lowered defenses, and even direct attack by Satan. Whatever the immediate cause of our illness, we can trace its original source to Satan, the author of all the evil in our world. The Good News is that Jesus is more powerful than the devil or any disease. He often brings physical healing in this life; and when he returns, he will put an end to all disease and disability.

13:18-21 The general expectation among Jesus' hearers was that the Messiah would come as a great king and leader, freeing the nation from Rome and restoring Israel's former glory. But Jesus said his Kingdom was beginning quietly. Like the tiny mustard seed that grows into an enormous tree, or the spoonful

of yeast that makes the bread dough double in size, the Kingdom of God would eventually push outward until the whole world was changed.

13:22 This is the second time Luke reminds us that Jesus was intentionally going to Jerusalem (the other time is in 9:51). Jesus knew he was on his way to die, but he continued preaching to large crowds. The prospect of death did not deter Jesus from his mission.

13:24, 25 Finding salvation requires more concentrated effort than most people are willing to put forth. Obviously we cannot save ourselves—there is no way we can work ourselves into God's favor. We "work hard to enter" through the narrow door by earnestly desiring to know Jesus and diligently striving to follow him whatever the cost. We dare not put off making this decision because the door will not stay open forever.

13:26, 27 The people were eager to know who would be in God's Kingdom. Jesus explained that, although many people know something about God, only a few have acknowledged their sins and accepted his forgiveness. We may not necessarily see the people we expect to find in the Kingdom of God. Some perfectly respectable religious leaders claiming allegiance to Jesus will not be there because they were not true followers and secretly were morally corrupt. Just listening to Jesus' words or admiring his miracles is not enough. We must turn from sin and trust in God to save us.

13:29
Ps 107:3
Isa 43:5; 49:12;
59:19
Rev 14:15; 21:13;
22:16

13:30
Matt 19:30; 20:16
Mark 10:31

28 "There will be weeping and gnashing of teeth, for you will see Abraham, Isaac, Jacob, and all the prophets in the Kingdom of God, but you will be thrown out. 29And people will come from all over the world—from east and west, north and south—to take their places in the Kingdom of God. 30And note this: Some who seem least important now will be the greatest then, and some who are the greatest now will be least important then.*"

Jesus Grieves over Jerusalem (154)

31At that time some Pharisees said to him, "Get away from here if you want to live! Herod Antipas wants to kill you!"

13:33
Matt 16:21

32Jesus replied, "Go tell that fox that I will keep on casting out demons and healing people today and tomorrow; and the third day I will accomplish my purpose. 33Yes, today, tomorrow, and the next day I must proceed on my way. For it wouldn't do for a prophet of God to be killed except in Jerusalem!

13:34-35
Luke 19:41-44

13:35
†Ps 118:26
Jer 12:7; 22:5
Luke 19:38

34"O Jerusalem, Jerusalem, the city that kills the prophets and stones God's messengers! How often I have wanted to gather your children together as a hen protects her chicks beneath her wings, but you wouldn't let me. 35And now, look, your house is abandoned. And you will never see me again until you say, 'Blessings on the one who comes in the name of the LORD!'*"

Jesus Heals a Man with Swollen Limbs (155)

14:1
Luke 7:36; 11:37

14:3
Luke 6:9

14:5
Matt 12:11

14 One Sabbath day Jesus went to eat dinner in the home of a leader of the Pharisees, and the people were watching him closely. 2There was a man there whose arms and legs were swollen.* 3Jesus asked the Pharisees and experts in religious law, "Is it permitted in the law to heal people on the Sabbath day, or not?" 4When they refused to answer, Jesus touched the sick man and healed him and sent him away. 5Then he turned to them and said, "Which of you doesn't work on the Sabbath? If your son* or your cow falls into a pit, don't you rush to get him out?" 6Again they could not answer.

Jesus Teaches about Humility (156)

14:7
Matt 23:6

14:8-11
Prov 25:6-7

7When Jesus noticed that all who had come to the dinner were trying to sit in the seats of honor near the head of the table, he gave them this advice: 8"When you are invited to a wedding feast, don't sit in the seat of honor. What if someone who is more distinguished than you has also been invited? 9The host will come and say, 'Give this person your seat.' Then you will be embarrassed, and you will have to take whatever seat is left at the foot of the table!

10 "Instead, take the lowest place at the foot of the table. Then when your host sees you, he will come and say, 'Friend, we have a better place for you!' Then you will be honored in front

13:30 Greek *Some are last who will be first, and some are first who will be last.*   **13:35** Ps 118:26.   **14:2** Or *who had dropsy.*   **14:5** Some manuscripts read *donkey.*

13:29 God's Kingdom will include people from every part of the world. Israel's rejection of Jesus as Messiah would not stop God's plan. True Israel includes all people who believe in Christ. This was an important fact for Luke to stress as he was directing his Good News to a Gentile audience (see also Romans 4:16-25; Galatians 3:6-9).

• **13:30** God's Kingdom will have many surprises. Some who are despised now will be greatly honored then; some influential people here will be left outside the gates. Many "great" people on this earth (in God's eyes) are virtually ignored by the rest of the world. What matters to God is not a person's earthly popularity, status, wealth, heritage, or power but his or her commitment to Christ. How do your values match those of the Bible? Put God in first place, and you will join people from all over the world who will take their places at the feast in the Kingdom of Heaven.

13:31-33 The Pharisees weren't interested in protecting Jesus from danger; they were trying to trap him themselves. The Pharisees urged Jesus to leave because they wanted to stop him from going to Jerusalem, not because they feared Herod. But Jesus' life, work, and death would not be determined by Herod or the Pharisees. His life was planned and directed by God himself, and his mission would unfold in God's time and according to God's plan.

13:33 Why was Jesus focusing on Jerusalem? Jerusalem, the city of God, symbolized the entire nation. It was Israel's largest city, the nation's spiritual and political capital, and Jews from around the world frequently visited it. But Jerusalem had a history of rejecting God's prophets (1 Kings 19:10; 2 Chronicles 24:19; Jeremiah 2:30; 26:20-23). It would reject the Messiah, just as it had rejected his forerunners.

14:1-6 Earlier Jesus had been invited to a Pharisee's home for discussion (7:36). This time a prominent Pharisee invited Jesus to his home specifically to trap him into saying or doing something for which he could be arrested. It may be surprising to see Jesus on the Pharisees' turf after he had denounced them so many times. But he was not afraid to face them, even though he knew that their purpose was to trick him into breaking their laws.

• **14:7-11** Jesus advised people not to rush for the best places at a feast. People today are just as eager to raise their social status, whether by being with the right people, dressing for success, or driving the right car. Whom do you try to impress? Rather than aiming for prestige, look for a place where you can serve. If God wants you to serve on a wider scale, he will invite you to take a higher place.

• **14:7-14** Jesus taught two lessons here. First, he spoke to the guests, telling them not to seek places of honor. Service is more important in God's Kingdom than status. Second, he told the host not to be exclusive about whom he invited. God opens his Kingdom to everyone.

of all the other guests. ¹¹For those who exalt themselves will be humbled, and those who humble themselves will be exalted."

¹²Then he turned to his host. "When you put on a luncheon or a banquet," he said, "don't invite your friends, brothers, relatives, and rich neighbors. For they will invite you back, and that will be your only reward. ¹³Instead, invite the poor, the crippled, the lame, and the blind. ¹⁴Then at the resurrection of the righteous, God will reward you for inviting those who could not repay you."

Jesus Tells the Parable of the Great Feast (**157**)

¹⁵Hearing this, a man sitting at the table with Jesus exclaimed, "What a blessing it will be to attend a banquet* in the Kingdom of God!"

¹⁶Jesus replied with this story: "A man prepared a great feast and sent out many invitations. ¹⁷When the banquet was ready, he sent his servant to tell the guests, 'Come, the banquet is ready.' ¹⁸But they all began making excuses. One said, 'I have just bought a field and must inspect it. Please excuse me.' ¹⁹Another said, 'I have just bought five pairs of oxen, and I want to try them out. Please excuse me.' ²⁰Another said, 'I now have a wife, so I can't come.'

²¹"The servant returned and told his master what they had said. His master was furious and said, 'Go quickly into the streets and alleys of the town and invite the poor, the crippled, the blind, and the lame.' ²²After the servant had done this, he reported, 'There is still room for more.' ²³So his master said, 'Go out into the country lanes and behind the hedges and urge anyone you find to come, so that the house will be full. ²⁴For none of those I first invited will get even the smallest taste of my banquet.'"

Jesus Teaches about the Cost of Being a Disciple (**158**)

²⁵A large crowd was following Jesus. He turned around and said to them, ²⁶"If you want to be my disciple, you must hate everyone else by comparison—your father and mother, wife and children, brothers and sisters—yes, even your own life. Otherwise, you cannot be my disciple. ²⁷And if you do not carry your own cross and follow me, you cannot be my disciple.

²⁸"But don't begin until you count the cost. For who would begin construction of a building without first calculating the cost to see if there is enough money to finish it? ²⁹Otherwise, you might complete only the foundation before running out of money, and then everyone would laugh at you. ³⁰They would say, 'There's the person who started that building and couldn't afford to finish it!'

14:15 Greek *to eat bread.*

14:11 Matt 23:12; Luke 18:14
14:14 Acts 24:15
14:20 Deut 24:5; 1 Cor 7:33
14:24 Matt 21:43; Acts 13:46
14:26 Deut 33:9; Matt 16:24; Mark 8:34; Luke 9:23; 18:29; John 12:25
14:27 Matt 10:38; 16:24; Mark 8:34; Luke 9:23

• **14:11** How can we humble ourselves? Some people try to give the appearance of humility in order to manipulate others. Others think that humility means putting themselves down. Truly humble people compare themselves only with Christ, realize their sinfulness, and understand their limitations. On the other hand, they also recognize their gifts and strengths and are willing to use them as Christ directs. Humility is not self-degradation; it is realistic self-assessment and commitment to serve.

14:15-24 The man sitting at the table with Jesus envisioned the glory of God's Kingdom, but he did not yet understand how to have a share in it. In Jesus' story, many people turned down the invitation to the banquet because the timing was inconvenient. We, too, may resist or delay responding to God's invitation, and our excuses may sound reasonable—work duties, family responsibilities, financial needs, or other reasons. Nevertheless, God's invitation is the most important event in your life, no matter how inconveniently it may be timed. Are you making excuses to avoid responding to God's call? Jesus reminds us that the time will come when God will pull his invitation and offer it to others—then it will be too late to get into the banquet.

14:16ff The custom was to send two invitations to a party: the first to announce the event and the second to tell the guests that everything was ready. The guests in Jesus' story insulted the host by making excuses when he issued the second invitation. In Israel's history, God's first invitation came from Moses and the prophets; the second came from his Son. The religious leaders accepted the first invitation. They believed that God had called them to be his people, but they insulted God by refusing to accept his Son. Thus, as the master in the story sent his servant into the streets to invite the needy to his banquet, so God sent his Son to a whole world of needy people to tell them that God's Kingdom had arrived and was ready for them.

• **14:16ff** In this chapter we read Jesus' words against seeking status and in favor of hard work and even suffering. Let us not lose sight of the end result of all our humility and self-sacrifice—a joyous banquet with our Lord! God never asks us to suffer for the sake of suffering. He never asks us to give up something good unless he plans to replace it with something even better. Jesus is not calling us to join him in a labor camp but in a feast—the wedding feast of the Lamb (Revelation 19:6-9), when God and his beloved church will be joined forever.

14:27 Jesus' audience was well aware of what it meant to carry one's own cross. When the Romans led a criminal to his execution site, he was forced to carry the cross on which he would die. This showed his submission to Rome and warned observers that they had better submit, too. Jesus made this statement to get the crowds to think through their enthusiasm for him. He encouraged those who were superficial either to go deeper or to turn back. Following Christ means total submission to him—perhaps even to the point of death. (See also the note on 9:23.)

• **14:28-30** When a builder doesn't count the cost or estimates it inaccurately, the building may be left uncompleted. Will you abandon the Christian life after a little while because you did not count the cost of commitment to Jesus? What are those costs? Christians may face loss of social status or wealth. They may have to give up control of their money, their time, or their career. They may be hated, separated from their family, and even put to death. Following Christ does not mean a trouble-free life. We must care-

31 "Or what king would go to war against another king without first sitting down with his counselors to discuss whether his army of 10,000 could defeat the 20,000 soldiers marching against him? 32And if he can't, he will send a delegation to discuss terms of peace while the enemy is still far away. 33So you cannot become my disciple without giving up everything you own.

34"Salt is good for seasoning. But if it loses its flavor, how do you make it salty again? 35Flavorless salt is good neither for the soil nor for the manure pile. It is thrown away. Anyone with ears to hear should listen and understand!"

14:33
Phil 3:7-8
14:34
Matt 5:13
Mark 9:50
14:35
Matt 11:15

Jesus Tells the Parable of the Lost Sheep (159)

15 Tax collectors and other notorious sinners often came to listen to Jesus teach. 2This made the Pharisees and teachers of religious law complain that he was associating with such sinful people—even eating with them!

3So Jesus told them this story: 4 "If a man has a hundred sheep and one of them gets lost, what will he do? Won't he leave the ninety-nine others in the wilderness and go to search for the one that is lost until he finds it? 5And when he has found it, he will joyfully carry it home on his shoulders. 6When he arrives, he will call together his friends and neighbors, saying, 'Rejoice with me because I have found my lost sheep.' 7In the same way, there is more joy in heaven over one lost sinner who repents and returns to God than over ninety-nine others who are righteous and haven't strayed away!

15:1
Matt 9:11
Luke 5:29
Gal 2:12

Jesus Tells the Parable of the Lost Coin (160)

8"Or suppose a woman has ten silver coins* and loses one. Won't she light a lamp and sweep the entire house and search carefully until she finds it? 9And when she finds it, she will call in her friends and neighbors and say, 'Rejoice with me because I have found my lost coin.' 10In the same way, there is joy in the presence of God's angels when even one sinner repents."

Jesus Tells the Parable of the Lost Son (161)

11To illustrate the point further, Jesus told them this story: "A man had two sons. 12The younger son told his father, 'I want my share of your estate now before you die.' So his father agreed to divide his wealth between his sons.

15:12
Deut 21:17

15:8 Greek *ten drachmas.* A drachma was the equivalent of a full day's wage.

---

fully count the cost of becoming Christ's disciples so that we will firmly hold to our faith and won't be tempted later to turn back.

14:34 Salt can lose its flavor. When it gets wet and then dries, nothing is left but a tasteless residue. Many Christians blend into the world and avoid the cost of standing up for Christ. But Jesus says if Christians lose their distinctive saltiness, they become worthless. Just as salt flavors and preserves food, we are to preserve the good in the world and bring new flavor to life. This requires careful planning, willing sacrifice, and unswerving commitment to Christ's Kingdom. But if a Christian fails to be "salty," he or she fails to represent Christ in the world. How salty are you?

• **15:2** Why were the Pharisees and teachers of religious law bothered that Jesus associated with these people? The religious leaders were always careful to stay "clean" according to Old Testament law. In fact, they went well beyond the law in their avoidance of certain people and situations and in their ritual washings. By contrast, Jesus took their concept of "cleanness" lightly. He risked defilement by touching those who had leprosy and by neglecting to wash in the Pharisees' prescribed manner, and he showed complete disregard for their sanctions against associating with certain classes of people. He came to offer salvation to sinners and to show that God loves them. Jesus didn't worry about the accusations. Instead, he continued going to those who needed him, regardless of the effect these rejected people might have on his reputation. How are you following Jesus' example?

• **15:3-6** It may seem foolish for the shepherd to leave 99 sheep to go search for just one. But the shepherd knew that the 99 would be safe in the sheepfold, whereas the lost sheep was in danger. Because each sheep was of high value, the shepherd knew that it was worthwhile to search diligently for the lost one. God's love for the individual is so great that he seeks out each one and rejoices

when he or she is found. Jesus associated with sinners because he wanted to bring the lost sheep—people considered beyond hope—the Good News of God's Kingdom. Before you were a believer, God sought you; and he is still seeking those who are yet lost.

• **15:4, 5** We may be able to understand a God who would forgive sinners who come to him for mercy. But a God who tenderly searches for sinners and then joyfully forgives them must possess an extraordinary love! This is the kind of love that prompted Jesus to come to earth to search for lost people and save them. This is the kind of extraordinary love that God has for you.

• **15:8-10** Palestinian women received 10 silver coins as a wedding gift. Besides their monetary value, these coins held sentimental value like that of a wedding ring, and to lose one would be extremely distressing. Just as a woman would rejoice at finding her lost coin, so the angels rejoice over a repentant sinner. Each individual is precious to God. He grieves over every loss and rejoices whenever one of his children is found and brought into the Kingdom. Perhaps we would have more joy in our churches if we shared Jesus' love and concern for the lost, diligently seeking them, and rejoicing when they come to the Savior.

15:12 The younger son's share of the estate would have been one-third, with the older son receiving two-thirds (Deuteronomy 21:17). In most cases he would have received this at his father's death, although fathers sometimes chose to divide up their inheritance early and retire from managing their estates. What is unusual here is that the younger one initiated the division of the estate. This showed arrogant disregard for his father's authority as head of the family.

¹³ "A few days later this younger son packed all his belongings and moved to a distant land, and there he wasted all his money in wild living. ¹⁴About the time his money ran out, a great famine swept over the land, and he began to starve. ¹⁵He persuaded a local farmer to hire him, and the man sent him into his fields to feed the pigs. ¹⁶The young man became so hungry that even the pods he was feeding the pigs looked good to him. But no one gave him anything.

¹⁷ "When he finally came to his senses, he said to himself, 'At home even the hired servants have food enough to spare, and here I am dying of hunger! ¹⁸I will go home to my father and say, "Father, I have sinned against both heaven and you, ¹⁹ and I am no longer worthy of being called your son. Please take me on as a hired servant." '

²⁰ "So he returned home to his father. And while he was still a long way off, his father saw him coming. Filled with love and compassion, he ran to his son, embraced him, and kissed him. ²¹His son said to him, 'Father, I have sinned against both heaven and you, and I am no longer worthy of being called your son.*'

²²"But his father said to the servants, 'Quick! Bring the finest robe in the house and put it on him. Get a ring for his finger and sandals for his feet. ²³And kill the calf we have been fattening. We must celebrate with a feast, ²⁴ for this son of mine was dead and has now returned to life. He was lost, but now he is found.' So the party began.

²⁵"Meanwhile, the older son was in the fields working. When he returned home, he heard music and dancing in the house, ²⁶and he asked one of the servants what was going on. ²⁷ 'Your brother is back,' he was told, 'and your father has killed the fattened calf. We are celebrating because of his safe return.'

²⁸ "The older brother was angry and wouldn't go in. His father came out and begged him, ²⁹but he replied, 'All these years I've slaved for you and never once refused to do a single thing you told me to. And in all that time you never gave me even one young goat for a feast with my friends. ³⁰Yet when this son of yours comes back after squandering your money on prostitutes, you celebrate by killing the fattened calf!'

³¹ "His father said to him, 'Look, dear son, you have always stayed by me, and everything I have is yours. ³² We had to celebrate this happy day. For your brother was dead and has come back to life! He was lost, but now he is found!' "

15:18
Ps 51:4

15:20
Gen 45:14-15;
46:29

15:22
Gen 41:42
Zech 3:4
Rev 6:11

15:24
Eph 2:1, 5; 5:14

15:31
Prov 29:3
John 17:10, 24

15:21 Some manuscripts add *Please take me on as a hired servant.*

15:15, 16 According to Moses' law, pigs were unclean animals (Leviticus 11:2-8; Deuteronomy 14:8). This meant that pigs could not be eaten or used for sacrifices. To protect themselves from defilement, Jews would not even touch pigs. For a Jew to stoop to feeding pigs was a great humiliation, and for this young man to eat food that the pigs had touched was to be degraded beyond belief. The younger son had truly sunk to the depths.

15:17 The younger son, like many who are rebellious and immature, wanted to be free to live as he pleased, and he had to hit bottom before he came to his senses. It often takes great sorrow and tragedy to cause people to look to the only One who can help them—Jesus. Are you trying to live life your own way, selfishly pushing aside any responsibility or commitment that gets in your way? Stop and look before you hit bottom. You will save yourself and your family much grief.

• **15:20** In the two preceding stories, the seeker actively looked for the coin and the sheep, which could not return by themselves. In this story, the father watched and waited. He was dealing with a human being with a will of his own, but he was ready to greet his son if he returned. In the same way, God's love is constant and patient and welcoming. He will search for us and give us opportunities to respond, but he will not force us to come to him. Like the father in this story, God waits patiently for us to come to our senses.

• **15:24** The sheep was lost because it foolishly wandered away (15:4); the coin was lost through no fault of its own (15:8); and the son left out of selfishness (15:12). God's great love reaches out and finds sinners no matter why or how they got lost.

• **15:25-31** The older brother found great difficulty in accepting his younger brother when he returned, and it is just as difficult to accept "younger brothers and sisters" today. People who repent after leading notoriously sinful lives are often held in suspicion; churches are sometimes unwilling to admit them to membership. Instead, we should rejoice like the angels in heaven when an unbeliever repents and turns to God. Like the father, accept repentant sinners wholeheartedly and give them the support and encouragement that they need to grow in Christ.

• **15:30** In the story of the lost son, the father's response is contrasted with the older brother's. The father forgave because he was filled with love. The son refused to forgive because he was bitter. His resentment rendered him just as lost to the father's love as his younger brother had been. Don't let anything keep you from forgiving others. If you are refusing to forgive people, you are missing a wonderful opportunity to experience joy and share it with others. Make your joy grow: Forgive somebody who has hurt you.

• **15:32** In Jesus' story, the older brother represents the Pharisees, who were angry and resentful that sinners were being welcomed into God's Kingdom. "After all," the Pharisees must have thought, "we have sacrificed and done *so much* for God." How easy it is to resent God's gracious forgiveness of others whom we consider to be far worse sinners than ourselves. But if our self-righteousness gets in the way of rejoicing when others come to Jesus, we are no better than the Pharisees.

Jesus Tells the Parable of the Shrewd Manager (**162**)

16:1
Luke 15:13, 30

16 Jesus told this story to his disciples: "There was a certain rich man who had a manager handling his affairs. One day a report came that the manager was wasting his employer's money. 2So the employer called him in and said, ' What's this I hear about you? Get your report in order, because you are going to be fired.'

3 "The manager thought to himself, 'Now what? My boss has fired me. I don't have the strength to dig ditches, and I'm too proud to beg. 4Ah, I know how to ensure that I'll have plenty of friends who will give me a home when I am fired.'

5 "So he invited each person who owed money to his employer to come and discuss the situation. He asked the first one, 'How much do you owe him?' 6The man replied, 'I owe him 800 gallons of olive oil.' So the manager told him, ' Take the bill and quickly change it to 400 gallons.*'

7 "'And how much do you owe my employer?' he asked the next man. 'I owe him 1,000 bushels of wheat,' was the reply. 'Here,' the manager said, 'take the bill and change it to 800 bushels.*'

16:8
John 12:36
Eph 5:8
1 Thes 5:5

8 "The rich man had to admire the dishonest rascal for being so shrewd. And it is true that the children of this world are more shrewd in dealing with the world around them than are the children of the light. 9Here's the lesson: Use your worldly resources to benefit others and make friends. Then, when your earthly possessions are gone, they will welcome you to an eternal home.*

16:10-12
Matt 25:20-30
Luke 19:17-26

10"If you are faithful in little things, you will be faithful in large ones. But if you are dishonest in little things, you won't be honest with greater responsibilities. 11And if you are untrustworthy about worldly wealth, who will trust you with the true riches of heaven? 12And if you are not faithful with other people's things, why should you be trusted with things of your own?

16:13
Matt 6:24

13 "No one can serve two masters. For you will hate one and love the other; you will be devoted to one and despise the other. You cannot serve both God and money."

16:14
Luke 23:35
1 Tim 3:3

14The Pharisees, who dearly loved their money, heard all this and scoffed at him. 15Then he said to them, "You like to appear righteous in public, but God knows your hearts. What this world honors is detestable in the sight of God.

16:15
Prov 24:12
Matt 23:28
Luke 8:9-14

16:16
Matt 11:12-13

16 "Until John the Baptist, the law of Moses and the messages of the prophets were your guides. But now the Good News of the Kingdom of God is preached, and everyone is eager to get in.* 17 But that doesn't mean that the law has lost its force. It is easier for heaven and earth to disappear than for the smallest point of God's law to be overturned.

16:17
Matt 5:18

16:6 Greek *100 baths . . . 50 [baths].* **16:7** Greek *100 korous . . . 80 [korous].* **16:9** Or *you will be welcomed into eternal homes.* **16:16** Or *everyone is urged to enter in.*

16:1-8 Our use of money is a good test of the lordship of Christ. (1) Money belongs to God, not us; let us use our resources wisely. (2) Money can be used for good or evil; let us use ours for good. (3) Money has a lot of power, let us use it carefully and thoughtfully. We must use our material goods in a way that will foster faith and obedience (see 12:33, 34).

16:9 We are to make wise use of the financial opportunities we have, not to earn heaven but to help people find Christ. If we use our money to help those in need or to help others find Christ, our earthly investment will bring eternal benefit. When we obey God's will, the unselfish use of possessions will follow.

16:10, 11 Our integrity is often put on the line in money matters. God calls us to be honest even in small details we could easily ignore. Heaven's riches are far more valuable than earthly wealth. But if we are not trustworthy with our money here (no matter how much or little we have), we will be unfit to handle the vast riches of God's Kingdom. See that you maintain your integrity in all matters, whether big or small.

16:13 Money can easily take God's place in your life. It can become your master. How can you tell if you are a slave to money? Ask yourself: Do I think and worry about it frequently? Do I give up doing what I should do or would like to do in order to make more money? Do I spend a great deal of my time caring for my possessions? Is it hard for me to give money away? Am I in debt?

Money is a hard and deceptive master. Wealth promises power and control, but often it cannot deliver. Great fortunes can be made—and lost—overnight, and no amount of money can provide health, happiness, or eternal life. How much better it is to let God be your master. His servants have peace of mind and security, both now and forever.

16:14 Because the Pharisees loved money, they took exception to Jesus' teaching. We live in an age that measures people's worth by how much money they make. Do you scoff at Jesus' warnings against serving money? Do you try to explain them away? Do you apply them to someone else? Unless we take Jesus' statements seriously, we may be acting like Pharisees ourselves.

16:15 The Pharisees acted piously to get praise from others, but God knew what was in their hearts. They considered their wealth a sign of God's approval. God detested their wealth because it caused them to abandon true spirituality. Though prosperity may earn people's praise, it must never substitute for devotion and service to God.

16:16, 17 John the Baptist's ministry was the dividing line between the Old and New Testaments (John 1:15-18). With the arrival of Jesus came the realization of all the prophets' hopes. Jesus emphasized that his Kingdom fulfilled the law (the Old Testament); it did not cancel it (Matthew 5:17). His was not a new system but the culmination of the old. The same God who worked through Moses was working through Jesus.

[18] "For example, a man who divorces his wife and marries someone else commits adultery. And anyone who marries a woman divorced from her husband commits adultery."

16:18
Matt 5:32; 19:9
Mark 10:11-12
1 Cor 7:10-11

Jesus Tells about the Rich Man and the Beggar (163)

[19]Jesus said, "There was a certain rich man who was splendidly clothed in purple and fine linen and who lived each day in luxury. [20]At his gate lay a poor man named Lazarus who was covered with sores. [21]As Lazarus lay there longing for scraps from the rich man's table, the dogs would come and lick his open sores.

[22] "Finally, the poor man died and was carried by the angels to be with Abraham.* The rich man also died and was buried, [23] and his soul went to the place of the dead.* There, in torment, he saw Abraham in the far distance with Lazarus at his side.

16:22
Matt 8:11

[24]"The rich man shouted, 'Father Abraham, have some pity! Send Lazarus over here to dip the tip of his finger in water and cool my tongue. I am in anguish in these flames.'

16:24
Luke 3:8

[25]"But Abraham said to him, 'Son, remember that during your lifetime you had everything you wanted, and Lazarus had nothing. So now he is here being comforted, and you are in anguish. [26]And besides, there is a great chasm separating us. No one can cross over to you from here, and no one can cross over to us from there.'

16:25
Luke 6:24

[27]"Then the rich man said, 'Please, Father Abraham, at least send him to my father's home. [28] For I have five brothers, and I want him to warn them so they don't end up in this place of torment.'

16:28
Acts 18:5

[29]"But Abraham said, 'Moses and the prophets have warned them. Your brothers can read what they wrote.'

16:29
Luke 24:27, 44
John 1:45; 5:45-47
Acts 15:21

[30]"The rich man replied, 'No, Father Abraham! But if someone is sent to them from the dead, then they will repent of their sins and turn to God.'

[31]"But Abraham said, 'If they won't listen to Moses and the prophets, they won't listen even if someone rises from the dead.'"

16:31
Matt 6:24
John 11:44-48

Jesus Tells about Forgiveness and Faith (164)

17 One day Jesus said to his disciples, "There will always be temptations to sin, but what sorrow awaits the person who does the tempting! [2]It would be better to be thrown into the sea with a millstone hung around your neck than to cause one of these little ones to fall into sin. [3]So watch yourselves!

17:1-3
Matt 18:7
Mark 9:42

"If another believer* sins, rebuke that person; then if there is repentance, forgive. [4]Even if that person wrongs you seven times a day and each time turns again and asks forgiveness, you must forgive."

17:3
Matt 18:15

16:22 Greek *into Abraham's bosom.*   **16:23** Greek *to Hades.*   **17:3** Greek *If your brother.*

16:18 Most religious leaders of Jesus' day permitted a man to divorce his wife for nearly any reason. Jesus' teaching about divorce went beyond Moses' (Deuteronomy 24:1-4). Stricter than any of the then-current schools of thought, Jesus' teachings shocked his hearers (see Matthew 19:10) just as they shake today's readers. Jesus says in no uncertain terms that marriage is a lifetime commitment. To leave your spouse for another person may be legal, but it is adultery in God's eyes. As you think about marriage, remember that God intends it to be a permanent commitment.

16:19-31 The Pharisees considered wealth to be a proof of a person's righteousness. Jesus startled them with this story in which a diseased beggar is rewarded and a rich man is punished. The rich man did not go to hell because of his wealth but because he was selfish, refusing to feed Lazarus, take him in, or care for him. The rich man was hard-hearted in spite of his great blessings. The amount of money we have is not as important as the way we use it. What is your attitude toward your money and possessions? Do you hoard them selfishly, or do you use them to help others?

16:20 This Lazarus is merely a character in a story and should not be confused with the Lazarus whom Jesus raised from the dead in John 11.

16:29-31 The rich man thought that his five brothers would surely believe a messenger who had been raised from the dead. But Jesus said that if they did not believe Moses and the proph-

ets, who spoke constantly of caring for the poor, not even a resurrection would convince them. Notice the irony in Jesus' statement; on his way to Jerusalem to die, he was fully aware that even when he had risen from the dead, most of the religious leaders would not accept him. They were set in their ways, and neither Scripture nor God's Son himself would shake them loose.

17:1-3 Jesus warned about God's wrath for those who offend, abuse, or lead astray the little ones. Jesus warns any predators who would hurt children in any way. How appropriate such a warning is in this day when corruption enters our homes every day in many television programs or on the internet. While Christians must guard against physical abuse, they also must be aware of and work against the mental and spiritual corruption that unfiltered television and unsupervised internet surfing can bring.

Jesus' warning envisions an additional group, however. The "little ones" can be new disciples. Indifference to the training and treatment of new Christians can leave them theologically vulnerable. Make the follow-through care of recent converts and new members a high priority in your church.

17:3, 4 To rebuke does not mean to point out every sin we see; it means to bring sin to a person's attention with the purpose of restoring him or her to God and to fellow humans. When you feel you must rebuke another Christian for a sin, check your attitudes before you speak. Do you love that person? Are you willing to forgive? Unless rebuke is tied to forgiveness, it will not help the sinning person.

17:5
Mark 9:24
17:6
Matt 17:20; 21:21

⁵The apostles said to the Lord, "Show us how to increase our faith."

⁶The Lord answered, "If you had faith even as small as a mustard seed, you could say to this mulberry tree, 'May you be uprooted and thrown into the sea,' and it would obey you!

⁷ "When a servant comes in from plowing or taking care of sheep, does his master say, 'Come in and eat with me'? ⁸No, he says, 'Prepare my meal, put on your apron, and serve me while I eat. Then you can eat later.' ⁹And does the master thank the servant for doing what he was told to do? Of course not. ¹⁰In the same way, when you obey me you should say, 'We are unworthy servants who have simply done our duty.'"

17:10
1 Cor 9:16

Jesus Heals Ten Men with Leprosy (169)

17:11
Luke 9:51-52;
13:22
17:12
Lev 13:46
17:14
Lev 14:2-3
Luke 5:14
17:16
Matt 10:5

17:19
Matt 9:22
Luke 7:50; 18:42

¹¹As Jesus continued on toward Jerusalem, he reached the border between Galilee and Samaria. ¹²As he entered a village there, ten lepers stood at a distance, ¹³crying out, "Jesus, Master, have mercy on us!"

¹⁴He looked at them and said, "Go show yourselves to the priests."* And as they went, they were cleansed of their leprosy.

¹⁵One of them, when he saw that he was healed, came back to Jesus, shouting, "Praise God!" ¹⁶He fell to the ground at Jesus' feet, thanking him for what he had done. This man was a Samaritan.

¹⁷Jesus asked, "Didn't I heal ten men? Where are the other nine? ¹⁸ Has no one returned to give glory to God except this foreigner?" ¹⁹And Jesus said to the man, "Stand up and go. Your faith has healed you.*"

17:14 See Lev 14:2-32.   **17:19** Or *Your faith has saved you.*

17:5, 6 The disciples' request was genuine; they wanted the faith necessary for such radical forgiveness. But Jesus didn't directly answer their question because the amount of faith is not as important as its genuineness. What is faith? It is complete trust and loyalty to God that results in a willingness to do his will. Faith is not something we use to put on a show for others. It is complete and humble obedience to God's will, readiness to do whatever he calls us to do. The amount of faith isn't as important as the right kind of faith—faith in our all-powerful God.

17:6 A mustard seed is small, but it is alive and growing. Almost invisible at first, the seed will begin to spread, first under the ground and then visibly. Like a tiny seed, a small amount of genuine faith in God will take root and grow. Although each change will be gradual and imperceptible, soon this faith will have produced major results that will uproot and destroy competing loyalties. We don't need more faith; a tiny seed of faith is enough if it is alive and growing.

17:7-10 If we have obeyed God, we have only done our duty, and we should regard it as a privilege. Do you sometimes feel that you deserve extra credit for serving God? Remember, obedience is not something extra we do; it is our duty. Jesus is not suggesting that our service is meaningless or useless, nor is he advocating doing away with rewards. He is attacking unwarranted self-esteem and spiritual pride.

17:11-14 Because leprosy was contagious, people who had leprosy were required to try to stay away from other people and to announce their presence if they had to come near. Sometimes leprosy would go into remission. If a leper thought his leprosy had gone away, he was supposed to present himself to a priest, who could declare him clean (Leviticus 14). Jesus sent the 10 lepers to the priest *before* they were healed—and they went! They responded in faith, and Jesus healed them on the way. Is your trust in God so strong that you act on what he says even before you see evidence that it will work?

17:16 Jesus healed all 10 lepers, but only one returned to thank him. It is possible to receive God's great gifts with an ungrateful spirit—9 of the 10 men did so. Only the thankful man, however, learned that his faith had played a role in his healing; and only grateful Christians grow in understanding God's grace. God does not demand that we thank him, but he is pleased when we do so. And he uses our responsiveness to teach us more about himself.

17:16 Not only was this man a leper, he was also a Samaritan—a race despised by the Jews as idolatrous half-breeds (see the note on 10:33). Once again Luke is pointing out that God's grace is for everybody.

LAST TRIP FROM GALILEE
Jesus left Galilee for the last time—he would not return before his death. He passed through Samaria, met and healed 10 men who had leprosy, and continued to Jerusalem. He spent some time east of the Jordan (Mark 10:1) before going to Jericho (Luke 19:1).

Jesus Teaches about the Coming of the Kingdom of God (170)

20One day the Pharisees asked Jesus, "When will the Kingdom of God come?"

Jesus replied, "The Kingdom of God can't be detected by visible signs.* 21You won't be able to say, 'Here it is!' or 'It's over there!' For the Kingdom of God is already among you.*"

22Then he said to his disciples, "The time is coming when you will long to see the day when the Son of Man returns,* but you won't see it. 23People will tell you, 'Look, there is the Son of Man,' or 'Here he is,' but don't go out and follow them. 24For as the lightning flashes and lights up the sky from one end to the other, so it will be on the day when the Son of Man comes. 25But first the Son of Man must suffer terribly* and be rejected by this generation.

26 "When the Son of Man returns, it will be like it was in Noah's day. 27In those days, the people enjoyed banquets and parties and weddings right up to the time Noah entered his boat and the flood came and destroyed them all.

28 "And the world will be as it was in the days of Lot. People went about their daily business—eating and drinking, buying and selling, farming and building—29until the morning Lot left Sodom. Then fire and burning sulfur rained down from heaven and destroyed them all. 30Yes, it will be 'business as usual' right up to the day when the Son of Man is revealed. 31On that day a person out on the deck of a roof must not go down into the house to pack. A person out in the field must not return home. 32Remember what happened to Lot's wife! 33If you cling to your life, you will lose it, and if you let your life go, you will save it. 34That night two people will be asleep in one bed; one will be taken, the other left. 35Two women will be grinding flour together at the mill; one will be taken, the other left.*"

37"Where will this happen, Lord?"* the disciples asked.

Jesus replied, "Just as the gathering of vultures shows there is a carcass nearby, so these signs indicate that the end is near."*

17:20
John 3:3; 18:36

17:23
Mark 13:21
Luke 17:21; 21:8

17:24
1 Tim 6:15

17:25
Matt 16:21
Mark 8:31
Luke 9:22

17:26-27
Matt 24:37-39

17:28
Gen 19:1-28

17:30
2 Thes 1:7

17:31
Matt 24:17-18
Mark 13:15-16

17:33
Matt 10:39; 16:25
Mark 8:35
Luke 9:24
John 12:25

17:35
Matt 24:41

17:37
Matt 24:28

Jesus Tells the Parable of the Persistent Widow (171)

18 One day Jesus told his disciples a story to show that they should always pray and never give up. 2 "There was a judge in a certain city," he said, "who neither feared God nor cared about people. 3A widow of that city came to him repeatedly, saying, 'Give me justice in this dispute with my enemy.' 4The judge ignored her for a while, but finally he said to himself, 'I don't fear God or care about people, 5but this woman is driving me crazy. I'm going to see that she gets justice, because she is wearing me out with her constant requests!' "

18:1
Rom 12:12
Col 4:2
1 Thes 5:17

18:5
Luke 11:7-8

17:20 Or *by your speculations.* 17:21 Or *is within you,* or *is in your grasp.* 17:22 Or *long for even one day with the Son of Man.* "Son of Man" is a title Jesus used for himself. 17:25 Or *suffer many things.* 17:35 Some manuscripts add verse 36, *Two men will be working in the field; one will be taken, the other left.* Compare Matt 24:40. 17:37a Greek *"Where, Lord?"* 17:37b Greek *"Wherever the carcass is, the vultures gather."*

17:20, 21 The Pharisees asked when God's Kingdom would come, not knowing that it had already arrived. The Kingdom of God is not like an earthly kingdom with geographical boundaries. Instead, it begins with the work of God's Spirit in people's lives and in relationships. We must resist looking to institutions or programs for evidence of the progress of God's Kingdom. Instead, we should look for what God is doing in people's hearts.

17:23, 24 Many will claim to be the Messiah, and many will claim that the Son of Man has returned—and people will believe them. Jesus warns us never to take such reports seriously, no matter how convincing they may sound. When Jesus returns, his power and presence will be evident to everyone. No one will need to spread the message because all will see for themselves.

17:23-36 Life will be going on as usual on the day Christ returns. No warning will sound. Most people will be going about their everyday tasks, indifferent to the demands of God. They will be as surprised by Christ's return as the people in Noah's day were by the Flood (Genesis 6–8) or the people in Lot's day by the destruction of Sodom (Genesis 19). We don't know the time of Christ's return, but we do know that he is coming. He may come today, tomorrow, or centuries in the future. Whenever Christ comes, we must be morally and spiritually ready. Live as if Jesus were returning today.

17:26-35 Jesus warned against false security. We are to abandon the values and attachments of this world in order to be ready for Christ's return. His return will happen suddenly,

and when he comes, there will be no second chances. Some will be taken to be with him; the rest will be left behind.

17:33 Those clinging to this life are those seeking to escape physical persecution. Those who live for themselves display these common attitudes: (1) *Materialism*—I want it and work hard to get it. All that I see is real. Unseen things are merely ideas and dreams. (2) *Individualism*—I work hard for me, and you work hard for you. I may make it; you may not. That's your problem, not mine. (3) *Skepticism*—Anything I'm not convinced about can't be wanted. Everything important to know I can figure out. Those who have these attitudes may protect themselves, but they will lose the spiritual dimension to their lives. Keep your commitment to Christ at full strength. Then you'll be ready when he returns.

17:37 To answer the disciples' question, Jesus quoted a familiar proverb. One vulture circling overhead does not mean much, but a gathering of vultures means that a carcass is nearby. Likewise, one sign of the end may not be significant, but when many signs occur, the Second Coming is near.

18:1 To persist in prayer and not give up does not mean endless repetition or painfully long prayer sessions. Constant prayer means keeping our requests continually before God as we live for him day by day, believing he will answer. When we live by faith, we are not to give up. God may delay answering, but his delays always have good reasons. As we persist in prayer, we grow in character, faith, and hope.

18:3 Widows and orphans were among the most vulnerable

18:7
Rev 6:10

18:8
1 Tim 4:1

⁶Then the Lord said, "Learn a lesson from this unjust judge. ⁷ Even he rendered a just decision in the end. So don't you think God will surely give justice to his chosen people who cry out to him day and night? Will he keep putting them off? ⁸I tell you, he will grant justice to them quickly! But when the Son of Man* returns, how many will he find on the earth who have faith?"

Jesus Tells the Parable of Two Men Who Prayed (172)

18:11
Matt 6:5

18:12
Matt 23:23

⁹Then Jesus told this story to some who had great confidence in their own righteousness and scorned everyone else: ¹⁰ "Two men went to the Temple to pray. One was a Pharisee, and the other was a despised tax collector. ¹¹The Pharisee stood by himself and prayed this prayer*: 'I thank you, God, that I am not a sinner like everyone else. For I don't cheat, I don't sin, and I don't commit adultery. I'm certainly not like that tax collector! ¹²I fast twice a week, and I give you a tenth of my income.'

18:14
Matt 23:12
Luke 14:11

¹³ "But the tax collector stood at a distance and dared not even lift his eyes to heaven as he prayed. Instead, he beat his chest in sorrow, saying, 'O God, be merciful to me, for I am a sinner.' ¹⁴ I tell you, this sinner, not the Pharisee, returned home justified before God. For those who exalt themselves will be humbled, and those who humble themselves will be exalted."

Jesus Blesses the Children (174/Matthew 19:13-15; Mark 10:13-16)

¹⁵One day some parents brought their little children to Jesus so he could touch and bless them. But when the disciples saw this, they scolded the parents for bothering him.

18:17
Matt 18:3

¹⁶Then Jesus called for the children and said to the disciples, "Let the children come to me. Don't stop them! For the Kingdom of God belongs to those who are like these children. ¹⁷ I tell you the truth, anyone who doesn't receive the Kingdom of God like a child will never enter it."

Jesus Speaks to the Rich Young Man (175/Matthew 19:16-30; Mark 10:17-31)

¹⁸Once a religious leader asked Jesus this question: "Good Teacher, what should I do to inherit eternal life?"

18:20
†Exod 20:13-16
†Deut 5:17-20

¹⁹ "Why do you call me good?" Jesus asked him. "Only God is truly good. ²⁰But to answer your question, you know the commandments: 'You must not commit adultery. You must not murder. You must not steal. You must not testify falsely. Honor your father and mother.'*"

²¹The man replied, "I've obeyed all these commandments since I was young."

18:8 "Son of Man" is a title Jesus used for himself.   **18:11** Some manuscripts read *stood and prayed this prayer to himself.*   **18:20** Exod 20:12-16; Deut 5:16-20.

---

of all God's people, and both Old Testament prophets and New Testament apostles insisted that these needy people be properly cared for. See, for example, Exodus 22:22-24; Isaiah 1:17; 1 Timothy 5:3; James 1:27.

18:6, 7 If godless judges respond to constant pressure, how much more will a great and loving God respond to us? If we know he loves us, we can believe he will hear our cries for help.

18:10 The people who lived near Jerusalem often would go to the Temple to pray. The Temple was the center of their worship.

18:11-14 The Pharisee did not go to the Temple to pray to God but to announce to all within earshot how good he was. The tax collector went not recognizing his sin and begging for mercy. Self-righteousness is dangerous. It leads to pride, causes a person to despise others, and prevents him or her from learning anything from God. The tax collector's prayer should be our prayer because we all need God's mercy every day. Don't let pride in your achievements cut you off from God.

18:15, 16 It was customary for a mother to bring her children to a rabbi for a blessing, and that is why these mothers gathered around Jesus. The disciples, however, thought the children were unworthy of the Master's time—less important than whatever else he was doing. But Jesus welcomed them because little children have the kind of faith and trust needed to enter God's Kingdom. It is important that we introduce our children to Jesus.

18:17 How does someone "receive the Kingdom of God like a child"? It means having the simple, trusting attitude that children show to adults on whom they depend. Jesus wants his people to enjoy prayer by delighting in his company. Find ways in a busy day to read the Bible enthusiastically, seek God's help in any problem, rely on him for guidance, and trust him explicitly. Children do all that with adults who love them. How much more should believers have that attitude toward Jesus, who loves them.

• **18:18ff** This leader sought reassurance, some way of knowing for sure that he had eternal life. He wanted Jesus to measure and grade his qualifications or to give him some task he could do to assure his own immortality. So Jesus gave him a task— the one thing the rich man knew he could not do. "Then who in the world can be saved?" the bystanders asked. "No one can, by his or her own achievements," Jesus' answer implied. "What is impossible for people is possible with God." Salvation cannot be earned—it is God's gift (see Ephesians 2:8-10).

18:18, 19 Jesus' question to the leader who came and called him "Good Teacher" was, in essence, "Do you know who I am?" Undoubtedly the man did not catch the implications of Jesus' reply—that the man was right in calling him good because Jesus truly is God.

22When Jesus heard his answer, he said, "There is still one thing you haven't done. Sell all your possessions and give the money to the poor, and you will have treasure in heaven. Then come, follow me."

23But when the man heard this he became very sad, for he was very rich.

24When Jesus saw this,* he said, "How hard it is for the rich to enter the Kingdom of God! 25In fact, it is easier for a camel to go through the eye of a needle than for a rich person to enter the Kingdom of God!"

26Those who heard this said, "Then who in the world can be saved?"

27He replied, "What is impossible for people is possible with God."

28Peter said, "We've left our homes to follow you."

29 "Yes," Jesus replied, "and I assure you that everyone who has given up house or wife or brothers or parents or children, for the sake of the Kingdom of God, 30will be repaid many times over in this life, and will have eternal life in the world to come."

Jesus Predicts His Death the Third Time (**177**/Matthew 20:17-19; Mark 10:32-34)

31Taking the twelve disciples aside, Jesus said, "Listen, we're going up to Jerusalem, where all the predictions of the prophets concerning the Son of Man will come true. 32He will be handed over to the Romans,* and he will be mocked, treated shamefully, and spit upon. 33They will flog him with a whip and kill him, but on the third day he will rise again."

34But they didn't understand any of this. The significance of his words was hidden from them, and they failed to grasp what he was talking about.

Jesus Heals a Blind Beggar (**179**/Matthew 20:29-34; Mark 10:46-52)

35As Jesus approached Jericho, a blind beggar was sitting beside the road. 36When he heard the noise of a crowd going past, he asked what was happening. 37They told him that Jesus the Nazarene* was going by. 38So he began shouting, "Jesus, Son of David, have mercy on me!"

39"Be quiet!" the people in front yelled at him.

But he only shouted louder, "Son of David, have mercy on me!"

40When Jesus heard him, he stopped and ordered that the man be brought to him. As the man came near, Jesus asked him, 41 "What do you want me to do for you?"

"Lord," he said, "I want to see!"

42And Jesus said, "All right, receive your sight! Your faith has healed you." 43Instantly the man could see, and he followed Jesus, praising God. And all who saw it praised God, too.

18:22
Matt 6:20

18:28
Matt 4:19

18:31
Ps 22
Isa 53
Luke 9:51;
24:25-27, 44

18:32
Matt 16:21
Luke 9:22, 44

18:38
Matt 9:27

18:41
Mark 10:36

18:42
Matt 9:22
Luke 7:50; 17:19

18:43
Luke 19:37

18:24 Some manuscripts read *When Jesus saw how sad the man was.*   **18:32** Greek *the Gentiles.*   **18:37** Or *Jesus of Nazareth.*

• **18:22, 23** This man's wealth made his life comfortable and gave him power and prestige. By telling him to sell everything he owned, Jesus was touching the very basis of his security and identity. The man did not understand that he would be even more secure if he followed Jesus than he was with all his wealth. Jesus does not ask believers to sell everything they have, although this may be his will for some. He does ask us all, however, to get rid of anything that has become more important in life than God. If your possessions take first place in your life, it would be better for you to get rid of them.

18:26-30 Peter and the other disciples had paid a high price— leaving their homes and jobs—to follow Jesus. But Jesus reminded Peter that following him has its benefits as well as its sacrifices. Any believer who has had to give up something to follow Christ will be repaid in this life as well as in the next. For example, if you must give up a secure job, you will find that God offers a secure relationship with himself now and forever. If you must give up your family's approval, you will gain the love of the family of God. The disciples had begun to pay the price of following Jesus, and he said they would be rewarded. Don't dwell on what you have given up; think about what you have gained and give thanks for it. You can never outgive God.

18:31-34 Some predictions about what would happen to Jesus are found in Psalm 41:9 (betrayal); Psalm 22:16-18 and Isaiah 53:4-7 (crucifixion); Psalm 16:10 (resurrection). The disciples didn't understand Jesus, apparently because they were focusing on what he had said about his death and were ignoring what he had said about his resurrection. Even though Jesus had spoken plainly, they would not grasp the significance of his words until they saw the risen Christ face to face.

18:35 Beggars often would wait along the roads near cities because that was where they could contact the most people. Usually disabled in some way, beggars were unable to earn a living. Medical help was not available for their problems, and people tended to ignore their obligation to care for the needy (Leviticus 25:35-38). Thus, beggars had little hope of escaping their degrading way of life. But this blind beggar took hope in the Messiah. He shamelessly cried out for Jesus' attention, and Jesus said that his faith allowed him to see. No matter how desperate your situation may seem, if you call out to Jesus in faith, he will help you.

18:38 The blind man called Jesus "Son of David," a title for the Messiah (Isaiah 11:1-3). This means that he understood Jesus to be the long-awaited Messiah. It is interesting to note that a poor and blind beggar could *see* that Jesus was the Messiah, while the religious leaders who saw his miracles were blinded to his identity and refused to recognize him as the Messiah.

Jesus Brings Salvation to Zacchaeus's Home (180)

19:1
Luke 18:35

19 Jesus entered Jericho and made his way through the town. ²There was a man there named Zacchaeus. He was the chief tax collector in the region, and he had become

19:4
1 Kgs 10:27
1 Chr 27:28

very rich. ³He tried to get a look at Jesus, but he was too short to see over the crowd. ⁴So he ran ahead and climbed a sycamore-fig tree beside the road, for Jesus was going to pass that way.

⁵When Jesus came by, he looked up at Zacchaeus and called him by name. "Zacchaeus!" he said. "Quick, come down! I must be a guest in your home today."

⁶Zacchaeus quickly climbed down and took Jesus to his house in great excitement and

19:7
Matt 9:11
Luke 5:30; 15:2

joy. ⁷But the people were displeased. "He has gone to be the guest of a notorious sinner," they grumbled.

19:8
Exod 22:1
Num 5:7
Luke 3:12-13

⁸Meanwhile, Zacchaeus stood before the Lord and said, "I will give half my wealth to the poor, Lord, and if I have cheated people on their taxes, I will give them back four times as much!"

19:9
Matt 9:13
Acts 16:31-34
1 Tim 1:15

⁹Jesus responded, "Salvation has come to this home today, for this man has shown himself to be a true son of Abraham. ¹⁰For the Son of Man* came to seek and save those who are lost."

Jesus Tells the Parable of the King's Ten Servants (181)

19:11-27
Matt 25:14-30

¹¹The crowd was listening to everything Jesus said. And because he was nearing Jerusalem,

19:11
Acts 1:6

he told them a story to correct the impression that the Kingdom of God would begin right

19:10 "Son of Man" is a title Jesus used for himself.

19:1-10 To finance their great world empire, the Romans levied heavy taxes on all nations under their control. The Jews opposed these taxes because they supported a secular government and its pagan gods, but they were still forced to pay. Tax collectors were among the most unpopular people in Israel. Jews by birth, they chose to work for Rome and were considered traitors. Besides, it was common knowledge that tax collectors were making themselves rich by gouging their fellow Jews. No wonder the people muttered when Jesus went home with the tax collector Zacchaeus. But despite the fact that Zacchaeus was both a cheater and a turncoat, Jesus loved him; and in response, this tax collector was converted. In every society, certain groups of people are considered "untouchable" because of their political views, their immoral behavior, or their lifestyle. We should not give in to social pressure to avoid these people. Jesus loves them, and they need to hear his Good News.

• **19:8** Judging from the crowd's reaction to him, Zacchaeus must have been a very crooked tax collector. After he met Jesus, however, he realized that his life needed straightening out. By giving to the poor and making restitution—with generous interest—to those he had cheated, Zacchaeus demonstrated inner change by outward action. Following Jesus in your head or heart alone is not enough. You must show your faith by changed behavior. Has your faith resulted in action? What changes do you need to make?

19:9, 10 When Jesus said Zacchaeus was a son of Abraham and yet was lost, he must have shocked his hearers in at least two ways: (1) They would not have liked to acknowledge that this unpopular tax collector was a fellow son of Abraham, and (2) they would not have wished to admit that sons of Abraham could be lost. But a person is not saved because of a good heritage or condemned by a bad one; faith is more important than genealogy. Jesus came to save all the lost, regardless of their background or previous way of life. Through faith, the lost can be forgiven and made new.

19:11ff The people still hoped for a political leader who would set up an earthly kingdom and get rid of Roman domination. Jesus' story showed that his Kingdom would not take this form right away. First, he would go away for a while, and his followers would need to be faithful and productive during his absence. Upon his return, Jesus would inaugurate a Kingdom more powerful and just than anything they could expect or imagine.

• **19:11ff** This story showed Jesus' followers what they were to do during the time between Jesus' departure and his second coming. Because we live in that time period, it applies directly to us. We have been given excellent resources to build and expand God's Kingdom. Jesus expects us to use these talents so that they multiply and the Kingdom grows. He asks each of us to account for what we do with his gifts. While awaiting the coming of the Kingdom of God in glory, we must do Christ's work.

away. ¹²He said, "A nobleman was called away to a distant empire to be crowned king and then return. ¹³Before he left, he called together ten of his servants and divided among them ten pounds of silver,* saying, 'Invest this for me while I am gone.' ¹⁴ But his people hated him and sent a delegation after him to say, 'We do not want him to be our king.'

19:12
Mark 13:34

¹⁵"After he was crowned king, he returned and called in the servants to whom he had given the money. He wanted to find out what their profits were. ¹⁶The first servant reported, 'Master, I invested your money and made ten times the original amount!'

¹⁷"'Well done!' the king exclaimed. 'You are a good servant. You have been faithful with the little I entrusted to you, so you will be governor of ten cities as your reward.'

19:17
Luke 16:10

¹⁸"The next servant reported, 'Master, I invested your money and made five times the original amount.'

¹⁹"'Well done!' the king said. 'You will be governor over five cities.'

²⁰"But the third servant brought back only the original amount of money and said, 'Master, I hid your money and kept it safe. ²¹I was afraid because you are a hard man to deal with, taking what isn't yours and harvesting crops you didn't plant.'

²² "'You wicked servant!' the king roared. 'Your own words condemn you. If you knew that I'm a hard man who takes what isn't mine and harvests crops I didn't plant, ²³why didn't you deposit my money in the bank? At least I could have gotten some interest on it.'

19:22
Job 15:6
Matt 12:37

²⁴"Then, turning to the others standing nearby, the king ordered, 'Take the money from this servant, and give it to the one who has ten pounds.'

²⁵"'But, master,' they said, 'he already has ten pounds!'

²⁶"'Yes,' the king replied, 'and to those who use well what they are given, even more will be given. But from those who do nothing, even what little they have will be taken away. ²⁷And as for these enemies of mine who didn't want me to be their king—bring them in and execute them right here in front of me.'"

19:26
Matt 13:12
Mark 4:25
Luke 8:18

19:27
Luke 19:14

3. Jesus' ministry in Jerusalem

Jesus Rides into Jerusalem on a Young Donkey
(**183**/Matthew 21:1-11; Mark 11:1-11; John 12:12-19)

²⁸After telling this story, Jesus went on toward Jerusalem, walking ahead of his disciples. ²⁹As he came to the towns of Bethphage and Bethany on the Mount of Olives, he sent two disciples ahead. ³⁰"Go into that village over there," he told them. "As you enter it, you will see a young donkey tied there that no one has ever ridden. Untie it and bring it here. ³¹If anyone asks, 'Why are you untying that colt?' just say, 'The Lord needs it.'"

³²So they went and found the colt, just as Jesus had said. ³³And sure enough, as they were untying it, the owners asked them, "Why are you untying that colt?"

³⁴And the disciples simply replied, "The Lord needs it." ³⁵So they brought the colt to Jesus and threw their garments over it for him to ride on.

19:13 Greek *ten minas;* one mina was worth about three months' wages.

LAST WEEK IN JERUSALEM
As they approached Jerusalem from Jericho (19:1), Jesus and the disciples came to the villages of Bethany and Bethphage, nestled on the eastern slope of the Mount of Olives, only a few miles outside Jerusalem. Jesus stayed in Bethany during the nights of that last week, entering Jerusalem during the day.

• **19:20-27** Why was the king so hard on this man who had not increased the money? He punished the man because (1) he didn't share his master's interest in the Kingdom, (2) he didn't trust his master's intentions, (3) his only concern was for himself, and (4) he did nothing to use the money. Like the king in this story, God has given you gifts to use for the benefit of his Kingdom. Do you want the Kingdom to grow? Do you trust God to govern it fairly? Are you as concerned for others' welfare as you are for your own? Are you willing to use faithfully what he has entrusted to you?

19:30-35 By this time Jesus was extremely well known. Everyone coming to Jerusalem for the Passover festival had heard of him, and, for a time, the popular mood was favorable toward him. "The Lord needs it" was all the disciples had to say, and the colt's owners gladly turned their animal over to them.

19:35-38 Christians celebrate this event on Palm Sunday. The people lined the road, praising God, waving palm branches, and throwing their cloaks in front of the colt as it passed before them. "Long live the King" was the meaning behind their joyful shouts, because they knew that Jesus was intentionally fulfilling the prophecy in Zechariah 9:9: "Look, your king is coming to you. He is righteous and victorious, yet he is humble, riding on a donkey—riding on a donkey's colt." To announce that he was indeed the Messiah,

19:36
2 Kgs 9:13

³⁶As he rode along, the crowds spread out their garments on the road ahead of him. ³⁷When he reached the place where the road started down the Mount of Olives, all of his followers began to shout and sing as they walked along, praising God for all the wonderful miracles they had seen.

19:38
†Pss 118:25-26;
148:1
Luke 2:14; 13:35

³⁸ "Blessings on the King who comes in the name of the LORD!
    Peace in heaven, and glory in highest heaven!"*

³⁹But some of the Pharisees among the crowd said, "Teacher, rebuke your followers for saying things like that!"

19:40
Hab 2:11

⁴⁰He replied, "If they kept quiet, the stones along the road would burst into cheers!"

19:43
Isa 29:3
Jer 6:6
Ezek 4:2
Luke 21:20

⁴¹But as he came closer to Jerusalem and saw the city ahead, he began to weep. ⁴² "How I wish today that you of all people would understand the way to peace. But now it is too late, and peace is hidden from your eyes. ⁴³Before long your enemies will build ramparts against your walls and encircle you and close in on you from every side. ⁴⁴They will crush you into

19:44
Ps 137:9
Luke 21:6

the ground, and your children with you. Your enemies will not leave a single stone in place, because you did not accept your opportunity for salvation."

Jesus Clears the Temple Again (**184**/Matthew 21:12-17; Mark 11:12-19)

⁴⁵Then Jesus entered the Temple and began to drive out the people selling animals for sacri-

19:46
†Isa 56:7
†Jer 7:11

fices. ⁴⁶He said to them, "The Scriptures declare, 'My Temple will be a house of prayer,' but you have turned it into a den of thieves."*

19:47
Matt 26:55
Luke 21:37; 22:53
John 18:20

⁴⁷After that, he taught daily in the Temple, but the leading priests, the teachers of religious law, and the other leaders of the people began planning how to kill him. ⁴⁸But they could think of nothing, because all the people hung on every word he said.

Religious Leaders Challenge Jesus' Authority
(**189**/Matthew 21:23-27; Mark 11:27-33)

20:2
John 2:18
Acts 4:7; 7:27

20 One day as Jesus was teaching the people and preaching the Good News in the Temple, the leading priests, the teachers of religious law, and the elders came up to him. ²They demanded, "By what authority are you doing all these things? Who gave you the right?"

20:4
Mark 1:4

³"Let me ask you a question first," he replied. ⁴"Did John's authority to baptize come from heaven, or was it merely human?"

20:6
Luke 7:29

⁵They talked it over among themselves. "If we say it was from heaven, he will ask why we didn't believe John. ⁶But if we say it was merely human, the people will stone us because they are convinced John was a prophet." ⁷So they finally replied that they didn't know.

⁸And Jesus responded, "Then I won't tell you by what authority I do these things."

19:38 Pss 118:26; 148:1. **19:46** Isa 56:7; Jer 7:11.

Jesus chose a *time* when all Israel would be gathered at Jerusalem, a *place* where huge crowds could see him, and a *way* of proclaiming his mission that was unmistakable. The people went wild. They were sure their liberation was at hand.

• **19:38** The people who were praising God for giving them a king had the wrong idea about Jesus. They expected him to be a national leader who would restore their nation to its former glory; thus, they were deaf to the words of their prophets and blind to Jesus' real mission. When it became apparent that Jesus was not going to fulfill their hopes, many people turned against him.

19:39, 40 The Pharisees thought the crowd's words were sacrilegious and blasphemous. They didn't want someone challenging their power and authority, and they didn't want a revolt that would bring the Roman army down on them. So they asked Jesus to keep his people quiet. But Jesus said that if the people were quiet, the stones would burst into cheers. Why? Not because Jesus was setting up a powerful political kingdom but because he was establishing God's eternal Kingdom, a reason for the greatest celebration of all.

19:41-44 The Jewish leaders had rejected their King (19:47). They had gone too far. They had refused God's offer of salvation in Jesus Christ when they were visited by God himself, and soon their nation would suffer. God did not turn away from the Jewish people who obeyed him, however, and he continues to offer salvation to the people he loves, both Jews and Gentiles.

Eternal life is within your reach; accept it while the opportunity is still offered.

19:43, 44 About 40 years after Jesus said these words, they came true. In A.D. 66, the Jews revolted against Roman control. Three years later Titus, son of the emperor Vespasian, was sent to crush the rebellion. Roman soldiers attacked Jerusalem and broke through the northern wall but still couldn't take the city. Finally, they laid siege to it, and in A.D. 70 they were able to enter the severely weakened city and burn it. Six hundred thousand Jews were killed during Titus's onslaught.

• **19:47** Who were the "other leaders of the people"? This group probably included wealthy leaders in politics, commerce, and law. They had several reasons for wanting to get rid of Jesus. He had damaged business in the Temple by driving the merchants out. In addition, he was preaching against injustice, and his teachings often favored the poor over the rich. Furthermore, his great popularity was in danger of attracting Rome's attention, and the leaders of Israel wanted as little as possible to do with Rome.

• **20:1-8** This group of leaders wanted to get rid of Jesus, so they tried to trap him with their question. If Jesus would answer that his authority came from God—if he stated openly that he was the Messiah and the Son of God—they would accuse him of blasphemy and bring him to trial. Jesus did not let himself be caught. Instead, he turned the question on them. Thus, he exposed their motives and avoided their trap.

Jesus Tells the Parable of the Evil Farmers (**191**/Matthew 21:33-46; Mark 12:1-12)

[9] Now Jesus turned to the people again and told them this story: "A man planted a vineyard, leased it to tenant farmers, and moved to another country to live for several years. [10] At the time of the grape harvest, he sent one of his servants to collect his share of the crop. But the farmers attacked the servant, beat him up, and sent him back empty-handed. [11] So the owner sent another servant, but they also insulted him, beat him up, and sent him away empty-handed. [12] A third man was sent, and they wounded him and chased him away.

20:9-19
Isa 5:1-7
20:10-12
2 Chr 36:15-16

[13] "'What will I do?' the owner asked himself. 'I know! I'll send my cherished son. Surely they will respect him.'

[14] "But when the tenant farmers saw his son, they said to each other, 'Here comes the heir to this estate. Let's kill him and get the estate for ourselves!' [15] So they dragged him out of the vineyard and murdered him.

20:14
Heb 1:2

"What do you suppose the owner of the vineyard will do to them?" Jesus asked. [16] "I'll tell you—he will come and kill those farmers and lease the vineyard to others."

"How terrible that such a thing should ever happen," his listeners protested.

[17] Jesus looked at them and said, "Then what does this Scripture mean?

20:17
†Ps 118:22
Acts 4:11

'The stone that the builders rejected
has now become the cornerstone.'*

[18] Everyone who stumbles over that stone will be broken to pieces, and it will crush anyone it falls on."

20:18
Isa 8:14-15
Dan 2:34, 35

[19] The teachers of religious law and the leading priests wanted to arrest Jesus immediately because they realized he was telling the story against them—they were the wicked farmers. But they were afraid of the people's reaction.

Religious Leaders Question Jesus about Paying Taxes
(**193**/Matthew 22:15-22; Mark 12:13-17)

[20] Watching for their opportunity, the leaders sent spies pretending to be honest men. They tried to get Jesus to say something that could be reported to the Roman governor so he would arrest Jesus. [21] "Teacher," they said, "we know that you speak and teach what is right and are not influenced by what others think. You teach the way of God truthfully. [22] Now tell us—is it right for us to pay taxes to Caesar or not?"

[23] He saw through their trickery and said, [24] "Show me a Roman coin.* Whose picture and title are stamped on it?"

"Caesar's," they replied.

[25] "Well then," he said, "give to Caesar what belongs to Caesar, and give to God what belongs to God."

20:25
Luke 23:2
Rom 13:6-7

[26] So they failed to trap him by what he said in front of the people. Instead, they were amazed by his answer, and they became silent.

20:17 Ps 118:22.   **20:24** Greek *a denarius.*

• **20:9-16** The characters in this story are easily identified. Even the religious leaders understood it. The owner of the vineyard is God; the vineyard is Israel; the tenant farmers are the religious leaders; the servants are the prophets and priests God sent to Israel; the son is the Messiah, Jesus; the others are the Gentiles. Jesus' parable indirectly answered the religious leaders' question about his authority; it also showed them that he knew about their plan to kill him.

20:17-19 Quoting Psalm 118:22, Jesus showed the unbelieving leaders that even their rejection of the Messiah had been prophesied in Scripture. Ignoring the cornerstone was dangerous. A person could be tripped or crushed (judged and punished). Jesus' comments were veiled, but the religious leaders had no trouble interpreting them. They immediately wanted to arrest him.

20:18 The word "broken" conjures up uniformly negative images: broken bones, broken hearts, broken toys. You don't want something you value to be broken. Conversely, in God's dictionary, brokenness is not only good but also essential. He uses only people whose hearts, volition, and pride have been broken. Jesus gives a double warning: those who stumble over that stone—himself—"will be broken to pieces," while it will crush anyone it falls on. God offers a choice of "brokennesses." Those who cast

themselves on Jesus, submitting their wills and all that they are to him, will be broken by him of arrogance, hard-heartedness, and self-centeredness. It is not a pleasant process but an absolutely necessary one. For those who do not submit to him, he will ultimately "fall on them," an experience that can only be described as "crushing." The choice is yours: broken before him, or crushed by him.

20:20-26 Jesus turned his enemies' attempt to trap him into a powerful lesson: As God's followers, we have legitimate obligations to both God and the government. But it is important to keep our priorities straight. When the two authorities conflict, our duty to God always must come before our duty to the government.

20:22 This was a loaded question. The Jews were enraged at having to pay taxes to Rome, thus supporting the pagan government and its gods. They hated the system that allowed tax collectors to charge exorbitant rates and keep the extra for themselves. If Jesus said they should pay taxes, they would call him a traitor to their nation and their religion. But if he said they should not, they could report him to Rome as a rebel. Jesus' questioners thought they had him this time, but he outwitted them again.

20:24 This Roman coin was a denarius, the usual pay for one day's work.

Religious Leaders Question Jesus about the Resurrection
(**194**/Matthew 22:23-33; Mark 12:18-27)

20:27
Acts 23:8

20:28
†Deut 25:5

27 Then Jesus was approached by some Sadducees—religious leaders who say there is no resurrection from the dead. 28 They posed this question: "Teacher, Moses gave us a law that if a man dies, leaving a wife but no children, his brother should marry the widow and have a child who will carry on the brother's name.* 29 Well, suppose there were seven brothers. The oldest one married and then died without children. 30 So the second brother married the widow, but he also died. 31 Then the third brother married her. This continued with all seven of them, who died without children. 32 Finally, the woman also died. 33 So tell us, whose wife will she be in the resurrection? For all seven were married to her!"

20:36
John 1:12
Gal 4:5-7
1 Jn 3:1-2

20:37
†Exod 3:6

34 Jesus replied, "Marriage is for people here on earth. 35 But in the age to come, those worthy of being raised from the dead will neither marry nor be given in marriage. 36 And they will never die again. In this respect they will be like angels. They are children of God and children of the resurrection.

37 "But now, as to whether the dead will be raised—even Moses proved this when he wrote about the burning bush. Long after Abraham, Isaac, and Jacob had died, he referred to the Lord* as 'the God of Abraham, the God of Isaac, and the God of Jacob.'* 38 So he is the God of the living, not the dead, for they are all alive to him."

39 "Well said, Teacher!" remarked some of the teachers of religious law who were standing there. 40 And then no one dared to ask him any more questions.

Religious Leaders Cannot Answer Jesus' Question
(**196**/Matthew 22:41-46; Mark 12:35-37)

20:42-43
†Ps 110:1

41 Then Jesus presented them with a question. "Why is it," he asked, "that the Messiah is said to be the son of David? 42 For David himself wrote in the book of Psalms:

'The LORD said to my Lord,
     Sit in the place of honor at my right hand
43 until I humble your enemies,
     making them a footstool under your feet.'*

44 Since David called the Messiah 'Lord,' how can the Messiah be his son?"

Jesus Warns against the Religious Leaders (**197**/Matthew 23:1-12; Mark 12:38-40)
45 Then, with the crowds listening, he turned to his disciples and said, 46 "Beware of these teachers of religious law! For they like to parade around in flowing robes and love to receive

20:28 See Deut 25:5-6.   **20:37a** Greek *when he wrote about the bush. He referred to the Lord.*   **20:37b** Exod 3:6.
20:42-43 Ps 110:1.

• **20:27-38** The Sadducees, a group of conservative religious leaders, honored only the Pentateuch—Genesis through Deuteronomy—as Scripture. They also did not believe in a resurrection of the dead because they could find no mention of it in those books. The Sadducees decided to try their hand at tricking Jesus, so they brought him a question that they probably had used successfully to stump the Pharisees. After addressing their question about marriage, Jesus answered their *real* question about the resurrection. Basing his answer on the writings of Moses—an authority they respected—he upheld belief in the resurrection.

20:34, 35 Jesus' statement does not mean that people will not recognize their spouses in heaven. It simply means that we must not think of heaven as an extension of life as we now know it. Our relationships in this life are limited by time, death, and sin. We don't know everything about our resurrection life, but Jesus affirms that relationships will be different from what we are used to here and now.

20:37, 38 Jesus answered the Sadducees' question, then he went beyond it to the real issue. People may ask you tough religious questions, such as "How can a loving God allow people to starve?" "If God knows what I'm going to do, do I have any free choice?" If they do, follow Jesus' example. First, answer them to the best of your ability; then look for the real issue: hurt over a personal tragedy, for example, or difficulty in making a decision. Often the spoken question is only a test, not of your ability to answer hard questions, but of your willingness to listen and care.

• **20:41-44** The Pharisees and Sadducees had asked their questions. Then Jesus turned the tables and asked them a question that went right to the heart of the matter—what they thought about the Messiah's identity. The Pharisees knew that the Messiah would be a descendant of David, but they did not understand that he would be more than a human descendant—he would be God in the flesh. Jesus quoted from Psalm 110:1 to show that David knew that the Messiah would be both human and divine. The Pharisees expected only a human ruler to restore Israel's greatness as in the days of David and Solomon.

The central issue of life is what we believe about Jesus. Other spiritual questions are irrelevant unless we first decide to believe that Jesus is who he said he is. The Pharisees and Sadducees could not do this. They remained confused over Jesus' identity.

20:45-47 The teachers of religious law loved the benefits associated with their position, and they sometimes cheated the poor in order to get even more benefits. Every job has its rewards, but gaining rewards should never become more important than doing the job faithfully. God will punish people who use their position of responsibility to cheat others. Use whatever resources you have been given to help others and not just yourself.

respectful greetings as they walk in the marketplaces. And how they love the seats of honor in the synagogues and the head table at banquets. 47Yet they shamelessly cheat widows out of their property and then pretend to be pious by making long prayers in public. Because of this, they will be severely punished."

A Poor Widow Gives All She Has (200/Mark 12:41-44)

21 While Jesus was in the Temple, he watched the rich people dropping their gifts in the collection box. 2Then a poor widow came by and dropped in two small coins.*

3"I tell you the truth," Jesus said, "this poor widow has given more than all the rest of them. 4For they have given a tiny part of their surplus, but she, poor as she is, has given everything she has."

Jesus Tells about the Future (201/Matthew 24:1-25; Mark 13:1-23)

5Some of his disciples began talking about the majestic stonework of the Temple and the memorial decorations on the walls. But Jesus said, 6"The time is coming when all these things will be completely demolished. Not one stone will be left on top of another!"

7"Teacher," they asked, "when will all this happen? What sign will show us that these things are about to take place?"

8He replied, "Don't let anyone mislead you, for many will come in my name, claiming, 'I am the Messiah,'* and saying, 'The time has come!' But don't believe them. 9And when you hear of wars and insurrections, don't panic. Yes, these things must take place first, but the end won't follow immediately." 10Then he added, "Nation will go to war against nation, and kingdom against kingdom. 11There will be great earthquakes, and there will be famines and plagues in many lands, and there will be terrifying things and great miraculous signs from heaven.

12"But before all this occurs, there will be a time of great persecution. You will be dragged into synagogues and prisons, and you will stand trial before kings and governors because you are my followers. 13But this will be your opportunity to tell them about me.* 14So don't worry in advance about how to answer the charges against you, 15for I will give you the right words and such wisdom that none of your opponents will be able to reply or refute you! 16Even those closest to you—your parents, brothers, relatives, and friends—will betray you. They will even kill some of you. 17And everyone will hate you because you are my followers.* 18But not a hair of your head will perish! 19By standing firm, you will win your souls.

21:6
Luke 19:44

21:8
Luke 17:23

21:10
2 Chr 15:6
Isa 19:2

21:12
Acts 12:4

21:13
Phil 1:12

21:14
Luke 12:11-12

21:15
Acts 6:10

21:18
Matt 10:30

21:2 Greek *two lepta* [the smallest of Jewish coins]. **21:8** Greek *claiming, 'I am.'* **21:13** Or *This will be your testimony against them.* **21:17** Greek *on account of my name.*

• **20:47** How strange to think that the teachers of religious law would receive the worst punishment. But behind their appearance of holiness and respectability, they were arrogant, crafty, selfish, and uncaring. Jesus exposed their evil hearts. He showed that despite their pious words, they were neglecting God's laws and doing as they pleased. Religious deeds do not cancel sin. Jesus said that God's most severe judgment awaited these teachers because they should have been living examples of mercy and justice.

21:1, 2 Jesus was in the area of the Temple called the Court of Women. In this area were seven boxes in which worshipers could deposit their Temple tax and six boxes for freewill offerings, like the one this woman gave. This widow was not only poor but had few resources for making money. Her small gift was a sacrifice, but she gave it willingly.

21:1-4 In contrast to the way most of us handle our money, this widow gave all she had to live on. When we consider ourselves generous in giving a small percentage of our income to the Lord, we resemble those who gave "a tiny part of their surplus." Here, Jesus admired the woman's generous and sacrificial giving. As believers, we should consider increasing our giving—whether money, time, or talents—to a point beyond mere convenience or comfort.

21:5, 6 The Temple the disciples were admiring was not Solomon's Temple—that had been destroyed by the Babylonians early in the sixth century B.C. This Temple had been built by Ezra after the return from exile later in the sixth century B.C., desecrated by the Seleucids in the second century B.C., reconsecrated by the

Maccabees soon afterward, and enormously expanded by Herod the Great over a 46-year period. It was a beautiful, imposing structure with a significant history, but Jesus said that it would be completely destroyed. This happened in A.D. 70 when the Roman army burned Jerusalem.

• **21:7ff** Jesus did not leave his disciples unprepared for the difficult years ahead. He warned them about false messiahs, natural disasters, and persecutions; however, he assured the disciples that he would be with them to protect them and make his Kingdom known through them. In the end, Jesus promised that he would return in power and glory to save them. Jesus' warnings and promises to his disciples also apply to us as we look forward to his return.

• **21:12, 13** These persecutions soon began. Luke recorded many of them in the book of Acts. Paul wrote from prison that he suffered gladly because it helped him know Christ better and do Christ's work for the church (Philippians 3:10; Colossians 1:24). The early church thrived despite intense persecution. In fact, late in the second century the church father Tertullian wrote, "The blood of Christians is seed," because opposition helped spread Christianity.

• **21:14-19** Jesus warned that in the coming persecutions his followers would be betrayed by their family members and friends. Christians of every age have had to face this possibility. It is reassuring to know that even when we feel completely abandoned, the Holy Spirit will stay with us. He will comfort us, protect us, and give us the words we need. This assurance can give us the courage and hope to stand firm for Christ no matter how difficult the situation.

21:18 Jesus was *not* saying that believers would be exempt from physical harm or death during the persecutions. Remember that

21:22
Deut 32:35
Dan 9:24-27
Hos 9:7

21:23
1 Cor 7:26, 28

21:24
Isa 5:5; 63:18
Dan 8:13
2 Pet 3:10, 12
Rev 11:2

20"And when you see Jerusalem surrounded by armies, then you will know that the time of its destruction has arrived. 21Then those in Judea must flee to the hills. Those in Jerusalem must get out, and those out in the country should not return to the city. 22For those will be days of God's vengeance, and the prophetic words of the Scriptures will be fulfilled. 23How terrible it will be for pregnant women and for nursing mothers in those days. For there will be disaster in the land and great anger against this people. 24They will be killed by the sword or sent away as captives to all the nations of the world. And Jerusalem will be trampled down by the Gentiles until the period of the Gentiles comes to an end.

Jesus Tells about His Return (**202**/Matthew 24:26-35; Mark 13:24-31)

21:26
†Isa 34:4

21:27
†Dan 7:13
Matt 26:64
Rev 1:7; 14:14

25"And there will be strange signs in the sun, moon, and stars. And here on earth the nations will be in turmoil, perplexed by the roaring seas and strange tides. 26People will be terrified at what they see coming upon the earth, for the powers in the heavens will be shaken. 27Then everyone will see the Son of Man* coming on a cloud with power and great glory.* 28So when all these things begin to happen, stand and look up, for your salvation is near!"

21:33
Isa 40:6-8
Matt 5:18

29Then he gave them this illustration: "Notice the fig tree, or any other tree. 30When the leaves come out, you know without being told that summer is near. 31In the same way, when you see all these things taking place, you can know that the Kingdom of God is near. 32I tell you the truth, this generation will not pass from the scene until all these things have taken place. 33Heaven and earth will disappear, but my words will never disappear.

Jesus Tells about Remaining Watchful (**203**/Matthew 24:36-51; Mark 13:32-37)

21:34
Matt 24:48-50
Rom 13:13
1 Thes 5:3

21:36
Mark 13:33

21:37
Luke 19:47; 22:39
John 8:1-2

34"Watch out! Don't let your hearts be dulled by carousing and drunkenness, and by the worries of this life. Don't let that day catch you unaware, 35like a trap. For that day will come upon everyone living on the earth. 36Keep alert at all times. And pray that you might be strong enough to escape these coming horrors and stand before the Son of Man."

37Every day Jesus went to the Temple to teach, and each evening he returned to spend the night on the Mount of Olives. 38The crowds gathered at the Temple early each morning to hear him.

21:27a "Son of Man" is a title Jesus used for himself.   21:27b See Dan 7:13.

---

many of the disciples were martyred. Rather he was saying that none of his followers would suffer spiritual or eternal loss. On earth, everyone will die, but believers in Jesus will be saved for eternal life.

21:24 The "period of the Gentiles" began with Babylon's destruction of Jerusalem in 586 B.C. and the exile of the Jewish people. Israel was no longer an independent nation but was under the control of Gentile rulers. In Jesus' day, Israel was governed by the Roman Empire, and a Roman general would destroy the city in A.D. 70. Jesus was saying that the domination of God's people by his enemies would continue until God decided to end it. The "period of the Gentiles" refers not just to the repeated destructions of Jerusalem but also to the continuing and mounting persecution of God's people until the end.

• **21:28** The picture of the coming persecutions and natural disasters is gloomy, but ultimately it is a cause not for worry but for great joy. As believers see these events happening, they will know that the return of their Messiah is near, and they can look forward to his reign of justice and peace. Rather than being terrified by what is happening in our world, we should confidently await Christ's return to bring justice and restoration to his people.

21:34-36 Jesus told the disciples to keep a constant watch for his return. Although nearly 2,000 years have passed since he spoke these words, their truth remains: Christ is coming again, and we need to watch and be spiritually fit. This means working faithfully at the tasks God has given us. Don't let your mind and spirit be dulled by careless living, drinking, or foolishly pursuing pleasure. Don't let the cares of this life weigh you down. Be ready to move at God's command.

• **21:36** Only days after telling the disciples to pray that they might escape persecution, Jesus himself asked God to spare him the agonies of the cross, if that was God's will (22:41, 42). It is abnormal to *want* to suffer, but as Jesus' followers, we must be willing to suffer if by doing so we can help build God's Kingdom. We have

two wonderful promises to help us as we suffer: God will always be with us (Matthew 28:20), and he will one day rescue us and give us eternal life (Revelation 21:1-4).

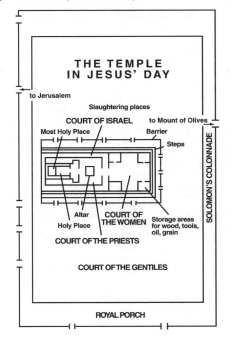

THE TEMPLE IN JESUS' DAY

C. DEATH AND RESURRECTION OF JESUS, THE SAVIOR (22:1—24:53)

The perfect man was a high ideal in Greek culture. Written with Greeks in mind, Luke's Gospel shows how Jesus was the perfect man given as the perfect sacrifice for the sin of all people. Christ is the ideal human—the perfect model for us to follow. We must stand in awe of his character, which met humanity's highest ideals as well as God's demand for an atonement for sin. He is, at one and the same time, our model and our Savior.

Religious Leaders Plot to Kill Jesus (**207**/Matthew 26:1-5; Mark 14:1-2)

22 The Festival of Unleavened Bread, which is also called Passover, was approaching. ²The leading priests and teachers of religious law were plotting how to kill Jesus, but they were afraid of the people's reaction.

Judas Agrees to Betray Jesus (**208**/Matthew 26:14-16; Mark 14:10-11)

³Then Satan entered into Judas Iscariot, who was one of the twelve disciples, ⁴and he went to the leading priests and captains of the Temple guard to discuss the best way to betray Jesus to them. ⁵They were delighted, and they promised to give him money. ⁶So he agreed and began looking for an opportunity to betray Jesus so they could arrest him when the crowds weren't around.

22:3
John 13:2, 27
Acts 1:17

22:5
Zech 11:12
1 Tim 6:10

Disciples Prepare for the Passover (**209**/Matthew 26:17-19; Mark 14:12-16)

⁷Now the Festival of Unleavened Bread arrived, when the Passover lamb is sacrificed. ⁸Jesus sent Peter and John ahead and said, "Go and prepare the Passover meal, so we can eat it together."

22:8
Exod 12:8-11

⁹"Where do you want us to prepare it?" they asked him.

¹⁰He replied, "As soon as you enter Jerusalem, a man carrying a pitcher of water will meet you. Follow him. At the house he enters, ¹¹say to the owner, 'The Teacher asks: Where is the guest room where I can eat the Passover meal with my disciples?' ¹²He will take you upstairs to a large room that is already set up. That is where you should prepare our meal." ¹³They went off to the city and found everything just as Jesus had said, and they prepared the Passover meal there.

22:10
1 Sam 10:2-7

Jesus and the Disciples Share the Last Supper
(**211**/Matthew 26:20-30; Mark 14:17-26; John 13:21-30)

¹⁴When the time came, Jesus and the apostles sat down together at the table.* ¹⁵Jesus said, "I have been very eager to eat this Passover meal with you before my suffering begins. ¹⁶For I tell you now that I won't eat this meal again until its meaning is fulfilled in the Kingdom of God."

22:15-20
1 Cor 11:23-26

22:16
Luke 14:15

¹⁷Then he took a cup of wine and gave thanks to God for it. Then he said, "Take this and share it among yourselves. ¹⁸For I will not drink wine again until the Kingdom of God has come."

22:14 Or *reclined together.*

22:1 All Jewish males over the age of 12 were required to go to Jerusalem for the Passover festival, which was followed by a seven-day celebration called the Festival of Unleavened Bread. For these festivals, Jews from all over the Roman Empire would converge on Jerusalem to celebrate one of the most important events in their history. To learn more about the Passover and the Festival of Unleavened Bread, see the first note on Mark 14:1.

22:3 Satan's part in the betrayal of Jesus does not remove any of the responsibility from Judas. Disillusioned because Jesus was talking about dying rather than about setting up his Kingdom, Judas may have been trying to force Jesus' hand and make him use his power to prove he was the Messiah. Or perhaps Judas, not understanding Jesus' mission, no longer believed that Jesus was God's chosen one. (For more information on Judas, see his Profile in Mark 14, p. 1655.) Whatever Judas thought, Satan assumed that Jesus' death would end his mission and thwart God's plan. Like Judas, he did not know that Jesus' death and resurrection were the most important parts of God's plan all along.

22:7, 8 The Passover meal included the sacrifice of a lamb because of the association with the Jews' exodus from Egypt. When the Jews were getting ready to leave, God told them to kill a lamb and paint its blood on the doorframes of their houses.

They then were to prepare the meat for food. Peter and John had to buy and prepare the lamb as well as the unleavened bread, herbs, wine, and other ceremonial food.

22:10 Ordinarily women, not men, would go to the well and bring home the water. So this man with the water pitcher would have stood out in the crowd.

• **22:14-18** The Passover commemorated Israel's escape from Egypt when the blood of a lamb painted on their doorframes had saved their firstborn sons from death. This event foreshadowed Jesus' work on the cross. As the spotless Lamb of God, his blood would be spilled in order to save his people from the penalty of death brought by sin.

22:17, 20 Luke mentions two cups of wine, while Matthew and Mark mention only one. In the traditional Passover meal, wine is served four times. Christ spoke the words about his body and his blood when he offered the fourth and last cup.

22:17-20 Christians differ in their interpretation of the meaning of the commemoration of the Lord's Supper. There are three main views: (1) The bread and wine actually become Christ's body and blood; (2) the bread and wine remain unchanged, yet Christ is spiritually present by faith in and through them; (3) the bread and wine, which remain unchanged, are lasting memorials of Christ's sacrifice. No matter which view they favor, all Christians agree

22:19
Luke 24:30
Acts 27:35

22:20
Exod 24:8
Jer 31:31-34
Heb 9:15-18

22:21
Ps 41:9
John 13:21

22:22
Acts 2:23; 4:28

¹⁹He took some bread and gave thanks to God for it. Then he broke it in pieces and gave it to the disciples, saying, "This is my body, which is given for you. Do this to remember me."

²⁰After supper he took another cup of wine and said, "This cup is the new covenant between God and his people—an agreement confirmed with my blood, which is poured out as a sacrifice for you.*

²¹"But here at this table, sitting among us as a friend, is the man who will betray me. ²² For it has been determined that the Son of Man* must die. But what sorrow awaits the one who betrays him." ²³The disciples began to ask each other which of them would ever do such a thing.

²⁴Then they began to argue among themselves about who would be the greatest among

22:19-20 Some manuscripts do not include 22:19b-20, *which is given for you . . . which is poured out as a sacrifice for you.* **22:22** "Son of Man" is a title Jesus used for himself.

JESUS' TRIAL	Event	Probable Reasons	References
	Trial before Annas (powerful ex-high priest)	Although no longer the high priest, he may have still wielded much power	John 18:13-23
	Trial before Caiaphas (the ruling high priest)	To gather evidence for the full high council hearing to follow	Matthew 26:57-68 Mark 14:53-65 Luke 22:54, 63-65 John 18:24
	Trial before the high council (Sanhedrin)	Formal religious trial and condemnation to death	Matthew 27:1 Mark 15:1 Luke 22:66-71
	Trial before Pilate (highest Roman authority)	All death sentences needed Roman approval	Matthew 27:2, 11-14 Mark 15:1-5 Luke 23:1-6 John 18:28-38
	Trial before Herod (ruler of Galilee)	A courteous and guilt-sharing act by Pilate because Jesus was from Galilee, Herod's district	Luke 23:7-12
	Trial before Pilate	Pilate's last effort to avoid condemning an obviously innocent man	Matthew 27:15-26 Mark 15:6-15 Luke 23:13-25 John 18:39–19:16

Jesus' trial was actually a series of hearings, carefully controlled to accomplish the death of Jesus. The verdict was predecided, but certain "legal" procedures were necessary. A lot of effort went into condemning and crucifying an innocent man. Jesus went through an unfair trial in our place so that we would not have to face a fair trial and receive the well-deserved punishment for our sins.

---

that the Lord's Supper commemorates Christ's death on the cross for our sins and points to the coming of his Kingdom in glory. When we partake of it, we show our deep gratitude for Christ's work on our behalf, and our faith is strengthened.

• **22:19** Jesus asked the disciples to eat the broken bread to remember him. He wanted them to remember his sacrifice, the basis for forgiveness of sins, and also his friendship, which they could continue to enjoy through the work of the Holy Spirit. Although the exact meaning of Communion has been strongly debated throughout church history, Christians still take bread and wine in order to remember their Lord and Savior, Jesus Christ. Do not neglect participating in the Lord's Supper. Let it remind you of what Christ did for you.

• **22:20** In Old Testament times, God agreed to forgive people's sins if they would bring animals for the priests to sacrifice. When this sacrificial system was inaugurated, the covenant between God and his people was sealed with the blood of animals (Exodus 24:8). But animal blood did not in itself remove sin (only God can forgive sin), and animal sacrifices had to be repeated day after day and year after year. Jesus instituted a "new covenant" (agreement) between God and his people. Under this new covenant, Jesus would die in the place of sinners. Unlike the blood of animals, his blood (because he is God) would remove the sins of all who put their faith in him. Jesus' sacrifice would never have to be repeated; it would be good for all eternity (Hebrews

9:23-28). The prophets looked forward to this new covenant that would fulfill the old sacrificial agreement (Jeremiah 31:31-34), and John the Baptist called Jesus "the Lamb of God who takes away the sin of the world" (John 1:29).

22:21 From the accounts of Mark and John, we know that the betrayer was Judas Iscariot. Although the other disciples were confused by Jesus' words, Judas knew what Jesus meant.

22:24 The most important event in human history was about to take place, and the disciples were still arguing about their prestige in the Kingdom! Looking back, we see that this was no time to worry about status. But the disciples, wrapped up in their own concerns, did not perceive what Jesus had been trying to tell them about his approaching death and resurrection. What are your major concerns today? Twenty years from now, as you look back, will these worries look petty and inappropriate? Get your eyes off yourself and get ready for Christ's coming into human history for the second time.

22:24-27 The world's system of leadership is very different from leadership in God's Kingdom. Worldly leaders are often selfish and arrogant as they claw their way to the top. (Some kings in the ancient world gave themselves the title "Benefactor," friend of the people). But among Christians, the leader is to be the one who *serves* best. There are different styles of leadership—some lead through public speaking, some through administering, some

them. 25Jesus told them, "In this world the kings and great men lord it over their people, yet they are called 'friends of the people.' 26But among you it will be different. Those who are the greatest among you should take the lowest rank, and the leader should be like a servant. 27Who is more important, the one who sits at the table or the one who serves? The one who sits at the table, of course. But not here! For I am among you as one who serves.

28 "You have stayed with me in my time of trial. 29And just as my Father has granted me a Kingdom, I now grant you the right 30to eat and drink at my table in my Kingdom. And you will sit on thrones, judging the twelve tribes of Israel.

Jesus Predicts Peter's Denial (212/John 13:31-38)

31 "Simon, Simon, Satan has asked to sift each of you like wheat. 32But I have pleaded in prayer for you, Simon, that your faith should not fail. So when you have repented and turned to me again, strengthen your brothers."

33Peter said, "Lord, I am ready to go to prison with you, and even to die with you."

34But Jesus said, "Peter, let me tell you something. Before the rooster crows tomorrow morning, you will deny three times that you even know me."

35 Then Jesus asked them, "When I sent you out to preach the Good News and you did not have money, a traveler's bag, or an extra pair of sandals, did you need anything?"

"No," they replied.

36 "But now," he said, "take your money and a traveler's bag. And if you don't have a sword, sell your cloak and buy one! 37For the time has come for this prophecy about me to be fulfilled: 'He was counted among the rebels.'* Yes, everything written about me by the prophets will come true."

38"Look, Lord," they replied, "we have two swords among us."

"That's enough," he said.

Jesus Agonizes in the Garden (223/Matthew 26:36-46; Mark 14:32-42)

39 Then, accompanied by the disciples, Jesus left the upstairs room and went as usual to the Mount of Olives. 40There he told them, "Pray that you will not give in to temptation."

41He walked away, about a stone's throw, and knelt down and prayed, 42 "Father, if you are willing, please take this cup of suffering away from me. Yet I want your will to be done, not mine." 43Then an angel from heaven appeared and strengthened him. 44He prayed more fervently, and he was in such agony of spirit that his sweat fell to the ground like great drops of blood.*

45At last he stood up again and returned to the disciples, only to find them asleep, exhausted from grief. 46 "Why are you sleeping?" he asked them. "Get up and pray, so that you will not give in to temptation."

22:37 Isa 53:12.   **22:43-44** Verses 43 and 44 are not included in many ancient manuscripts.

22:26 Matt 23:11; Mark 9:35; 1 Pet 5:5
22:27 John 13:4-16
22:31 Job 1:6-12; Amos 9:9
22:32 John 17:9, 15; 21:15
22:33 John 11:16
22:35 Matt 10:9-10; Luke 9:3
22:37 †Isa 53:12
22:40 Matt 6:13

through relationships—but every Christian leader needs a servant's heart. Ask the people you lead how you can serve them better.

22:31, 32 Satan wanted to crush Simon Peter and the other disciples like grains of wheat. He hoped to find only chaff and blow it away. But Jesus assured Peter that his faith, although it would falter, would not be destroyed. It would be renewed, and Peter would become a powerful leader.

22:33, 34 Jesus told the disciples that one of them would betray him and that calamity awaited the traitor (22:22). Jesus then told Peter that he would deny that he knew Jesus. Later, however, Peter would repent and receive a commission to feed Jesus' lambs (John 21:15). Betraying and denying—one is just about as bad as the other. But Judas and Peter had entirely different fates because one repented.

22:35-38 Here Jesus reversed his earlier advice regarding how to travel (9:3). The disciples were to bring bags, money, and swords. They would be facing hatred and persecution and would need to be prepared. When Jesus said, "That's enough," he may have meant it was not time to think of using swords. In either case, mention of a sword vividly communicated the trials they would soon face.

22:39 The Mount of Olives was located just to the east of Jerusalem. Jesus went up the southwestern slope to an olive grove called Gethsemane, which means "oil press."

22:40 Jesus asked the disciples to pray that they would not fall into temptation because he knew that he would soon be leaving them. Jesus also knew that they would need extra strength to face the temptations ahead—temptations to run away or to deny their relationship with him. They were about to see Jesus die. Would they still think he was the Messiah? The disciples' strongest temptation would undoubtedly be to think they had been deceived.

• **22:41, 42** Was Jesus trying to get out of his mission? It is never wrong to express our true feelings to God. Jesus exposed his dread of the coming trials, but he also reaffirmed his commitment to do what God wanted. The cup he spoke of meant the terrible agony he knew he would endure—not only the horror of the crucifixion but, even worse, the total separation from God that he would have to experience in order to die for the world's sins.

• **22:44** Only Luke tells us that Jesus' sweat resembled drops of blood. Jesus was in extreme agony, but he did not give up or give in. He went ahead with the mission for which he had come.

22:46 These disciples were asleep. How tragic it is that many Christians act as though they are sound asleep when it comes to devotion to Christ and service for him. Don't be found insensitive to or unprepared for Christ's work.

Jesus Is Betrayed and Arrested
(**224**/Matthew 26:47-56; Mark 14:43-52; John 18:1-11)

47 But even as Jesus said this, a crowd approached, led by Judas, one of the twelve disciples. Judas walked over to Jesus to greet him with a kiss. 48 But Jesus said, "Judas, would you betray the Son of Man with a kiss?"

49 When the other disciples saw what was about to happen, they exclaimed, "Lord, should we fight? We brought the swords!" 50 And one of them struck at the high priest's slave, slashing off his right ear.

51 But Jesus said, "No more of this." And he touched the man's ear and healed him.

52 Then Jesus spoke to the leading priests, the captains of the Temple guard, and the elders who had come for him. "Am I some dangerous revolutionary," he asked, "that you come with swords and clubs to arrest me? 53 Why didn't you arrest me in the Temple? I was there every day. But this is your moment, the time when the power of darkness reigns."

22:53
Luke 19:47
John 7:30

Peter Denies Knowing Jesus
(**227**/Matthew 26:69-75; Mark 14:66-72; John 18:25-27)

54 So they arrested him and led him to the high priest's home. And Peter followed at a distance. 55 The guards lit a fire in the middle of the courtyard and sat around it, and Peter joined them there. 56 A servant girl noticed him in the firelight and began staring at him. Finally she said, "This man was one of Jesus' followers!"

57 But Peter denied it. "Woman," he said, "I don't even know him!"

58 After a while someone else looked at him and said, "You must be one of them!"

"No, man, I'm not!" Peter retorted.

59 About an hour later someone else insisted, "This must be one of them, because he is a Galilean, too."

60 But Peter said, "Man, I don't know what you are talking about." And immediately, while he was still speaking, the rooster crowed.

22:61
Luke 7:13

61 At that moment the Lord turned and looked at Peter. Suddenly, the Lord's words

---

22:47 A kiss was and still is the traditional greeting among men in certain parts of the world. In this case, it was also the agreed-upon signal to point out Jesus (Matthew 26:48). It is ironic that a gesture of greeting would be the means of betrayal. It was a hollow gesture because of Judas's treachery. Have any of your religious practices become empty gestures? We still betray Christ when our acts of service or giving are insincere or carried out merely for show.

22:50 We learn from the Gospel of John that the man who cut off the servant's ear was Peter (John 18:10).

• **22:53** The religious leaders had not arrested Jesus in the Temple for fear of a riot. Instead, they came secretly at night, under the influence of the power of darkness, Satan himself. Although it looked as if Satan was getting the upper hand, everything was proceeding according to God's plan. It was time for Jesus to die.

• **22:54** Jesus was immediately taken to the high priest's home, even though this was the middle of the night. The Jewish leaders were in a hurry—they wanted to complete the execution before the Sabbath and get on with the Passover celebration. This residence was a palace with outer walls enclosing a courtyard, where servants and soldiers warmed themselves around a fire.

22:55 Peter's experiences in the next few hours would change his life. He would change from a halfhearted follower to a repentant disciple, and finally to the kind of person Christ could use to build his church. For more information on Peter, see his Profile in Matthew 27, p. 1603.

22:60 Sin, like cancer, has a way of growing if unchecked. Notice the progression of Peter's denials: In 22:57, he denied knowing Jesus; in 22:58, he denied being one of his followers; in 22:60, he denied even knowing what they were talking about. Sin has a way of spreading. As it does, the cover-up gets bigger as well. The time to get a grip on sin and its cancerous effects is in the very beginning, before it has time to multiply its poisons in your life. Better yet, kill it before it even begins. Confess your sins or your desire to sin to the Lord, and ask his help to avoid Peter's mistakes.

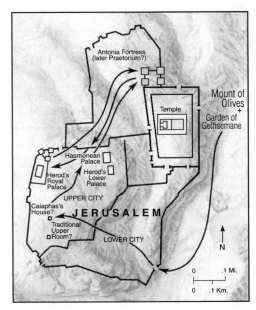

JESUS' TRIAL   Taken from Gethsemane, Jesus first appeared before the Jewish high council, which had convened at daybreak at Caiaphas's house. From there he went to Pilate, the Roman governor; then to Herod, tetrarch of Galilee, who was visiting in Jerusalem; and back to Pilate, who, in desperation, sentenced Jesus to die.

flashed through Peter's mind: "Before the rooster crows tomorrow morning, you will deny three times that you even know me." 62And Peter left the courtyard, weeping bitterly.

63The guards in charge of Jesus began mocking and beating him. 64They blindfolded him and said, "Prophesy to us! Who hit you that time?" 65And they hurled all sorts of terrible insults at him.

The Council of Religious Leaders Condemns Jesus (**228**/Matthew 27:1-2; Mark 15:1)
66At daybreak all the elders of the people assembled, including the leading priests and the teachers of religious law. Jesus was led before this high council,* 67and they said, "Tell us, are you the Messiah?"

But he replied, "If I tell you, you won't believe me. 68And if I ask you a question, you won't answer. 69But from now on the Son of Man will be seated in the place of power at God's right hand.*"

70They all shouted, "So, are you claiming to be the Son of God?"

And he replied, "You say that I am."

71"Why do we need other witnesses?" they said. "We ourselves heard him say it."

22:69
Ps 110:1
Dan 7:13
Acts 7:56
22:70
Matt 4:3

Jesus Stands Trial before Pilate
(**230**/Matthew 27:11-14; Mark 15:2-5; John 18:28-37)

23 Then the entire council took Jesus to Pilate, the Roman governor. 2They began to state their case: "This man has been leading our people astray by telling them not to pay their taxes to the Roman government and by claiming he is the Messiah, a king."

3So Pilate asked him, "Are you the king of the Jews?"

Jesus replied, "You have said it."

4Pilate turned to the leading priests and to the crowd and said, "I find nothing wrong with this man!"

5Then they became insistent. "But he is causing riots by his teaching wherever he goes—all over Judea, from Galilee to Jerusalem!"

23:2
John 19:12

23:4
1 Tim 6:13

Jesus Stands Trial before Herod (**231**)
6"Oh, is he a Galilean?" Pilate asked. 7When they said that he was, Pilate sent him to Herod Antipas, because Galilee was under Herod's jurisdiction, and Herod happened to be in Jerusalem at the time.

8Herod was delighted at the opportunity to see Jesus, because he had heard about him and had been hoping for a long time to see him perform a miracle. 9He asked Jesus question after question, but Jesus refused to answer. 10Meanwhile, the leading priests and the teachers of religious law stood there shouting their accusations. 11Then Herod and his soldiers began mocking and ridiculing Jesus. Finally, they put a royal robe on him and sent him back to Pilate. 12(Herod and Pilate, who had been enemies before, became friends that day.)

23:8
Luke 9:9
23:9
John 19:9

23:12
Acts 4:27

22:66 Greek *before their Sanhedrin.* **22:69** See Ps 110:1.

22:62 Peter wept bitterly, not only because he realized that he had denied his Lord, the Messiah, but also because he had turned away from a very dear friend, a person who had loved and taught him for three years. Peter had said that he would *never* deny Christ, despite Jesus' prediction (Mark 14:29-31; Luke 22:33, 34). But when frightened, he went against all he had boldly promised. Unable to stand up for his Lord for even 12 hours, he had failed as a disciple and as a friend. We need to be aware of our own breaking points and not become overconfident or self-sufficient. If we fail him, we must remember that Christ can use those who recognize their failure. From this humiliating experience Peter learned much that would help him later when he assumed leadership of the young church.

• **22:70** Jesus in effect agreed that he was the Son of God when he simply turned the high priest's question around by saying, "You say that I am." And Jesus identified himself with God by using a familiar title for God found in the Old Testament: "I AM" (Exodus 3:14). The high priest recognized Jesus' claim and could accuse him of blasphemy. For any other reason this claim would have been blasphemy, but in this case it was true. Blasphemy, the sin of claiming to be God or of attacking God's authority and majesty in any way, was punishable by death. The Jewish leaders had the evidence they wanted.

23:1 Pilate was the Roman governor of Judea, where Jerusalem was located. He had a reputation for seeming to take special pleasure in harassing the Jews. For example, Pilate had taken money from the Temple treasury and had used it to build an aqueduct. And he had insulted the Jewish religion by bringing imperial images into the city. As Pilate well knew, such acts could backfire. If the people were to lodge a formal complaint against his administration, Rome might remove him from his post. Pilate was already beginning to feel insecure in his position when the Jewish leaders brought Jesus to trial. Would he continue to badger the Jews and risk his political future, or would he give in to their demands and condemn a man who, he was quite sure, was innocent? That was the question facing Pilate that springtime Friday morning nearly 2,000 years ago. For more about Pilate, see his Profile in Mark 15, p. 1661.

23:7 Herod Antipas was in Jerusalem that weekend for the Passover celebration. (This was the Herod who had killed John the Baptist.) Pilate hoped to pass Jesus off on Herod because he knew that Jesus had lived and worked in Galilee. But Herod was not much help. He was curious about Jesus and enjoyed making fun of him. But when Herod sent Jesus back to Pilate, it was with the verdict of "not guilty." For more about Herod Antipas, see his Profile in Mark 6, p. 1629.

23:12 Herod was the part-Jewish ruler of Galilee and Perea. Pilate was the Roman governor of Judea and Samaria. Those four

Pilate Hands Jesus Over to Be Crucified
(232/Matthew 27:15-26; Mark 15:6-15; John 18:39–19:16)
13 Then Pilate called together the leading priests and other religious leaders, along with the people, 14and he announced his verdict. "You brought this man to me, accusing him of leading a revolt. I have examined him thoroughly on this point in your presence and find him innocent. 15Herod came to the same conclusion and sent him back to us. Nothing this man has done calls for the death penalty. 16So I will have him flogged, and then I will release him."*

23:16
John 19:1
Acts 16:37
23:18
Acts 3:13-14

18Then a mighty roar rose from the crowd, and with one voice they shouted, "Kill him, and release Barabbas to us!" 19(Barabbas was in prison for taking part in an insurrection in Jerusalem against the government, and for murder.) 20Pilate argued with them, because he wanted to release Jesus. 21But they kept shouting, "Crucify him! Crucify him!"

22For the third time he demanded, "Why? What crime has he committed? I have found no reason to sentence him to death. So I will have him flogged, and then I will release him."

23But the mob shouted louder and louder, demanding that Jesus be crucified, and their voices prevailed. 24So Pilate sentenced Jesus to die as they demanded. 25As they had requested, he released Barabbas, the man in prison for insurrection and murder. But he turned Jesus over to them to do as they wished.

Jesus Is Led Away to Be Crucified
(234/Matthew 27:32-34; Mark 15:21-24; John 19:17)
26As they led Jesus away, a man named Simon, who was from Cyrene,* happened to be coming in from the countryside. The soldiers seized him and put the cross on him and

23:16 Some manuscripts add verse 17, *Now it was necessary for him to release one prisoner to them during the Passover celebration.* Compare Matt 27:15; Mark 15:6; John 18:39.   **23:26** *Cyrene* was a city in northern Africa.

---

provinces, together with several others, had been united under Herod the Great. But when Herod died in 4 B.C., the kingdom was divided among his sons. Archelaus, the son who had received Judea and Samaria, was removed from office within 10 years, and his provinces were then ruled by a succession of Roman governors, of whom Pilate was the fifth.

Herod Antipas had two advantages over Pilate: He came from a hereditary part-Jewish monarchy and he had held his position much longer. But Pilate had two advantages over Herod: He was a Roman citizen and an envoy of the emperor, and his position was created to replace that of Herod's ineffective half brother. It is not surprising that the two men were uneasy around each other. Jesus' trial, however, brought them together. Because Pilate recognized Herod's authority over Galilee, Herod stopped feeling threatened by the Roman politician. And because neither man knew what to do in this predicament, their common problem united them.

23:13-25 Pilate wanted to release Jesus, but the crowd loudly demanded his death; so Pilate sentenced Jesus to die. No doubt Pilate did not want to risk losing his position, which may already have been shaky, by allowing a riot to occur in his province. As a career politician, he knew the importance of compromise, and he saw Jesus more as a political threat than as a human being with rights and dignity.

When the stakes are high, it is difficult to stand up for what is right, and it is easy to see our opponents as problems to be solved rather than as people to be respected. Had Pilate been a man of real courage, he would have released Jesus no matter what the consequences. But the crowd roared, and Pilate buckled. We are like Pilate when we know what is right but decide not to do it. When you have a difficult decision to make, don't discount the effects of peer pressure. Realize beforehand that the right decision could have unpleasant consequences: social rejection, career derailment, public ridicule. Then think of Pilate and resolve to stand up for what is right no matter what other people pressure you to do.

• **23:15** Jesus was tried six times, by both Jewish and Roman authorities, but he was never convicted of a crime deserving death. Today, no one can find fault in Jesus. But just like Pilate, Herod, and the religious leaders, many still refuse to acknowledge him as Lord.

23:18, 19 Barabbas had been part of a rebellion against the Roman government (Mark 15:7). As a political insurgent, he was no doubt a hero among some of the Jews. How ironic it is that Barabbas, who was released, was guilty of the very crime Jesus was accused of (23:14).

23:18, 19 Who was Barabbas? Jewish men had names that identified them with their fathers. Simon Peter, for example, is called Simon son of John (Matthew 16:17). Barabbas is never identified by his given name, and this name is not much help either—*barabbas* means "son of *Abba*" (or "son of daddy"). He could have been anybody's son—and that's just the point. Barabbas, son of an unnamed father, committed a crime. Because Jesus died in his place, this man was set free. We, too, are sinners and criminals who have broken God's holy law. Like Barabbas, we deserve to die. But Jesus has died in our place, for our sins, and we have been set free. We don't have to be "very important people" to accept our freedom in Christ. In fact, thanks to Jesus, God adopts us all as his own sons and daughters and gives us the right to call him our dear Father (see Galatians 4:4-6).

• **23:22** When Pilate said he would have Jesus flogged, he was referring to a punishment that could have killed Jesus. The usual procedure was to bare the upper half of the victim's body and tie his hands to a pillar before whipping him with a three-pronged whip. The number of lashes was determined by the severity of the crime; up to 40 were permitted under Jewish law. After being flogged, Jesus also endured other agonies as recorded in Matthew and Mark. He was slapped, struck with fists, and mocked. A crown of thorns was placed on his head, and he was beaten with a stick and stripped before being hung on the cross.

23:23, 24 Pilate did not want to give Jesus the death sentence. He thought the Jewish leaders were simply jealous men who wanted to get rid of a rival. When they threatened to report Pilate to Caesar (John 19:12), however, Pilate became frightened. Historical records indicate that Pilate had already been warned by Roman authorities about tensions in this region. The last thing he needed was a riot in Jerusalem at Passover time, when the city was crowded with Jews from all over the empire. So Pilate turned Jesus over to the mob to do with as they pleased.

made him carry it behind Jesus. 27A large crowd trailed behind, including many grief-stricken women. 28But Jesus turned and said to them, "Daughters of Jerusalem, don't weep for me, but weep for yourselves and for your children. 29For the days are coming when they will say, 'Fortunate indeed are the women who are childless, the wombs that have not borne a child and the breasts that have never nursed.' 30People will beg the mountains, 'Fall on us,' and plead with the hills, 'Bury us.'* 31For if these things are done when the tree is green, what will happen when it is dry?*"

23:29
Luke 21:23

23:30
Isa 2:19
†Hos 10:8
Rev 6:16

Jesus Is Placed on the Cross
(235/Matthew 27:35-44; Mark 15:25-32; John 19:18-27)

32Two others, both criminals, were led out to be executed with him. 33When they came to a place called The Skull,* they nailed him to the cross. And the criminals were also crucified—one on his right and one on his left.

23:32
Isa 53:12
Matt 27:38
Mark 15:27
John 19:18

34Jesus said, "Father, forgive them, for they don't know what they are doing."* And the soldiers gambled for his clothes by throwing dice.*

23:34
†Ps 22:18

35The crowd watched and the leaders scoffed. "He saved others," they said, "let him save himself if he is really God's Messiah, the Chosen One." 36The soldiers mocked him, too, by offering him a drink of sour wine. 37They called out to him, "If you are the King of the Jews, save yourself!" 38A sign was fastened above him with these words: "This is the King of the Jews."

23:35
Ps 22:17

23:36
Pss 22:7; 69:21
Matt 27:48

39One of the criminals hanging beside him scoffed, "So you're the Messiah, are you? Prove it by saving yourself—and us, too, while you're at it!"

23:30 Hos 10:8.   **23:31** Or *If these things are done to me, the living tree, what will happen to you, the dry tree?*   **23:33** Sometimes rendered *Calvary*, which comes from the Latin word for "skull."   **23:34a** This sentence is not included in many ancient manuscripts.   **23:34b** Greek *by casting lots.* See Ps 22:18.

23:27-29 Luke alone mentions the tears of the Jewish women while Jesus was being led through the streets to his execution. Jesus told them not to weep for him but for themselves. He knew that in only about 40 years, Jerusalem and the Temple would be destroyed by the Romans.

23:31 This proverb is difficult to interpret. Some feel it means:

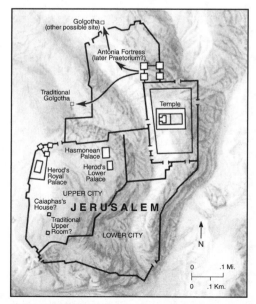

Golgotha □
(other possible site)

Antonia Fortress
(later Praetorium?)

Traditional
Golgotha □

Temple

Hasmonean
Palace

Herod's
Royal
Palace

Herod's
Lower
Palace

UPPER CITY

Caiaphas's
House? □   **JERUSALEM**

Traditional
Upper
Room? □   LOWER CITY

N

0   .1 Mi.
0   .1 Km.

JESUS LED AWAY TO DIE As Jesus was led away through the streets of Jerusalem, he could no longer carry his cross, and Simon of Cyrene was given the burden. Jesus was crucified, along with common criminals, on a hill outside Jerusalem.

If the innocent Jesus (green tree) suffered at the hands of the Romans, what would happen to the guilty Jews (dry tree)?

23:32, 33 The place called The Skull, or Golgotha, was probably a hill outside Jerusalem along a main road. The Romans executed people publicly as examples to the people.

23:32, 33 When James and John asked Jesus for the places of honor next to him in his Kingdom, he told them they didn't know what they were asking (Mark 10:35-39). Here, as Jesus was preparing to inaugurate his Kingdom through his death, the places on his right and on his left were taken by dying men—criminals. As Jesus explained to his two position-conscious disciples, a person who wants to be close to Jesus must be prepared to suffer and die. The way to the Kingdom is the way of the cross.

23:34 Jesus asked God to forgive the people who were putting him to death—Jewish leaders, Roman politicians and soldiers, bystanders—and God answered that prayer by opening up the way of salvation even to Jesus' murderers. Jesus was suffering the most horrible, painful death ever devised by sinful man, and he looked at the people responsible for his suffering and prayed for their forgiveness. The Roman officer and soldiers who witnessed the Crucifixion said, "This man truly was the Son of God!" (Matthew 27:54). Soon many priests were converted to the Christian faith (Acts 6:7). Because we are all sinners, we all played a part in putting Jesus to death. The good news is that God is gracious. He will forgive us and give us new life through his Son.

23:34 Roman soldiers customarily divided up the clothing of executed criminals among themselves. When they gambled for Jesus' clothes, they fulfilled the prophecy in Psalm 22:18.

23:38 This sign was meant to be ironic. A king, stripped and executed in public view, had obviously lost his kingdom forever. But Jesus, who turns the world's wisdom upside down, was just coming into his Kingdom. His death and resurrection would strike the deathblow to Satan's rule and establish Christ's eternal authority over the earth. Few people reading the sign that bleak afternoon understood its real meaning, but the sign was absolutely true. All was not lost. Jesus is King of the Jews—and of the Gentiles and the whole universe.

23:39-43 As this man was about to die, he turned to Christ for forgiveness, and Christ accepted him. This shows that our deeds

23:43
2 Cor 12:3-4
Rev 2:7

⁴⁰But the other criminal protested, "Don't you fear God even when you have been sentenced to die? ⁴¹We deserve to die for our crimes, but this man hasn't done anything wrong." ⁴²Then he said, "Jesus, remember me when you come into your Kingdom." ⁴³And Jesus replied, "I assure you, today you will be with me in paradise."

Jesus Dies on the Cross (236/Matthew 27:45-56; Mark 15:33-41; John 19:28-37)

23:45
Exod 26:31-33
Heb 9:3, 8;
10:19-20
23:46
†Ps 31:5

⁴⁴By this time it was about noon, and darkness fell across the whole land until three o'clock. ⁴⁵The light from the sun was gone. And suddenly, the curtain in the sanctuary of the Temple was torn down the middle. ⁴⁶Then Jesus shouted, "Father, I entrust my spirit into your hands!"* And with those words he breathed his last.

23:48
Luke 18:13
23:49
Ps 38:11

⁴⁷When the Roman officer* overseeing the execution saw what had happened, he worshiped God and said, "Surely this man was innocent.*" ⁴⁸And when all the crowd that came to see the crucifixion saw what had happened, they went home in deep sorrow.* ⁴⁹But Jesus' friends, including the women who had followed him from Galilee, stood at a distance watching.

Jesus Is Laid in the Tomb (237/Matthew 27:57-61; Mark 15:42-47; John 19:38-42)

23:53
Luke 19:30

⁵⁰Now there was a good and righteous man named Joseph. He was a member of the Jewish high council, ⁵¹but he had not agreed with the decision and actions of the other religious leaders. He was from the town of Arimathea in Judea, and he was waiting for the Kingdom of God to come. ⁵²He went to Pilate and asked for Jesus' body. ⁵³Then he took the body down from the cross and wrapped it in a long sheet of linen cloth and laid it in a new tomb that had been carved out of rock. ⁵⁴This was done late on Friday afternoon, the day of preparation,* as the Sabbath was about to begin.

23:55
Luke 8:2; 23:49
23:56
Exod 12:16; 20:10
Lev 23:8

⁵⁵As his body was taken away, the women from Galilee followed and saw the tomb where his body was placed. ⁵⁶Then they went home and prepared spices and ointments to anoint his body. But by the time they were finished the Sabbath had begun, so they rested as required by the law.

Jesus Rises from the Dead (239/Matthew 28:1-7; Mark 16:1-8; John 20:1-10)

24:1
John 20:19
1 Cor 16:2

24 But very early on Sunday morning* the women went to the tomb, taking the spices they had prepared. ²They found that the stone had been rolled away from the

23:46 Ps 31:5.   **23:47a** Greek *the centurion*.   **23:47b** Or *righteous*.   **23:48** Greek *went home beating their breasts*.
23:54 Greek *It was the day of preparation*.   **24:1** Greek *But on the first day of the week, very early in the morning*.

---

don't save us—our faith in Christ does. It is never too late to turn to God. Even in his misery, Jesus had mercy on this criminal who decided to believe in him. Our lives will be much more useful and fulfilling if we turn to God early, but even those who repent at the very last moment will be with God in paradise.

23:42, 43 The dying criminal had more faith than the rest of Jesus' followers put together. Although the disciples continued to love Jesus, their hopes for the Kingdom were shattered. Most of them had gone into hiding. As one of his followers sadly said two days later, "We had hoped he was the Messiah who had come to rescue Israel" (24:21). By contrast, the criminal looked at the man who was dying next to him and said, "Jesus, remember me when you come into your Kingdom." By all appearances, the Kingdom was finished. How awe-inspiring is the faith of this man who alone saw beyond the present shame to the coming glory!

23:44 Darkness covered the entire land for about three hours in the middle of the day. All nature seemed to mourn over the stark tragedy of the death of God's Son.

23:45 This significant event symbolized Christ's work on the cross. The Temple had three parts: the courts for all the people; the Holy Place, where only priests could enter; and the Most Holy Place, where the high priest alone could enter once a year to atone for the sins of the people. It was in the Most Holy Place that the Ark of the Covenant, and God's presence with it, rested. The curtain that was torn was the one that closed off the Most Holy Place from view. At Christ's death, the barrier between God and humanity was split in two. Now all people can approach God directly through Christ (Hebrews 9:1-14; 10:19-22).

23:50-52 Joseph of Arimathea was a wealthy and honored member of the Jewish high council. He was also a secret disciple of Jesus (John 19:38). The disciples who had publicly followed Jesus

fled, but Joseph boldly took a stand that could have cost him dearly. He cared enough about Jesus to ask for his body so he could give it a proper burial.

23:53 The tomb was likely a man-made cave cut out of one of the many limestone hills in the area around Jerusalem. Such a tomb was large enough to walk into. After burial, a large stone would have been rolled across the entrance (John 20:1).

23:55 The Galilean women followed Joseph to the tomb, so they knew exactly where to find Jesus' body when they returned after the Sabbath with their spices and perfumes. These women could not do "great" things for Jesus—they were not permitted to stand up before the Jewish high council or the Roman governor and testify on his behalf—but they did what they could. They stayed at the cross when most of the disciples had fled, and they got ready to anoint their Lord's body. Because of their devotion, they were the first to know about the Resurrection. As believers, we may feel we can't do much for Jesus. But we are called to take advantage of the opportunities given us, doing what we *can* do and not worrying about what we cannot do.

24:1 The women brought spices to the tomb as we would bring flowers—as a sign of love and respect. The women went home and kept the Sabbath as the law required, from sundown Friday to sundown Saturday, before gathering up their spices and perfumes and returning to the tomb.

• **24:1-9** The two angels (appearing as "two men . . . clothed in dazzling robes") asked the women why they were looking in a tomb for someone who was alive. Often we run into people who are looking for God among the dead. They study the Bible as a mere historical document and go to church as if going to a memorial service. But Jesus is not among the dead—he lives! He reigns in the hearts of Christians, and he is the head of his church. Do you look for Jesus

entrance. ³So they went in, but they didn't find the body of the Lord Jesus. ⁴As they stood there puzzled, two men suddenly appeared to them, clothed in dazzling robes.

24:3
Mark 16:19
Acts 1:21; 4:33

⁵The women were terrified and bowed with their faces to the ground. Then the men asked, "Why are you looking among the dead for someone who is alive? ⁶He isn't here! He is risen from the dead! Remember what he told you back in Galilee, ⁷that the Son of Man* must be betrayed into the hands of sinful men and be crucified, and that he would rise again on the third day."

24:4
Acts 1:10
24:6
Matt 16:21
Luke 9:22

⁸Then they remembered that he had said this. ⁹So they rushed back from the tomb to tell his eleven disciples—and everyone else—what had happened. ¹⁰It was Mary Magdalene, Joanna, Mary the mother of James, and several other women who told the apostles what had happened. ¹¹But the story sounded like nonsense to the men, so they didn't believe it. ¹²However, Peter jumped up and ran to the tomb to look. Stooping, he peered in and saw the empty linen wrappings; then he went home again, wondering what had happened.

24:8
John 2:22
24:10
Matt 27:56
Luke 8:1-3
24:11
Mark 16:11
24:12
John 20:3-7

Jesus Appears to Two Believers Traveling on the Road (243/Mark 16:12-13)

¹³That same day two of Jesus' followers were walking to the village of Emmaus, seven miles* from Jerusalem. ¹⁴As they walked along they were talking about everything that had happened. ¹⁵As they talked and discussed these things, Jesus himself suddenly came and began walking with them. ¹⁶But God kept them from recognizing him.

24:15
Matt 18:20
24:16
John 20:14; 21:4

¹⁷He asked them, "What are you discussing so intently as you walk along?"

They stopped short, sadness written across their faces. ¹⁸Then one of them, Cleopas, replied, "You must be the only person in Jerusalem who hasn't heard about all the things that have happened there the last few days."

24:18
John 19:25

¹⁹ "What things?" Jesus asked.

"The things that happened to Jesus, the man from Nazareth," they said. "He was a prophet who did powerful miracles, and he was a mighty teacher in the eyes of God and all the people. ²⁰But our leading priests and other religious leaders handed him over to be condemned to death, and they crucified him. ²¹We had hoped he was the Messiah who had come to rescue Israel. This all happened three days ago.

24:20
Luke 23:13
24:21
Luke 1:68
Acts 1:6

24:7 "Son of Man" is a title Jesus used for himself.   **24:13** Greek *60 stadia* [11.1 kilometers].

---

among the living? Do you expect him to be active in the world and in the church? Look for signs of his power—they are all around you.

• **24:6, 7** The angels reminded the women that Jesus had accurately predicted all that had happened to him (9:22, 44; 18:31-33).

• **24:6, 7** The resurrection of Jesus from the dead is the central fact of Christian history. On it, the church is built; without it, there would be no Christian church today. Jesus' resurrection is unique. Other religions have strong ethical systems, concepts about paradise and the afterlife, and various holy scriptures. Only Christianity has a God who became human, literally died for his people, and was raised again in power and glory to rule his church forever.

Why is the Resurrection so important? (1) Because Christ was raised from the dead, we know that the Kingdom of Heaven has broken into earth's history. Our world is now headed for redemption, not disaster. God's mighty power is at work destroying sin, creating new lives, and preparing us for Jesus' second coming. (2) Because of the Resurrection, we know that death has been conquered and we, too, will be raised from the dead to live forever with Christ. (3) The Resurrection gives authority to the church's witness in the world. Look at the early evangelistic sermons in the book of Acts: The apostles' most important message was the proclamation that Jesus Christ had been raised from the dead! (4) The Resurrection gives meaning to the church's sacrament of the Lord's Supper. Like Jesus' followers on the Emmaus Road, we break bread with our risen Lord, who comes in power to save us. (5) The Resurrection helps us find meaning even in great tragedy. No matter what happens to us as we walk with the Lord, the Resurrection gives us hope for the future. (6) The Resurrection assures us that Christ is alive and ruling his Kingdom. He is not a legend; he is alive and real. (7) God's power that brought Jesus back from the dead is available to us so that we can live for him in an evil world.

Christians can look very different from one another, and they can hold widely varying beliefs about politics, lifestyle, and even theology. But one central belief unites and inspires all true Chris-

tians: Jesus Christ rose from the dead! (For more on the importance of the Resurrection, see 1 Corinthians 15:3-7, 12-58.)

• **24:11, 12** People who hear about the Resurrection for the first time may need time before they can comprehend this amazing story. Like the disciples, they may pass through four stages of belief: (1) At first, they may think it is a fairy tale, impossible to believe. (2) Like Peter, they may check out the facts but still be puzzled about what happened. (3) Only when they encounter Jesus personally will they be able to accept the fact of the Resurrection. (4) Then, as they commit themselves to Jesus and devote their lives to serving him, they will begin fully to understand the reality of his presence with them.

24:12 From John 20:3, 4, we learn that another disciple ran to the tomb with Peter. That other disciple was almost certainly John, the author of the fourth Gospel.

24:13ff The two followers returning to Emmaus at first missed the significance of history's greatest event because they were too focused on their disappointments and problems. In fact, they didn't recognize Jesus when he was walking beside them. To compound the problem, they were walking in the wrong direction—away from the fellowship of believers in Jerusalem. We are likely to miss Jesus and withdraw from the strength found in other believers when we become preoccupied with our dashed hopes and frustrated plans. Only when we are looking for Jesus in our midst will we experience the power and help he can bring.

24:18 The news about Jesus' crucifixion had spread throughout Jerusalem. Because this was Passover week, Jews visiting the city from all over the Roman Empire now knew about his death. This was not a small, insignificant event, affecting only the disciples—the whole nation was interested.

24:21 These followers from Emmaus had been counting on Jesus to redeem Israel, that is, to rescue the nation from its enemies. Most Jews believed that the Old Testament prophecies pointed to a

24:22-23
Matt 28:1-8
Mark 16:1-8

22 "Then some women from our group of his followers were at his tomb early this morning, and they came back with an amazing report. 23 They said his body was missing, and they had seen angels who told them Jesus is alive! 24Some of our men ran out to see, and sure enough, his body was gone, just as the women had said."

24:26
Matt 26:24
Luke 24:7, 44
John 12:23-24;
13:31-32
Acts 17:3
Heb 2:10; 5:5

25 Then Jesus said to them, "You foolish people! You find it so hard to believe all that the prophets wrote in the Scriptures. 26Wasn't it clearly predicted that the Messiah would have to suffer all these things before entering his glory?" 27 Then Jesus took them through the writings of Moses and all the prophets, explaining from all the Scriptures the things concerning himself.

28By this time they were nearing Emmaus and the end of their journey. Jesus acted as if he were going on, 29but they begged him, "Stay the night with us, since it is getting late." So he went home with them. 30As they sat down to eat,* he took the bread and blessed it. Then he broke it and gave it to them. 31Suddenly, their eyes were opened, and they recognized him. And at that moment he disappeared!

32 They said to each other, "Didn't our hearts burn within us as he talked with us on the road and explained the Scriptures to us?" 33And within the hour they were on their way back to Jerusalem. There they found the eleven disciples and the others who had gathered with them, 34who said, "The Lord has really risen! He appeared to Peter.*"

24:34
1 Cor 15:5

Jesus Appears to His Disciples (**244**/John 20:19-23)

35 Then the two from Emmaus told their story of how Jesus had appeared to them as they were walking along the road, and how they had recognized him as he was breaking the bread. 36And just as they were telling about it, Jesus himself was suddenly standing there

24:30 Or *As they reclined.*   **24:34** Greek *Simon.*

---

military and political Messiah; they didn't realize that the Messiah had come to redeem people from slavery to sin. When Jesus died, therefore, they lost all hope. They didn't understand that Jesus' death offered the greatest hope possible.

• **24:24** These followers knew that the tomb was empty but didn't understand that Jesus had risen, and they were filled with sadness. Despite the women's witness, which was verified by some of the disciples, and despite the biblical prophecies of this very event, they still didn't believe. Today the Resurrection still catches people by surprise. In spite of 2,000 years of evidence and witness, many people refuse to believe. What more will it take? For these disciples it took the living Jesus in their midst. For many people today, it takes the presence of alive Christians.

• **24:25** Even though these Jewish men knew the biblical prophecies well, they failed to understand that Christ's suffering was his path to glory. They could not understand why God had not intervened to save Jesus from the cross. They were so caught up in the world's admiration of political power and military might that they were blind to God's Kingdom values—that the last will be first, and that life grows out of death. The world has not changed its values. The suffering servant is no more popular today than he was 2,000 years ago. But we have not only the witness of the Old Testament prophets; we also have the witness of the New Testament apostles and the history of the Christian church testifying to Jesus' victory over death. Will we confront the values of our culture and put our faith in Jesus? Or will we foolishly continue to ignore this Good News?

24:25-27 After the two followers had explained their sadness and confusion, Jesus responded by going to Scripture and applying it to his ministry. When we are puzzled by questions or problems, we, too, can go to Scripture and find authoritative help. If we, like these two, do not understand what the Bible means, we can turn to other believers who know the Bible and have the wisdom to apply it to our situation.

24:27 Beginning with the promised offspring in Genesis (Genesis 3:15) and going through the suffering servant in Isaiah (Isaiah 53), the pierced one in Zechariah (Zechariah 12:10), and the messenger of the covenant in Malachi (Malachi 3:1), Jesus reintroduced these disciples to the Old Testament. Christ is the thread woven through all the Scriptures, the central theme that binds them together. Following are several key passages Jesus may have mentioned on

this walk to Emmaus: Genesis 3; 12; Psalms 22; 69; 110; Isaiah 53; Jeremiah 31; Zechariah 9; 13; Malachi 3.

24:33, 34 Paul also mentions that Jesus appeared to Peter alone (1 Corinthians 15:5). This appearance is not further described in the Gospels. Jesus showed individual concern for Peter because Peter felt completely unworthy after denying his Lord. But Peter repented, and Jesus approached him and forgave him. Soon God would use Peter in building Christ's church (see the first half of the book of Acts).

• **24:36-43** Jesus' body wasn't a figment of the imagination or the appearance of a ghost—the disciples touched him, and he ate food. On the other hand, his body wasn't a restored human body like Lazarus's (John 11)—he was able to appear and disappear. Jesus' resurrected body was immortal. This is the kind of body we will be given at the resurrection of the dead (see 1 Corinthians 15:42-50).

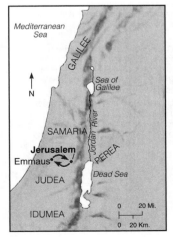

ON THE ROAD TO EMMAUS
After Jesus' death, two of his followers were walking from Jerusalem back toward Emmaus when a stranger joined them. During dinner in Emmaus, Jesus revealed himself to them and then disappeared. They immediately returned to Jerusalem to tell the disciples the good news that Jesus was alive!

among them. "Peace be with you," he said. 37But the whole group was startled and frightened, thinking they were seeing a ghost!

38"Why are you frightened?" he asked. "Why are your hearts filled with doubt? 39Look at my hands. Look at my feet. You can see that it's really me. Touch me and make sure that I am not a ghost, because ghosts don't have bodies, as you see that I do." 40As he spoke, he showed them his hands and his feet.

41Still they stood there in disbelief, filled with joy and wonder. Then he asked them, "Do you have anything here to eat?" 42They gave him a piece of broiled fish, 43and he ate it as they watched.

Jesus Appears to the Disciples in Jerusalem (249)

44Then he said, "When I was with you before, I told you that everything written about me in the law of Moses and the prophets and in the Psalms must be fulfilled." 45Then he opened their minds to understand the Scriptures. 46And he said, "Yes, it was written long ago that the Messiah would suffer and die and rise from the dead on the third day. 47It was also written that this message would be proclaimed in the authority of his name to all the nations,* beginning in Jerusalem: 'There is forgiveness of sins for all who repent.' 48You are witnesses of all these things.

49"And now I will send the Holy Spirit, just as my Father promised. But stay here in the city until the Holy Spirit comes and fills you with power from heaven."

24:44
Luke 24:27

24:47
Acts 2:38; 10:43;
13:38; 26:18

24:48
John 15:27

24:49
Acts 2:1-4

Jesus Ascends into Heaven (250/Mark 16:19-20)

50Then Jesus led them to Bethany, and lifting his hands to heaven, he blessed them. 51While he was blessing them, he left them and was taken up to heaven. 52So they worshiped him and then returned to Jerusalem filled with great joy. 53And they spent all of their time in the Temple, praising God.

24:50-53
Mark 16:19
Acts 1:4-14

24:53
Acts 2:46; 3:1; 5:42

24:44 Many days may have elapsed between verses 43 and 44 because Jesus and his followers traveled to Galilee and back before he returned to heaven (Matthew 28:16; John 21). In his second book, Acts, Luke makes it clear that Jesus spent 40 days with his disciples between his resurrection and ascension.

24:44-46 The writings by Moses, the prophets, and in the Psalms refers to the entire Old Testament. In other words, the entire Old Testament points to the Messiah. For example, his role as prophet was foretold in Deuteronomy 18:15-20; his sufferings were prophesied in Psalm 22 and Isaiah 53; his resurrection was predicted in Psalm 16:9-11 and Isaiah 53:10, 11.

24:45 Jesus opened these people's minds to understand the Scriptures. The Holy Spirit still does this in our life today when we study the Bible. Have you ever wondered how to understand a difficult Bible passage? Besides reading surrounding passages, asking other people, and consulting reference works, pray that the Holy Spirit will open your mind to understand, giving you the needed insight to put God's Word into action in your life.

24:47 Luke wrote to the Greek-speaking world. He wanted them to know that Christ's message of God's love and forgiveness should go to all the world. We must never ignore the worldwide scope of Christ's Good News. God wants all the world to hear the Good News of salvation.

• **24:50-53** As the disciples stood and watched, Jesus began rising into the air, and soon he disappeared into heaven. Seeing Jesus leave must have been frightening, but the disciples knew that Jesus would keep his promise to send the Holy Spirit to be with them. This same Jesus, who lived with the disciples, who died and was buried, and who rose from the dead, loves us and

promises to be with us always. We can get to know him better by studying the Scriptures, praying, and allowing the Holy Spirit to make us more like Jesus.

24:51 Jesus' physical presence left the disciples when he returned to heaven (Acts 1:9), but the Holy Spirit soon came to comfort them and empower them to spread the Good News of salvation (Acts 2:1-4). Today Jesus' work of salvation is complete, and he is sitting at God's right hand, where he has authority over heaven and earth.

24:53 Luke's Gospel portrays Jesus as a perfect life lived according to God's plan. As a child, he was obedient to his parents and amazed the religious leaders in the Temple. As an adult, he served God and others through preaching and healing, and finally, as a condemned man, he suffered without complaint. This portrayal of Jesus was well suited to Luke's Greek audience, who placed high value on being an example and improving oneself, and who often discussed the meaning of perfection. The Greeks, however, had a difficult time understanding the spiritual importance of the physical world. To them, the spiritual was always more important than the physical. To help them understand the God-man, who united the spiritual and the physical, Luke emphasized that Jesus was not a phantom but a real human being who healed people and fed them because he was concerned with their physical health as well as the state of their souls.

As believers living according to God's plan, we, too, should obey our Lord in every detail as we seek to bring wholeness to people's bodies and souls. If others want to know how to live a perfect life, we can point them to Jesus.

STUDY QUESTIONS

Thirteen lessons for individual or group study

HOW TO USE THIS BIBLE STUDY

It's always exciting to get more than you expect. And that's what you'll find in this Bible study guide—much more than you expect. Our goal was to write thoughtful, practical, dependable, and application-oriented studies of God's word.

This study guide contains the complete text of the selected Bible book. The commentary is accurate, complete, and loaded with unique charts, maps, and profiles of Bible people.

With the Bible text, extensive notes and features, and questions to guide discussion, Life Application Bible Studies have everything you need in one place.

The lessons in this Bible study guide will work for large classes as well as small-group studies. To get everyone involved in your discussions, encourage participants to answer the questions before each meeting.

Each lesson is divided into five easy-to-lead sections. The section called "Reflect" introduces you and the members of your group to a specific area of life touched by the lesson. "Read" shows which chapters to read and which notes and other features to use. Additional questions help you understand the passage. "Realize" brings into focus the biblical principle to be learned with questions, a special insight, or both. "Respond" helps you make connections with your own situation and personal needs. The questions are designed to help you find areas in your life where you can apply the biblical truths. "Resolve" helps you map out action plans for that day.

Begin and end each lesson with prayer, asking for the Holy Spirit's guidance, direction, and wisdom.

Recommended time allotments for each section of a lesson are as follows:

Segment	60 minutes	90 minutes
Reflect on your life	*5 minutes*	*10 minutes*
Read the passage	*10 minutes*	*15 minutes*
Realize the principle	*15 minutes*	*20 minutes*
Respond to the message	*20 minutes*	*30 minutes*
Resolve to take action	*10 minutes*	*15 minutes*

All five sections work together to help a person learn the lessons, live out the principles, and obey the commands taught in the Bible.

Also, at the end of each lesson, there is a section entitled "More for studying other themes in this section." These questions will help you lead the group in studying other parts of each section not covered in depth by the main lesson.

But don't just listen to God's word. You must do what it says. Otherwise, you are only fooling yourselves. For if you listen to the word and don't obey, it is like glancing at your face in a mirror. You see yourself, walk away, and forget what you look like. But if you look carefully into the perfect law that sets you free, and if you do what it says and don't forget what you heard, then God will bless you for doing it (James 1:22-25).

LESSON 1
TO TELL THE TRUTH
LUKE INTRODUCTION

REFLECT
on your life

1 What nonfiction book have you read lately? How do you know that what the author has written is true?

_____

_____

_____

_____

_____

2 Which of these sources of information do you trust the least: television news, radio news, newspapers, news magazines, tabloid magazines? Why?

_____

_____

_____

_____

3 Which of those news sources do you trust the most? Why?

_____

_____

_____

_____

Read the introduction to Luke, Luke 1:1-4, and the following notes:

❏ 1:1, 2   ❏ 1:1-4   ❏ 1:3, 4

READ
the passage

4 What reasons did Luke give for writing his Gospel (1:1-4)?

_____

_____

_____

_____

5 Why is his account reliable and trustworthy (1:3)?

_____

_____

_____

_____

6 Who is Luke's audience—to whom did he write this book (1:3)?

_____

_____

_____

7 What is the significance of the introductory words to Luke's Gospel?

_____

REALIZE
the principle

_____

_____

Luke wrote that he had "carefully investigated everything from the beginning" so that he could "write a careful account" (1:3). Certainly Luke's investigation would have included interviews with eyewitnesses to Christ's life as well as checking and rechecking any written reports against the facts. As a Gentile, Luke could have been objective in his research. As a doctor, he would have been meticulous. As we read and study Luke's biography of Christ, we can be confident that it is an accurate account. Written to Theophilus, the Gospel of Luke is for all those who love God.

8 Christians believe that Luke and the other Bible writers were inspired and guided by the Holy Spirit as they wrote (2 Timothy 3:16; 2 Peter 1:20-21), so that all of the Bible is accurate. Why, then, is it important that Luke was a careful historian?

_____

_____

_____

9 In 1 John 1:1-2, John wrote about being an eyewitness to the Word of life. What might have motivated Luke and John to begin their books with these strong claims of accuracy?

_____

_____

_____

_____

_____

10 Luke had to research and discover Jesus Christ for himself in order to share him effectively with others. For Luke, firsthand knowledge was essential to faith. Think back to when God became more than a word to you—when you discovered that he wanted a personal relationship with you. What first got your attention? How did you know it was true?

_____

_____

_____

_____

_____

ESPOND
the message

11 Suppose you were to write a brief story of your personal experience with Christ—the "Gospel according to _____ [your name]." What would you say were your reasons for turning to Christ? How would you describe your life since then?

_____

_____

_____

_____

12 Whom would you like to reach with your Gospel (for example, unbelievers at work, in the neighborhood, at school, or in your family)?

_____

_____

_____

_____

13 What questions about Christianity would they want answered?

_____

_____

_____

14 What would make you a credible, reliable witness to them?

_____

_____

_____

15 Name someone you know who would be encouraged to learn that Luke took pains to record history accurately.

_____

_____

RESOLVE
to take action

16 Write a brief prayer of thanks for the reliability of the Bible.

_____

_____

_____

A What qualifications did Luke have for writing a Gospel to a Gentile audience? What special qualifications has God given you to spread the gospel of Jesus Christ?

B Why was the theme of "the perfect human" especially appropriate for a Greek audience? What themes in Luke strike a responsive chord in you?

C How is the Greek culture of the first century similar to ours today? Why is Luke's message especially appropriate for people in our world?

MORE
for studying
other themes
in this section

LESSON 2
ALL SET
LUKE 1:1– 4:13

REFLECT
n your life

1 Describe some steps parents might take to prepare a child for first grade.

_____

_____

_____

2 How might a child respond to these preparations?

_____

_____

_____

READ
he passage

Read Luke 1:1–4:13, the profiles of Zechariah and Mary, and the following notes:

❐ 1:13   ❐ 1:17   ❐ 1:18-20   ❐ 1:38   ❐ 2:8   ❐ 2:8-15   ❐ 2:49, 50   ❐ 2:52

❐ 3:15   ❐ 3:16   ❐ 3:23   ❐ 4:2

3 What was the angel's message to Zechariah (1:11-17)? How did Zechariah respond (1:18)?

_____

_____

_____

4 What was the angel's message to Mary (1:26-37)? How did she respond (1:38, 46-55)?

_____

_____

_____

5 What was the angel's message to the shepherds (2:8-14)? How did they respond (2:15-18)?

_____

_____

_____

6 What was John the Baptist's message (3:2-3, 7-18)? How did the people respond (3:10, 12, 14-15)?

_____

_____

_____

7 How did God prepare the world for Christ's coming?

_____

_____

_____

_____

REALIZE
the principle

8 How did God prepare Jesus for his public ministry?

_____

_____

_____

God the Father did not spring his plan of salvation on the world. He prepared everyone involved at each step. He sent an angel to Zechariah and then to Mary. He sent John the Baptist to the people. And he allowed Jesus to experience temptation directly before ministering to others. God prepared each one for what was ahead, even if none of them knew exactly what it meant or what the future held. We may not know what God is doing in our life now, but we don't have to. Whatever God is doing, he is preparing us for what he *will* do. If we will trust him and are faithful to what he has given us to do now, we will be ready when his plans for our future unfold.

9 Why was it important for God to prepare the world for Christ's coming and ministry?

_____

_____

_____

10 How does God prepare people for his work today?

_____

_____

_____

11 How does God's work in our life invite us to trust him for the future?

_____

_____

_____

RESPOND
to the message

12 What past experiences has God used to prepare you for the work you do today? (Try to recall a specific example.)

_____

_____

_____

_____

13 What present experience requires you to trust God because you don't understand its purpose?

_____

_____

_____

_____

14 How might your present experience be preparing you for the future?

_____

_____

_____

15 How can you show your trust in God through this time of preparation?

_____

_____

_____

_____

16 In what area of your life can you work on trusting God to reveal his unfolding plan?

_____

_____

_____

17 How can you show your trust in God and his plan for you over the next few days or weeks?

_____

_____

_____

A Why did Zechariah and Elizabeth suffer for not having a child? How did God use their suffering to bring them joy? How is their experience similar to an experience you have had?

B Read Mary's song (1:46-55) and Zechariah's prophecy (1:68-79). What do their words reveal about their understanding of God's character and plan? How do you celebrate when you realize God has included you in his plan?

C When an angel suddenly appeared to the shepherds, they were at first terribly frightened (2:9). Later, when they returned to their fields after seeing the baby Jesus, they were "glorifying and praising God for all they had heard and seen" (2:20). What marvelous works of God cause you to praise him?

D What enabled Simeon to "die in peace" (2:25-32)? In what ways is he an example of faithfulness? In what ways can you demonstrate the same kind of faithfulness in your life?

E What do we learn about Jesus as an adolescent (2:41-52)? What does this teach us about a balanced life? How might this affect our relationships?

F What was unusual about John the Baptist's ministry (3:1-20)? What basic message did he preach, and how did he get his point across? In what ways is your life like his?

G Why was Jesus baptized (3:21-22)? What did he show us by way of example?

LESSON 3
WILL THE REAL JESUS PLEASE STAND UP?
LUKE 4:14–6:11

REFLECT
on your life

1 Describe a time when your reputation did not accurately describe you.

_____

_____

_____

_____

2 How did that reputation cause people to react to you?

_____

_____

_____

READ
the passage

Read Luke 4:14–6:11 and the following notes:

❏ 4:24 ❏ 4:39 ❏ 4:40 ❏ 5:8 ❏ 5:11 ❏ 5:18, 19 ❏ 5:21 ❏ 5:28, 29

3 How did people respond to Jesus after each of the following events?

Teaching in the synagogue (4:14-30): _____

_____

Teaching in Capernaum (4:31-32): _____

_____

Driving out the demon (4:33-37):_____

_____

Healing the sick (4:38-41): _____

_____

Providing many fish (5:1-11): _____

_____

Healing the man with leprosy (5:12-16): _____

_____

Forgiving the sins of the paralyzed man (5:17-26): _____

_____

Eating at Levi's (Matthew's) house (5:27-32): _____

_____

Picking grain and healing on the Sabbath (6:1-11): _____

_____

4 What may account for the differences in how people responded to Jesus?

_____

_____

_____

_____

REALIZE
the principle

The people who met Jesus all met the same person, and he did something for each of them. He taught them the truth, healed them, drove out demons, forgave their sins. Yet they responded in different ways. Jesus' hometown friends said, "You're no better than we are. We know your family." The Pharisees rejected him because he didn't fit their system—he threatened their secure religious world. Some in the crowds were curious. Some were amazed. Some left everything and followed him. Jesus gets the same range of responses today. Some people don't know who he is. Others know who he is but aren't willing to follow him for whatever reason. As Jesus confronts you today, how will you respond?

5 What ideas do people in your neighborhood or workplace have about Jesus today?

_____

_____

_____

_____

6 Who today responds to Christ with . . .

outrage?_____

disinterest? _____

curiosity? _____

amazement? _____

7 What would it mean for you to leave everything and follow Christ?

RESPOND
to the message

_____

_____

_____

_____

8 What has it cost you to follow Christ?

_____

_____

_____

_____

_____

9 What keeps you from responding to Christ in total commitment?

_____

_____

_____

_____

_____

10 Take time now to write out a brief prayer of commitment to follow Christ.

RESOLVE
to take action

_____

_____

_____

_____

_____

11 Whom can you enlist to hold you accountable for this commitment?

_____

_____

A What did Jesus show about his priorities by healing on the Sabbath? (See Luke 4:31-35, 38-41; 6:6-11.) With whom did these priorities clash (6:7-11)? How do Christ's actions affect your sense of what's most important?

MORE
for studying
other themes
in this section

B Why were tax collectors such as Levi despised by the Jews (5:27-32)? Who is despised for similar reasons in our society? How can Christians reach out to them?

C What was Levi risking and/or giving up when he followed Jesus (5:27-32)? What risks and/or sacrifices are involved for you in following Jesus?

LESSON 4
UPSIDE DOWN
LUKE 6:12–8:3

1 If you were a detective checking out a person's values, what would you investigate? What would you collect as evidence?

_____

_____

_____

_____

2 According to the world's values, what brings happiness? What gives meaning to life?

_____

_____

_____

_____

Read Luke 6:12–8:3 and the following notes:

❐ 6:20-23 ❐ 6:21 ❐ 6:24 ❐ 6:26 ❐ 6:27 ❐ 6:37, 38 ❐ 6:45

❐ 7:11-15 ❐ 7:44ff ❐ 8:2, 3

3 Whom does God bless, or who should rejoice (6:20-23)?

_____

_____

_____

4 For whom are sorrows waiting (6:24-26)?

_____

_____

_____

5 What actions did Christ tell his followers to take in loving others (6:27-42)?

_____

_____

_____

6 To what kinds of people did Jesus minister (7:1–8:3)?

_____

_____

_____

7 Why would Jesus' words about blessings have been a surprise to the disciples?

_____

_____

_____

_____

REALIZE
the principle

8 In Luke 6 Jesus gave his disciples many specific instructions. How do these instructions differ from the ways people usually act?

_____

_____

_____

9 Why would it be unusual for someone to reach out to a Roman officer, a widow, or an immoral woman, as Jesus did (Luke 7)?

_____

_____

_____

_____

At this point in his life, Jesus "had it all." Crowds followed him. People shook their heads in amazement at his teaching. Almost everyone liked him. He was a genuine celebrity. According to all of the world's values, he had a bright future. But then Jesus surprised everyone with remarkable statements and deeds reflecting what is really important in life. Blessings come to those who are poor, hungry, sad, and hated, he said—not to those who are rich, prosperous, and popular. He told his disciples that God wanted them to love their enemies and do good to them. He told them not to judge but to forgive. Then he demonstrated these values by reaching out to a Roman officer, a widow, an immoral woman, and others of low status. Jesus seldom told people what they expected to hear; his values opposed the world's. But God's values are right and true.

10 How do Jesus' values compare to our world's values today?

_____

_____

_____

_____

_____

11 Describe a time when God gave you joy in difficult circumstances.

R
RESPOND
ɔ the message

_____

_____

_____

_____

12 What people do you find it difficult to treat with kindness, compassion, or generosity (6:27-42)?

_____

_____

_____

_____

13 How can you reach out to people others have rejected, such as a person with AIDS, a former prisoner, or a disabled child?

_____

_____

_____

_____

14 In what ways does Jesus challenge your values (your sense of what's important)?

_____

_____

_____

_____

15 Name someone to whom you can demonstrate Christ's love (someone who doesn't like you, is a social misfit, or owes you something). How can you show that love this week?

RESOLVE
to take action

_____

_____

_____

A Who were the Jews' enemies in Jesus' day? Why was it difficult for the Jews to show love to their enemies (6:27-36)? What difficulties do you have showing love to your enemies?

MORE
for studying
other themes
in this section

B How can you acknowledge the truth about someone's sin without judging the person (6:37-42)? How can you help someone without being judgmental?

C What are some examples of "good fruit" (6:43-45)? What kind of fruit are you producing?

D What kind of person builds a "house without a foundation" (6:46-49)? What does Jesus identify as a solid foundation for our life? How can you build on this foundation?

E Why was Jesus amazed at the Roman officer's faith (7:1-10)? Why did Jesus heal the officer's slave? How does your faith compare with that of the officer?

F Why did John the Baptist have doubts about Jesus (7:18-23)? What did John do about those doubts? What can you do when you're confused or have doubts about God?

LESSON 5
ALL-POWERFUL LORD
LUKE 8:4–9:50

REFLECT
on your life

1 List several important people you have met. Over what or whom do these people have power or control?

_____

_____

_____

_____

_____

READ
the passage

Read Luke 8:4–9:50 and the following notes:

❒ 8:23   ❒ 8:23-25   ❒ 8:27, 28   ❒ 8:30   ❒ 8:33   ❒ 8:43-48   ❒ 8:45, 46

❒ 8:56   ❒ 9:13, 14   ❒ 9:16, 17   ❒ 9:27   ❒ 9:29, 30

2 What evidence of Jesus' power do you see in each of the following events?

Calming the storm (8:22-25): _____

_____

_____

Healing the demon-possessed man (8:26-39) and the boy with an evil spirit

(9:37-43): _____

_____

_____

Healing the woman with a hemorrhage (8:43-48): _____

_____

_____

_____

Raising Jairus's daughter (8:40-42, 49-56): _____

_____

_____

Feeding more than five thousand people (9:12-17): _____

_____

_____

Being transfigured (9:28-36): _____

_____

_____

3 What do you think the disciples learned about Jesus as they watched him perform these miracles?

_____

_____

_____

_____

REALIZE
the principle

Jesus' disciples and the crowds who followed him saw dramatic demonstrations of power. Jesus cured diseases and disabilities with a word or a touch. He spoke with authority to demons and drove them out of their victims. He brought dead people back to life. He revealed his power over nature itself. Jesus is God—he has power over every aspect of your life. He also has power over all the things you fear—natural disasters, Satan, hunger, death—everything. The question is, have you turned your fears over to him? You can turn over to God everything you feel threatened by and know you are in good hands.

4 How would you answer Jesus' question, "Who do you say I am" (9:20)?

_____

_____

_____

5 How does knowing what Jesus is really like affect how you relate to him?

_____

_____

_____

_____

6 What dampens your faith in Christ?

_____

_____

_____

7 Describe a time when you have seen Christ's power demonstrated in your life.

_____

_____

_____

_____

8 To what do you feel vulnerable (accidents, sickness, death, demons, something else)?

_____

_____

_____

9 Which areas of your life (or what problems in your life) are you reluctant to give control of to God? Why?

_____

_____

_____

10 How could you tell someone who is afraid to give control of his/her life to God?

_____

_____

_____

11 What fears do you need to turn over to Christ's control?

_____

_____

_____

12 How can the knowledge of Christ's power over your fears enhance your prayers this week?

_____

_____

_____

_____

A Why did Jesus speak to the crowds in parables (8:4-18)? What can you do to be more receptive to what Christ is telling you?

MORE
for studying
other themes
in this section

B Note the parable of the four soils (8:4-15). What kind of soil are you today? At what times in your life were you more like another type of soil? What does it take to be fertile soil?

C Who are Jesus' mother and brothers (8:19-21)? How can a person become part of God's family?

D Why did Jesus tell the formerly demon-possessed man to tell others of his healing (8:38-39) but asked Jairus and his wife not to tell anyone about their daughter coming back to life (8:56)? When is it best to tell of God's work in your life, and when is it best to let it speak for itself?

E What were Jesus' instructions to his disciples as he sent them out to preach (9:1-6)? What did he require of them that he also requires of you?

F How did the disciples respond to the hunger of the crowd (9:10-17)? What did they ask Jesus to do about it? What did Jesus do to stretch their faith in him? When have you seen God provide in unexpected ways?

G Who did the people think Jesus was (9:18-20)? Who do people today think he is? To whom can you reveal the truth about Christ? How can you do it?

H How are we to shoulder our cross daily (9:23)? give up our life for Christ's sake (9:24)? lose the world and gain our very soul (9:25)?

I How did Peter respond to what he saw on the mountain (9:28-36)? What is important about what God said from the cloud? What does this experience reveal to you about Jesus?

J Why did the disciples argue (9:46-48)? What does it take to be great in God's sight? What adjustments might this involve for you?

LESSON 6
THE PRICE IS RIGHT
LUKE 9:51–11:13

1 What is the most expensive purchase you have ever made?

_____

_____

2 Why did you make it?

_____

_____

_____

_____

3 How did you get the money to pay for it?

_____

_____

_____

Read Luke 9:51–11:13, the profiles of James and Martha, and the following notes:

❐ 9:51   ❐ 9:59   ❐ 9:62   ❐ 10:3   ❐ 10:23, 24   ❐ 10:27-37   ❐ 10:33

❐ 10:38-42   ❐ 11:4

4 Following Jesus is costly. What is the significance of the cost Jesus asked his disciples to pay?

No place to lay his head (9:57-58):_____

_____

Let the spiritually dead care for their own dead (9:59-60):_____
_____

No one looks back (9:61-62):_____
_____

As lambs among wolves (10:3): _____
_____

Love with all your heart (10:26-28):_____
_____

A neighbor to the man who was beaten and robbed (10:29-37): _____
_____

The one thing worth being concerned about (10:38-42): _____
_____

Forgive as we are forgiven (11:4):_____
_____

5 What price did James pay for his dedication to Jesus (see profile of James)?
_____ Death _____
_____
_____
_____

Jesus called many people to follow him. Some came right away; some started and then turned back; others refused entirely. To those who followed, Jesus made it clear that there would be a price to pay. Our commitment to Christ may affect our relationships, our job status, or our position in the community. Following Christ costs something. Even today, in many places of the world, following Christ can mean rejection, imprisonment, or even death. We may not be called to die for our faith, but Jesus does ask us to pattern our life after his. Obeying him will always involve sacrifice of some kind.

REALIZE
the principle

6 What did following Christ (or doing what was right) cost . . .

the disciples? _____

the seventy-two messengers? _____

the Good Samaritan?_____

Mary? _____

7 What makes faith in Christ worth dying for?

The reward of eternal life
& Him in Heaven

8 What might following Jesus (as described in Luke 9:51–11:13) cost a person in his/her . . .

lifestyle? _____

decisions? _____

relationships? _____

goals? _____

finances? _____

9 Following Christ means doing what God tells us to do. What has God told you to do that you are hesitating over because of the cost?

_____

_____

_____

10 What can you do this week to obey Christ in this area?

_____

_____

_____

A Why did James and John want to "call down fire from heaven" on a Samaritan village (9:51-55)? When are you tempted to condemn people or retaliate?

B What instructions did Jesus give to the seventy-two messengers (10:2-11)? Why was their mission successful? In what ways was their mission like the one God has given you?

C In the parable of the Good Samaritan, two people passed by the injured man without helping him, while another stopped to help (10:25-37). What do each man's actions show about him? Who needs your help? To whom can you be a Good Samaritan?

D How was Martha serving Jesus (10:38-42)? Why was she upset? When are you tempted to choose something good over what is best?

E Why did Jesus give this prayer to his disciples (11:1-4)? What is the significance of each phrase? How can your prayers reflect these priorities?

F Why did Jesus teach us to be persistent in prayer (11:5-13)? About what do you need to be persistent in prayer?

LESSON 7
IT'S WHAT'S INSIDE THAT COUNTS
LUKE 11:14–13:17

REFLECT
on your life

1 Finish these sentences:

A hypocritical peace activist is one who _____

_____

A hypocritical environmentalist is one who _____

_____

A hypocritical police officer is one who _____

_____

A hypocritical aerobics instructor is one who _____

_____

A hypocritical scientist is one who _____

_____

A hypocritical doctor is one who _____

_____

A hypocritical religious leader is one who _____

_____

READ
the passage

Read Luke 11:14–13:17 and the following notes:

❐ 11:37-39   ❐ 11:41   ❐ 11:42-52   ❐ 11:44   ❐ 11:46   ❐ 11:52

❐ 12:1, 2   ❐ 12:8, 9   ❐ 13:10-17

2 Who were the Pharisees?

_____

_____

3 List some ways the Pharisees demonstrated hypocrisy (11:37-52):

_____

_____

_____

4 What did Jesus say about hypocrisy (11:14–12:3; 13:10-17)?

_____

_____

Jesus had harsh words for the Pharisees and experts in religious law. They accused him of being allied with Satan. He condemned them for their blatant hypocrisy. They accosted him for working on the Sabbath. He criticized them for caring more about their traditions than about obeying God. As a result, "the teachers of religious law and the Pharisees became hostile and tried to provoke him with many questions" (11:53). The Pharisees and law experts were hypocrites because they claimed to be holy but were filled with sin. They went through religious motions but had no spiritual depth. They pretended to be devoted to God but were only concerned about themselves. In short, they focused on outward appearances and not on the inner condition of their heart. Jesus warned us to beware of hypocrites and hypocrisy in our own life.

REALIZE
the principle

5 What does it mean to focus on the inner condition of your heart?

_____

_____

_____

6 What is so bad about religious hypocrisy?

_____

_____

7 What are some examples of religious hypocrisy today?

_____

_____

8 What might a Christian hypocrite look like?

_____

_____

RESPOND
to the message

9 Why is it easy to say one thing and live the opposite?

_____

_____

_____

10 How can a Christian avoid being hypocritical?

_____

_____

_____

_____

11 What are some of the hindrances to living what you profess to believe?

_____

_____

_____

_____

12 How can you focus on the inner condition of your heart over outward appearances?

_____

_____

_____

RESOLVE
to take action

13 What areas of your life do you need to make more consistent with your Christian faith?

_____

_____

_____

_____

14 How will you know when you've made progress?

_____

_____

_____

A How did Jesus answer the charge that he was in league with Satan (11:14-23)?

MORE
for studying
other themes
in this section

B What is the danger for a person who makes a dramatic change in lifestyle (11:24-26)?

C How was Jonah a sign for the nation of Israel (11:29-32)? What lessons can we learn from God's treatment of Nineveh and other nations in the past?

D How does what you see and focus on affect your thoughts and motives (11:33-36)? What do a person's eyes reveal about him/her?

E How much does God know about you (12:6-7)? How can God's love and care for you free you from fear?

F In what situations do you find it difficult to admit that you're a Christian (12:8-12)? What can you do to become more bold in your witness for Christ?

G How do people store up things for themselves (12:13-21)? What does God say about greed? What can you do to "have a rich relationship with God"?

H What do people worry about most (12:22-34)? How does worry hurt us? What is God's antidote for worry?

I Why should believers be well prepared and ready for Christ's return (12:35-48)? How should they live to be ready? What changes can you make so that you will be ready for Christ's return?

J How does (or can) faith in Christ bring division among people (12:49-53)? How should you respond when someone you love strongly opposes your faith?

K What kind of fruit is God looking for Christians to bear (13:6-9)? How can you be more productive for God?

LESSON 8
MOVIN' UP
LUKE 13:18–14:35

REFLECT
on your life

1 What are some signs of status?

_____

_____

_____

_____

2 Why is status important to some people?

_____

_____

_____

_____

READ
the passage

Read Luke 13:18–14:35 and the following notes:

❏ 13:30   ❏ 14:7-11   ❏ 14:7-14   ❏ 14:11   ❏ 14:16ff   ❏ 14:28-30

3 Why did Jesus tell the parable of the wedding feast (14:7-14)?

_____

_____

_____

4 Why did Jesus tell the parable of the banquet (14:15-24)?

_____

_____

_____

5 What do these parables have in common?

_____

_____

_____

6 What did Jesus say about those who seek honor and status for themselves (14:8-9, 11)?

_____

_____

_____

_____

7 Why is status a problem for some?

_____

_____

_____

REALIZE
the principle

The people of Jesus' time made distinctions among themselves on the basis of status. Pharisees and experts in the law had high status. Rich people and those with authority had high status. Healthy people had high status. Meanwhile, almost everyone else—the poor, disabled, uneducated, and powerless—had low status. Jesus criticized the people for caring about these differences. He wanted his disciples to see things God's way, to realize that status doesn't matter to God—it matters only to the world. We should show concern for all people, especially those who have low or no status.

8 In your world, who are the people to be seen with?

_____

_____

_____

_____

9 What are the places to be?

_____

_____

_____

10 What makes a person great in God's eyes?

_____

_____

_____

11 Whom do you know who is great in God's eyes yet has low status in the world's eyes?

_____

_____

_____

12 What part of your image have you tried to protect?

_____

_____

_____

13 Describe a time when you tried to raise your own status.

_____

_____

_____

_____

14 Describe a time when you avoided people because of their low status.

_____

_____

_____

15 Name one status-seeking behavior you would like to eliminate from your life now.

_____

_____

_____

16 What person of low status (poor, disabled, or uneducated) can you reach out to this week? How will you reach out to this person?

_____

_____

_____

_____

A How is the Kingdom of God like a mustard seed (13:18-19)? How is the Kingdom of God like yeast (13:20-21)? How does this affect our expectations of the way God works in the world?

B In what sense is the door to heaven narrow (13:22-30)? Why will some who associated with Jesus be unable to enter? Who might these people be today? What's the difference between associating with Jesus and knowing him? How can a person enter the narrow door?

C Why was Jesus determined to go to Jerusalem (13:31-35)? Why did God's people find it difficult to listen to God's prophets? Why did Jesus grieve over this fact? What can you do to reach those who oppose God?

D What excuses do people make today for not accepting Christ's invitation to salvation, i.e., his "banquet" (14:15-24)? What can you do to "go out into the country lanes and behind the hedges and urge anyone you find to come" (14:23)?

E What would happen if we didn't love Jesus more than our families and even more than our life (14:26)? How does this affect your relationships at home?

F Why must a person count the cost before following Jesus (14:28-33)? What will it cost you to follow Christ completely?

MORE
for studying
other themes
in this section

LESSON 9
LOST AND FOUND
LUKE 15:1–17:37

REFLECT
on your life

1 What is the most valuable possession you've ever lost?

_____

_____

2 What did you do to try to find it?

_____

_____

_____

_____

_____

READ
the passage

Read Luke 15:1–17:37 and the following notes:

❒ 15:2   ❒ 15:3-6   ❒ 15:4, 5   ❒ 15:8-10   ❒ 15:20   ❒ 15:24   ❒ 15:25-31

❒ 15:30   ❒ 15:32

3 What would a shepherd do when one of his sheep strayed away (15:4)?

_____

_____

4 What would he do after he found it (15:5-6)?

_____

_____

_____

5 What would a woman do if she lost a silver coin (15:8)?

_____

_____

_____

6 What would she do when she found it (15:9)?

_____

_____

_____

7 What did the father do when his son returned home (15:11-32)?

_____

_____

_____

8 What has God done to find sinners (16:27-31)?

_____

_____

9 At what point will God stop seeking sinners (17:22-37)?

_____

_____

10 Why do you think Jesus told the three parables in chapter 15?

_____

_____

_____

REALIZE
the principle

In their desire to remain pure and holy, the Pharisees wanted nothing to do with "sinners." They thought that religious people who observed all the Pharisees' traditions should not associate with ungodly people (those who did not observe these traditions). What the Pharisees did not know or did not care about was that God seeks out sinners. Through these three parables, Jesus pointed out that the Pharisees lacked a key element of God's heart—compassion for people who do not know God. God wants everyone to come to him. Those who truly know God desire the same thing.

11 How can a person become spiritually lost?

_____

_____

_____

12 What might cause a Christian to develop a callous attitude toward those who do not know God?

_____

_____

_____

13 Whom do you know that is lost?

RESPOND
to the message

_____

_____

_____

_____

14 What can you do to help bring them to the Father?

_____

_____

_____

_____

15 How can you avoid becoming exclusive about your relationship with God, like the older brother in the parable of the lost son?

_____

_____

_____

16 Name the lost people for whom you can pray regularly.

RESOLVE
to take action

_____

_____

_____

A How did the shrewd manager protect himself against his employer (16:1-8)? How does your use of money reflect your commitment to God?

MORE
for studying
other themes
in this section

B How can a Christian use money and possessions to help bring people to the Father (16:9)? What reward awaits the Christian who does this? How can you use your money and possessions to "make friends"?

C Why is it important to be faithful or trustworthy in small matters (16:10-13)? What has God entrusted to you? How can you be faithful (or responsible) in these areas?

D How do some people try to serve "both God and money" (16:10-13)? Why is this impossible? How can money come between a person and God?

E Why did the Pharisees scoff at Jesus' teaching on money (16:14-15)? In what areas are you tempted to rationalize your disobedience of God's law?

F Why would the story of the rich man and Lazarus have upset the Pharisees (16:19-31)? Why did the rich man long for paradise?

G How did Jesus answer the disciples' request for more faith (17:5-10)? What are you tempted to put off for lack of faith? What is your simple duty in that area?

H Why did the one leper return to thank Jesus (17:11-19)? What good things has God done for you? Why is it important to remember to thank God? What can you thank God for today?

I Why will many people not be ready for Christ's return (17:20-37)? How can a person get ready? What do you need to do now to prepare?

LESSON 10
TRUE RICHES
LUKE 18:1–19:27

1 What does a single person give up when he/she gets married?

_____

_____

_____

_____

2 Why would a person willingly give all that up for marriage?

_____

_____

_____

_____

Read Luke 18:1–19:27 and the following notes:

❐ 18:18ff   ❐ 18:22, 23   ❐ 19:8   ❐ 19:11ff   ❐ 19:20-27

3 Why did the rich man go away sad (18:18-23)?

_____

_____

_____

4 Why did Zacchaeus receive Christ's forgiveness (19:1-10)?

_____

_____

_____

5 Based on each man's past, which of them would seem to be the most likely to follow Christ (18:20-21; 19:2, 7)? Why?

_____

_____

_____

6 What does God want us to do with our money and other resources (19:11-27)?

_____

_____

_____

The rich young man came to Jesus confident of his religious credentials, but he went away sad because he didn't love Christ as much as he loved his money. In contrast, Zacchaeus was willing to pay any price to follow Christ, even if it meant paying back four times the amount he had extorted. When confronted by Christ, each of these men made a choice about money—one served it; the other used it to serve God. Money can be either our master or our servant, but it cannot be both. When we choose to serve God with our money and resources, we gain the proper perspective and free ourselves from the tyranny of greed.

REALIZE
the principle

7 Why is money so important to some people?

_____

_____

_____

8 In addition to money, what else can easily take God's place in people's lives today?

_____

_____

_____

9 In what ways are you like the rich young man?

_____

_____

_____

RESPOND
to the message

10 In what ways are you like Zacchaeus?

_____

_____

_____

_____

11 Name something that would be difficult for you to give up to follow Christ.

_____

_____

_____

12 What resources can you invest for the Kingdom?

_____

_____

_____

_____

_____

13 How can you invest them?

_____

_____

_____

_____

_____

RESOLVE
to take action

14 How will you use your money and possessions to serve God this week?

_____

_____

_____

_____

_____

A Why is it important to persist in prayer (18:1-8)? How can you be more persistent in your prayer life?

MORE
for studying
other themes
in this section

B What is the difference between the prayer of the Pharisee and the prayer of the tax collector (18:9-14)? Why was the tax collector justified? How can you make your prayers more like his?

C Why did Jesus welcome the little children (18:15-17)? How can we come to God as little children?

D How did Jesus answer the rich man's question, "What should I do to inherit eternal life?" (18:18-22). Why was this answer difficult for the man to accept (18:23-24)? What barriers can stand in the way of your willingness to do what God wants?

E What did Jesus predict would happen to him (18:31-34)? Why were the disciples surprised when Jesus rose from the dead? What statement of Jesus' have you just recently come to understand?

F What did the blind beggar ask for (18:41)? What did he receive (18:42, 43)? How did this affect the man (18:43)? What blessings has God given you that inspire you to respond as this man did? How can you show that response this week?

LESSON 11
OPPOSITION
LUKE 19:28–21:38

REFLECT
on your life

1 What motivational sports slogans have you heard?

_____

_____

_____

_____

2 What are some possible reactions to overwhelming opposition?

_____

_____

_____

_____

READ
the passage

Read Luke 19:28–21:38 and the following notes:

❏ 19:38   ❏ 19:47   ❏ 20:1-8   ❏ 20:9-16   ❏ 20:27-38   ❏ 20:41-44   ❏ 20:47

❏ 21:7ff   ❏ 21:12, 13   ❏ 21:14-19   ❏ 21:28   ❏ 21:36

3 What people opposed Jesus (19:39, 47; 20:1, 19, 27, 46)?

_____

_____

_____

_____

_____

4 What tactics did the religious leaders use to try to trap Jesus (20:1-8, 19-40)?

_____

_____

_____

_____

_____

5 What kinds of persecution did Jesus tell his followers to expect (21:5-19)?

_____

_____

_____

_____

6 Why did the religious leaders try to trap Jesus instead of admitting that he was the Messiah?

REALIZE
the principle

_____

_____

_____

_____

After Jesus' triumphal entry into Jerusalem, the opposition intensified. The Pharisees, teachers of religious law, Sadducees, and leading priests united against him and used a variety of tricks and traps to find some legal way to apprehend him. Jesus eluded their verbal traps while continuing to fascinate the crowds. But the opposition was real and would eventually lead to his arrest.

Jesus warned his followers to prepare themselves for similar treatment. Following him, he told them, would invite persecution from all sides, even from those closest to them. It would take a conscious effort for them to stand firm in their devotion to Christ. Following Christ today invites persecution just as surely as it did then. Knowing this is the first step in standing firm against opposition to our faith.

7 How did Jesus' warning in 21:17 come true for the disciples?

_____

_____

_____

_____

8 Why was persecution a positive sign?

_____

_____

_____

9 How are true believers persecuted by religious leaders today?

RESPOND
to the message

_____

_____

_____

10 How are Christians persecuted by the government? family? friends?

_____

_____

_____

_____

11 Where might you face opposition (even persecution) for what you believe?

_____

_____

_____

12 Describe a time when you were tempted to be silent or to compromise your faith because of opposition.

_____

_____

_____

13 What truths will help you remain loyal to Christ when people oppose you because of your faith?

RESOLVE
to take action

_____

_____

_____

A What is the significance of the following events of Jesus' triumphal entry (19:28-46)?

MORE
for studying
other themes
in this section

- His entering the city on a colt

- The people joyfully praising God

- Jesus' telling the Pharisees that if the crowd were to keep quiet, the stones would burst into cheers

- His weeping for and words about Jerusalem

- His driving the merchants from the Temple

B How did the religious leaders react when Jesus said, "The stone that the builders rejected has now become the cornerstone" (20:17)? How should they have reacted? What can you do to avoid making the same mistake as the religious leaders?

C What lessons can we learn from the poor widow's offering (21:1-4)? How does her example challenge you to handle your finances differently?

D What signs will signal the end of this age (21:8-31)? What can we do in the meantime (21:34-36)? What will you do to prepare for this time?

LESSON 12
IN OUR PLACE
LUKE 22:1–23:56

REFLECT
on your life

1 Check two or three experiences that you would consider to be the most painful.

❏ Being betrayed by a close associate

❏ Saying good-bye to close friends

❏ Having a very close friend turn his/her back on you

❏ Struggling with a difficult decision

❏ Being deserted by friends and associates

❏ Being falsely accused

❏ Being mocked in public

❏ Being convicted of a crime you didn't commit

❏ Being tortured

❏ Dying a slow death

❏ Being executed publicly

❏ Being totally alone

2 Why did you select these experiences?

_____

_____

_____

_____

READ
the passage

Read Luke 22:1–23:56 and the following notes:

❏ 22:14-18 ❏ 22:19 ❏ 22:20 ❏ 22:41, 42 ❏ 22:44 ❏ 22:53 ❏ 22:54

❏ 22:70 ❏ 23:15 ❏ 23:22

3 Each of the following people or groups played a key role in the final hours of Jesus' life on earth. Briefly describe each person's part in the drama (22:1–23:25).

Judas:_____

_____

The twelve disciples: _____

_____

Peter: _____

_____

The religious leaders: _____

_____

Herod: _____

_____

Pilate: _____

_____

4 Why was Jesus in such agony when he went to pray (22:39-46)?

_____

_____

_____

_____

In the final hours of his life on earth, Jesus suffered unimaginable emotional and physical pain, including desertion and betrayal by friends, public humiliation, and physical torture. But the greatest suffering he endured was bearing the sins of the world on a rugged Roman cross. Suspended between heaven and earth, Jesus took our place, paying the penalty for our sins. He hung there totally alone, separated even from his Father. In dying for us, Jesus did more than we can comprehend. He not only took our sins away but also made it possible for us to have a relationship with God.

REALIZE
the principle

5 What crimes was Jesus accused of during his trials (22:66–23:25)?

_____

_____

_____

_____

6 Why did Jesus have to die in order for God's plan to be accomplished?

_____

_____

_____

7 Why was Jesus' pain on the cross so excruciating?

RESPOND
to the message

_____

_____

_____

8 How would you explain to an unbeliever the reason for Jesus' death?

_____

_____

_____

9 How have you responded to Jesus' sacrifice for *your* sins?

_____

_____

_____

10 How can you celebrate or remember Christ's sacrifice for you?

_____

_____

_____

_____

11 What can you do this week to express your gratitude to Christ for all he did for you?

RESOLVE
to take action

_____

_____

_____

_____

A Why do you think Judas betrayed Jesus? Why did Peter deny him? When are you tempted to deny your relationship with Jesus?

MORE
for studying
other themes
in this section

B What is the significance of Jesus' words to his disciples regarding the bread and the cup during the Last Supper (22:14-20)? Why do Christians still celebrate this event? Why do you take Communion? What do you do to prepare yourself for Communion?

C When Jesus was arrested, where were the people who had cheered him a few days earlier? Where would you have been? Why?

D Why did the religious leaders have to take Jesus to Pilate, the Roman governor (23:1)? What did they accuse Jesus of doing (23:2)? Why were these accusations different from the ones used before the Jewish council (22:66-71)? How did Jesus respond to these accusations? How do you respond when falsely accused of something?

E Why did Pilate give in to the religious leaders' demands to have Jesus crucified? How are you pressured to do wrong each day? How can you resist that pressure?

F How did each of the crucified criminals respond to Jesus (23:39-43)? What does this teach us about salvation?

G Why did Jesus tell the women of Jerusalem, "Don't weep for me, but weep for yourselves and for your children" (23:28)? For what do you weep?

H What was significant about the words exchanged between Jesus and the criminal on the cross (23:42-43)? In what ways do you identify with this criminal?

LESSON 13
ALIVE!
LUKE 24:1-53

1 What causes your peers to despair and lose hope?

_____

_____

_____

_____

_____

2 To what or to whom do people look for hope today?

_____

_____

_____

_____

_____

Read Luke 24:1-53 and the following notes:

❏ 24:1-9   ❏ 24:6, 7   ❏ 24:11, 12   ❏ 24:24   ❏ 24:25   ❏ 24:36-43   ❏ 24:50-53

3 Who were the first people to discover Jesus' resurrection? Why were they convinced it was true?

_____

_____

_____

4 Fill in the chart below:

What some expected from Jesus	What happened
(a) Jesus would rescue Israel from Roman oppression and set up a kingdom in Israel (24:21).	_____ _____ _____
(b) Jesus would save himself from the cross (23:35).	_____ _____
(c) Crucifying Jesus would put an end to this troublemaker (23:4-5).	_____ _____

5 What were the different reactions to the news of Jesus' resurrection (24:1-53)?

_____

_____

_____

_____

_____

When Jesus died, the disciples despaired. Lost and leaderless, they huddled in fear behind closed doors. But when Jesus appeared to them, their lives changed forever. Why? Because suddenly they had hope. When they saw that Jesus was alive, they knew that all he had taught them was true. They now realized that he was the Messiah, the one who had come to bring salvation to the world, and they were assured of their own resurrection and place in heaven. Suddenly the future looked brighter than they had ever imagined. The Resurrection continues to bring hope to those who despair today.

REALIZE
the principle

6 As Jesus explained to the two believers on the road to Emmaus, he had fulfilled all of Scripture and accomplished all that God had planned. What difference does it make to the world that Jesus is who he said he is?

_____

_____

_____

_____

_____

_____

7 How did the Resurrection give the disciples hope?

_____

_____

_____

_____

8 What difference does it make that Jesus is alive today?

_____

_____

_____

_____

ESPOND
the message

9 If you had been one of Jesus' followers nearly two thousand years ago, how would you have reacted to his death on the cross?

_____

_____

_____

10 How would you have reacted to the amazing news of his resurrection?

_____

_____

_____

11 How does the Resurrection give you hope?

_____

_____

_____

12 When do you most need to remember the truth of the Resurrection?

_____

_____

_____

13 Think of one way you can keep the hope of the Resurrection in your thoughts this week.

_____

_____

_____

_____

A Why is the Resurrection central to the Christian faith? How does the truth about the Resurrection impact you?

B What did it take to convince the disciples that Jesus had indeed risen from the dead (24:36-40)? What assures you of the truth of the Resurrection?

C How did Jesus spend his time with the disciples after the Resurrection (24:45)? How did Jesus prepare the disciples to be his witnesses? In what ways have you been prepared to witness for Christ?

D How did the disciples respond to Christ's ascension (24:50-53)? What motivates you to worship and praise God?

Take Your Bible Study to the Next Level

The **Life Application Study Bible** helps you apply truths in God's Word to everyday life. It's packed with nearly 10,000 notes and features that make it today's #1–selling study Bible.

Life Application Notes: Thousands of Life Application notes help explain God's Word and challenge you to apply the truth of Scripture to your life.

Personality Profiles: You can benefit from the life experiences of over a hundred Bible figures.

Book Introductions: These provide vital statistics, an overview, and a timeline to help you quickly understand the message of each book.

Maps: Over 200 maps next to the Bible text highlight important Bible places and events.

Christian Worker's Resource: Enhance your ministry effectiveness with this practical supplement.

Charts: Over 260 charts help explain difficult concepts and relationships.

Harmony of the Gospels: Using a unique numbering system, the events from all four Gospels are harmonized into one chronological account.

Daily Reading Plan: This reading plan is your guide to reading through the entire Bible in one unforgettable year.

Topical Index: A master index provides instant access to Bible passages and features that address the topics on your mind.

Dictionary/Concordance: With entries for many of the important words in the Bible, this is an excellent starting place for studying the Bible text.

Available in the New Living Translation, New International Version, King James Version, and New King James Version. Take an interactive tour of the *Life Application Study Bible* at
www.NewLivingTranslation.com/LASB

CP0271